22

The Complex Image

THE COMPLEX IMAGE

Faith and Method in American Autobiography

Joseph Fichtelberg

upp

UNIVERSITY OF
PENNSYLVANIA PRESS

Philadelphia

Excerpt from *Memories of a Catholic
    Girlhood*, copyright 1957, 1985 by Mary
    McCarthy, reprinted by permission of
    Harcourt Brace Jovanovich, Inc.

Library of Congress Cataloging-in-Publication Data

Fichtelberg, Joseph.
    The complex image: faith and method in American autobiography /
Joseph Fichtelberg.
        p.   cm.
    Includes index.
    ISBN 0-8122-8146-2
    1. American prose literature—History and criticism.
2. Autobiography.   3. Authors, American—Biography—History and
criticism.   4. United States—Biography—History and criticism.
I. Title.
PS366.A88F53   1989
810.9'492—dc20   89-14704
                                                                CIP

For Fannie

Contents

Acknowledgments

Like the texts I examine, this book is more than the sum of its revisions. To those who have helped in the process, I express my gratitude. At Columbia University, Andrew Delbanco, Alfred Hornung, Carl Hovde, Gillian Lindt, Eric McKitrick, and Joseph Ridgely offered sensitive criticism of my dissertation; the readers at the University of Pennsylvania Press helped to turn the dissertation into a book. Walter Kendrick aided in translating difficult passages from Nietzsche, and Philip Sicker and Richard Giannone helped the manuscript through its final stages. The staffs of several libraries have been most helpful: Butler Library and Rare Book Reading Room, Columbia University; Houghton Library, Harvard University; The Beinecke Rare Book and Manuscript Library, Yale University; Friends Historical Library, Swarthmore College; The New York Public Library. My thanks to the editors of *Early American Literature* for permission to reprint a revised portion of Chapter 4. A portion of Chapter 5 has appeared in *Mid-Hudson Language Studies*, volume 12, no. 1. Thanks also to Columbia University's Elliot V. K. Dobbie Fund for help with publication costs. I am grateful for permission to quote from the following:

From *The Autobiography of Alice B. Toklas* by Gertrude Stein. Copyright 1933 and renewed © 1961 by Alice B. Toklas. Reprinted by permission of Random House, Inc., and of the estate of Gertrude Stein.

From Gertrude Stein's manuscript of *The Autobiography of Alice B. Toklas*, The Collection of American Literature, Beinecke Rare Book and Manuscript Library, Yale University. Permission granted by the estate of Gertrude Stein.

From *The Autobiography of W. E. B. Du Bois* by W. E. B. Du Bois. Reprinted by permission of International Publishers Co., Inc.

From *God's Plot: The Paradoxes of Puritan Piety; Being the Autobiography & Journal of Thomas Shepard*, edited by Michael McGiffert. Copyright © 1972 by Michael McGiffert. Reprinted by permission of Michael McGiffert.

From *The Autobiography of Benjamin Franklin; A Genetic Text*, edited by J. A. Leo Lemay and P. M. Zall. Copyright © 1981 by the University of Tennessee Press. Reprinted by permission of the University of Tennessee Press.

From *Specimen Days* by Walt Whitman, edited by Floyd Stovall. Copyright © 1963 by New York University Press. Reprinted by permission of New York University Press.

Others sustained my work in a different way. The late Adam Munz taught by example: his courage and compassion are abiding influences on all who knew him. To my parents and brother, my wife, Patti, and my late grandmother, to whose memory this book is dedicated, my debt cannot be easily expressed. If, as James Olney maintains, literary criticism is concealed autobiography, this study is as much theirs as it is mine.

A new era begins for me with this date. From these days I discover in my life something important, the only important thing that ever happened to me: the description I made of a part of it.... I also know that that part which I recounted was not the most important. It was made the most important because I fixed it in words. And now what am I? Not he who lived but he who described. Oh, the only important part of life is the regathering.[1]

Italo Svevo, *Further Confessions of Zeno*

1 | *Varieties of Self: The Case of Friedrich Nietzsche*

If autobiographies, as Wilhelm Dilthey believed, "mak[e] the great historian," then anthologies of autobiography may well inspire the critical theorist.[1] Undoubtedly the best recent anthology is James Olney's *Autobiography: Essays Theoretical and Critical*,[2] a work exhibiting the more important trends of the last twenty-five years. Its fifteen articles, ranging from philosophical to topical treatments, allow one to survey what Dilthey might have called the "categories" of critical comment on the genre—as well as the omissions.

Three essays—those of Olney, Louis Renza, and Michael Sprinker—seem exemplary. Although the topic of Olney's "Some Versions of Memory/Some Versions of Bios: The Ontology of Autobiography" is the writer's life or *bios*, underlying that concern is a more basic commitment to the unity of the subject, that entity standing within or behind or above its handiwork, defining itself against the flow of life. With the openness that has characterized all his work, Olney puts no limit on possible *bioi*, the three he investigates challenging conventional notions of the genre. Richard Wright's *Black Boy* displays the writer's creative use of memory to shape the present moment. Since the past is lost, Olney maintains, the autobiographer must impose a pattern on memory; Wright's pattern—fear, panic, flight, and violence—reproduces the fictional elements of *Native Son*. Is the novel therefore autobiography? If one considers *bios* as "a process the whole of which the autobiographer is in a position to see" (240), the answer is yes, since the same pattern seems to stamp all Wright's work of the early 1940s. For even if Wright had tried to be faithful to his past, he had still to transport it "into a realm of order where events bear to one another a relationship of significance rather than of chronology" (247). That is, the autobiographer must seek essences, timeless truths.[3]

Olney pursues this Platonism in his other versions of *bios*. Paul Valéry's monumental poem *La Jeune Parque*, though bearing no discernible relationship to ordinary life, is nevertheless autobiography if one considers life in its radical sense—as "pure, atemporal consciousness," "bright, shining, ticking, sufficient unto itself" (252, 242). For Valéry intended to give a truer picture of his mental life during the Great War than a record of mundane events would allow. Like his contemporary, Gertrude Stein, he preferred "an eternal present" (255), a transcript of consciousness. Occupying a middle ground between Wright's reworked memory and Valéry's pure poetry is W. B. Yeats's archetypal *Autobiographies*. Here Olney's guide is Plotinus, who bids the higher soul "fle[e] multiplicity" and "escape the unbounded by drawing all to unity" in pure forms (259). Hence Yeats's weak memory and fanciful anecdotes serve a higher purpose, not to record life as it was, but life as it was meant to be, as an ideal order. In all three cases, then, Olney stresses the autobiographer's desire to make sense of his present being; pattern is all.

But Olney's phenomenological approach, sensitive though it may be, has several serious consequences. His formalism tends to sever autobiography from time—this in a genre that Dilthey thought the essence of history.[4] The past as encoded in the text's production—the writer's moving through time as he captures his "timeless" present—also figures little in Olney's discussion. How might events in a writer's quotidian life affect a project begun six months before? How does the language he has already used influence what he has yet to record? Indeed, Olney largely avoids questions of textuality. Although he does acknowledge in passing the reciprocal action of "the self shaping and shaped by . . . language" (258), often he seems to be unaware of how language qualifies even the most strenuous efforts to escape time—including Olney's attempts. Consciousness, that pure, nonreferential medium, nevertheless "glows" and "ticks," and memory is an "Ariadne's thread" (241)—a metaphor not only for memory, but for the labyrinth of language enclosing time, memory, and all the autobiographer or critic can know of consciousness.[5] But this critical blindness may well serve a deeper purpose, for it is the only way to save a self threatened with fragmentation. If it is true that "in trying to remember the past in the present the autobiographer imagines another person, another world into existence" (245); if the "I" of authorship bears no direct relationship to the historical "I" (a point students of Émile

Benveniste have used to attack the very notion of autobiography),[6] then only a link to some transcendental realm can ground the self. Consciousness, archetype, and form are the terms Olney uses to preserve *autos*, refined out of existence by the same shifting perspective that makes *bios* ultimately unknowable—the Heraclitean stream of language and time.

Louis Renza's essay, "The Veto of the Imagination: A Theory of Autobiography," which follows Olney's in the anthology, takes the split autobiographical self as its starting point. But where Olney sought to close the gap, Renza wants to widen it, insisting that "writing about [one's] own existence ironically entails a denial of this existence...as a secure referential source for such writing" (279). Renza demarcates three modes of autobiography, each contending with difference in a manner that betrays its impotence. The memoirist, opting for a narrative of highly public events, attempts to repress his anxiety over an inaccessible past, an evasion that merely underscores his concern. The confessional autobiographer establishes an exemplary "I" he cannot hope to satisfy, thus focusing his anxiety on an inaccessible or atemporal " 'dummy' ego" (284). St. Teresa's penitent, Franklin's successful tradesman, Henry Adams's manikin are all denials of this crippling difference. Most extreme is the narcissistic mode, in which the autobiographer dwells on himself to the exclusion of all else, in a vain attempt to preserve the essence of his fleeting identity. His failure often finds expression in paranoia—the projected alienation he feels not only from his past, but from his text. For language, too, is an Other, destroying, as it gives expression to self-presence. Is autobiography, then, possible? Renza's answer is inconclusive: perhaps it is "a unique, self-defining mode of self-referential expression, one that allows, then inhibits, its ostensible project of self-representation" (295). But the tentativeness of that project forces Renza to revise his assessment: autobiography may be no more than a fragmentary prelude to an impossible act of self-consciousness.

Despite his radical critique of the form, however, Renza, tracing the writer's vain attempts at self-presence, seems to share Olney's nostalgia for the subject. More radical than either approach is Sprinker's "Fictions of the Self: The End of Autobiography." Relying on Michel Foucault's discussions of authorship, Sprinker denies the autobiographer a self beyond his textual productions. Foucault's author is merely "the projection onto the texts, in more or less psychological terms, of the traits, connections, continuities, and exclusions" a reader finds there.[7] Hence, as Olney might maintain, any work is potentially autobiographical, insofar as it evinces textual patterns, repetitions that convey an organizing impulse. Sprinker discusses Kierkegaard's philosophical meditations and Freud's *The Interpretation of Dreams* as autobiographical; similarly, he *rejects* Nietzsche's *Ecce Homo* as illusory autobiography, treating instead the more diffuse *Will to Power*, in which Nietzsche's sharp attacks on the subject are mirrored in the work's all but anonymous construction. The unassimilated journal entries, edited by a sister whom Nietzsche once likened to a "Hell-machine,"[8] become as valid an expression of self as an authentic retrospection, for what constitutes autobiography is textual repetition:

> Just as dream interpretation returns again and again to the navel of the dream, so autobiography must return perpetually to the elusive center of selfhood buried in the unconscious . . . for no autobiography can take place except within the boundaries of a writing where concepts of subject, self, and author collapse into the act of producing a text. (342)

The autobiographer both affirms and loses himself in the labyrinth of language.

These approaches—Olney's unity, Renza's difference, and Sprinker's multiplicity—I take to represent the three possible responses to the problem of the subject in autobiography, a problem of which the American autobiographers I shall treat were acutely aware.[9] Pushed to their limits, the approaches seem to be incompatible: the self is either concentrated or dispersed, or constituted in the play of difference. But Sprinker's discussion of repetition raises another possibility, implicit but never confronted by the essayists. In Valéry's quest for pure consciousness, for example, he reported what "a devil of a time" he had "with the *words*. I made more than a hundred drafts. The transitions cost me infinite trouble" (257). How does this obsessive rewriting affect Valéry's "self-portrait": does it confirm, upset, or complicate that pure intuition he sought? Renza refers to "the magical power" of Samuel Pepys to banish the past, making his life a series of eternally present diary entries. But what is the effect of this continuous return to the scene of writing? How does the constant rereading, rewriting, reperusal of the past affect Pepys's text? Sprinker comes closest to addressing the problem in his discussion of Kierkegaard and Freud. For the former, repetition is a kind of self-overcoming in which the author recovers "what recollection has lost by means of a transumption of the recollected object into an atemporal order—'eternity, which is the true repetition' " (330).[10] Freud's dreams similarly lead back to the nodal point of the unconscious, a supertemporal structure open, but ultimately impervious, to time. The writer's reworking of material rooted in the past paradoxically leads him out of time, to the realm of Platonic knowledge where all recollection repeats the *eidos*. But must the critic of autobiography sacrifice time? Is there no way to reconcile subjectivity, language, and the past? I suggest that an answer lies in the autobiographer who, more than anyone else, has defined these problems for us—Friedrich Nietzsche.

NIETZSCHE AS AUTOBIOGRAPHER

That Nietzsche should have written an autobiography at all is not the least of his paradoxes, for his critique of the subject is well known. Two years before *Ecce Homo* he had stated categorically, "there is no 'being' behind doing, effecting, becoming; 'the doer' is merely a fiction added to the deed . . . our entire science still lies under the misleading influence of language and has not disposed of that little changeling, 'the subject.' "[11] "No subject 'atoms,' " he wrote a year later. "The sphere of a subject constantly growing or decreasing, the center of the system constantly shifting; in cases where it cannot organize the appropriate mass, it breaks into two parts."[12] That same year, he attacked the notion in even stronger terms:

> The subject: this is the term for our belief in a unity underlying all the different impulses of the highest feeling of reality; we understand this belief as the *effect* of one cause—we believe so firmly in our belief that for its sake we imagine "truth," "reality," "substantiality" in general.—"The subject" is the fiction that many similar states in us are the effect of one substratum: but it is we who first created the "similarity" of these states; our adjusting them and making them similar is the fact, not their similarity (—which ought rather, to be denied—). (*WP* §485, 268–69)

In place of this phantom unity, Nietzsche posited "a multiplicity of subjects," each the expression of a local drive or will, competing for dominance in the body (*WP* §490, 270). The very question of essence, he maintained, implies perspective, "and already presupposes a multiplicity" (*WP* §556, 301). There could be no privileged position in a world of conflicting forces and constant change.

Nevertheless, as Stanley Corngold has noted,[13] Nietzsche was by no means so adamant as these statements suggest. To every assertion of multiplicity it is possible to oppose one of unity: "At the bottom of us, 'right deep down,' " there was "some granite of spiritual fate," Nietzsche thought, "a mighty commander, an unknown sage . . . called Self." "Whenever a cardinal problem is at stake, there speaks an unchangeable 'this is I.' "[14] And in *Ecce Homo* he writes of "that nethermost self [*unterste Selbst*] which had, as it were, been buried and grown silent under the continual pressure of having to listen to other selves," awakening as it pursued its own thoughts (287–88).[15] But Nietzsche often proposed a third view as well, a processual self that emerges as *Übermensch* after repeated encounters with the historically impotent. The "higher nature of the great man," he wrote in 1888, "lies in being different, in incommunability, in distance of rank" (*WP* §876, 468); he occupies "the pinnacle of the whole species of man: so high, so superior that everything would perish from envy of him" (*WP* §877, 469). He alone is individual, in contrast to the "herd"; indeed, it is precisely through "the presence of opposites and the feelings they occasion" that he develops at all (*WP* §967, 507). The *Übermensch* alone can claim authenticity: "I teach: that there are higher and lower men, and that a single individual can under certain circumstances justify the existence of whole millennia—that is, a full, rich, great, whole human being in relation to countless incomplete fragmentary men" (*WP* §997, 518). That Nietzsche considered himself a candidate for the position, *Ecce Homo* makes fairly clear; nevertheless, it is just as easy to read the text as a study in multiplicity, or in unity.[16] In fact, the work's chief interest lies in its providing a philosophical basis for the self in textuality, a grounding that, like Nietzsche's attempt "to say *who I am*" (*EH* 217), is all-inclusive.

Given the vigor of Nietzsche's thought, it is not surprising that critics are often reluctant to treat *Ecce Homo* as autobiography. One of his best biographers denies the text that status, and both Derrida and Rodolphe Gasché treat it as a modernist alternative to autobiography.[17] Although Nietzsche boldly announces his autobiographical intent—"Seeing that before long I must confront humanity with the most difficult demand ever made of it, it seems indispensable to me to say *who I am*" (217)—the text itself bears few features we normally associate with the genre. There is no chronological account of his childhood and youth, no discussion of his philological work, little talk of contemporaries or events. Instead, the text reads like an apology in which the author strives to convince us that he, Nietzsche, is the most momentous unknown of the nineteenth century. Accordingly, *Ecce Homo* unfolds, much like the late philosophical texts, in groups of numbered paragraphs bound together by chapter headings—"Why I Am So Wise," "Why I Am So Clever," "Why I Write Such Good Books," "Why I Am A Destiny." Between the latter two sections lies a chronological appraisal of his writings, from *The Birth of Tragedy* to *The Case of Wagner*, and preceding the text proper are an extended foreword and a single page that Derrida has called an "exergue or . . . flysheet."[18] The man is the sum of his works.

Yet Nietzsche's largely topical account of himself is not without precedent. Jerome Cardan divides *The Book of My Life* into some fifty chapters, including such issues as "Erudition, or the Appearance of It," "Successes in My Practice," "Concerning My Health," "Books I Have Written," "Things of Worth Which I Have Achieved in Various Studies," and so on.[19] Similarly, Montaigne's *Essays* presents himself through the lenses of nearly one hundred diverse subjects. One might also associate *Ecce Homo* with the topical structure of Thoreau's *Walden*, and—insofar as the writings of Nietzsche's American master are autobiographical—with Emerson's *Essays*. Moreover, in the course of presenting himself, Nietzsche gives enough autobiographical detail to make this text more than philosophy: he offers recollections of his father; of his military service; of his professorship in Basel, his travels in Europe, and the circumstances of his books; and of the two signal friends of his life—Lou Salomé and Richard Wagner. As a summary of his career, the text is given added weight by its finality: saying who he was had no more urgent need than just before he was silenced forever. *Ecce Homo*, then, intends no more than the role Georg Misch assigned to all autobiographies: it seeks to give Nietzsche's life "philosophical dignity."[20]

If Nietzsche is the bearer of good news for humanity, one ought to be able to chart the growth of his prophetic power. Read in this way, *Ecce Homo* could resemble a spiritual autobiography—the progress of a thinker from isolation to saving truth. That truth appears in the sections devoted to *Thus Spoke Zarathustra*, attended by all the trappings of conversion. "Has anyone at the end of the nineteenth century a clear idea of what poets of strong ages have called *inspiration*?" Nietzsche asks. It is more than the idea "that one is merely incarnation, merely mouthpiece, merely a medium of overpowering forces":

> The concept of revelation—in the sense that suddenly, with indescribable certainty and subtlety, something becomes *visible*, audible, something that shakes one to the last depths and throws one down—that merely describes the facts. One hears, one does not seek; one accepts, one does not ask who gives; like lightning, a thought flashes up, with necessity, without hesitation regarding its form—I never had any choice. (300)

Nietzsche's valuation of *Zarathustra* was—to use one of his favorite adjectives—"tremendous" (*ungeheuer*). He reckons the place and the hour of revelation—that "holy spot" (302) in Sils-Maria, "6000 feet beyond man and time" in August 1881 (295). And although he denies his will to prophecy, the account, with its biblical ladder on which Zarathustra "ascends and descends" (304), its boast that the most inspired poets are "not even worthy of tying the shoelaces of Zarathustra" (304), leaves little doubt that Nietzsche considered this his highest achievement. Not only was Zarathustra able to resolve all philosophical contradiction ("in him all opposites are blended into a new unity. The highest and the lowest energies of human nature, what is sweetest, most frivolous, and most terrible wells forth from one fount with immortal assurance," 305), but he is seemingly capable of resolving Nietzsche's contradictions as well. Like Zarathustra, Nietzsche melds opposites. He was the greatest Nay-sayer, yet the "bringer of glad tidings"; the "most terrible human being that has existed so far" and the "most beneficial" (327); a mere man, yet no man at all, but "dynamite" (326). It was Zarathustra who first recognized the corrosion of morality, and Nietzsche, Zarathustra's *Döppelganger* (225), who confirmed it. "Am I understood?—The self-overcoming of morality, out of truthfulness; the self-overcoming of the moralist, into his opposite—into me—that is what the name of Zarathustra means in my mouth" (328). *Zarathustra* was Nietzsche's experience of unity.

Preceding this climax in the text is a long foreground in which Nietzsche gradually confronts error, a process he portrays as a detachment from the herd. In *Ecce Homo*, "herd" usually means "German." Thus, Nietzsche invents Polish noblemen to supplement his Saxon ancestors, and Russian fatalism to counter German decadence (225, 231). German climate and food conspired to deny him "welcome memories...from [his] whole childhood and youth" (241); German literature was provincial, German politics atavistic (243, 320–21). Haunting his struggles with the German spirit is Richard Wagner, benefactor and father-figure, the break with whom was an epoch in Nietzsche's life.[21] In Tribschen, where they first met, the young Basel professor revered the musician "as a *foreign* land, as an antithesis, as an incarnate protest against all 'German virtues' " (247), and found his wife, Cosima, one of the most brilliant women in Europe (243). And yet, as mentor Wagner was always ambiguous. If he was revolutionary, he was also poisonous (322); if he was the century's greatest musician he was also its greatest decadent (248). Again and again Nietzsche returns to the paradox of Wagner—the master's subtle cosmopolitanism crippled by his anti-Semitism (284–85), his appeal to the intellect compromised by his appeal to the *canaille*. "What did I never forgive Wagner?" Nietzsche asks. "That he *condescended* to the Germans—that he became *reichsdeutsch*" (248). Success had tainted his genius.

The break came at Bayreuth after Nietzsche, long pleading illness, fell victim to the "Wagnerian morass" (227):

> Wherever was I? There was nothing I recognized; I scarcely recognized Wagner. In vain did I leaf through my memories. Tribschen—a distant isle of the blessed: not a trace of any similarity. The incomparable days when the foundation stone was laid . . . not a trace of any similarity. *What had happened?*—Wagner had been translated into German! The Wagnerian had become master over Wagner.—*German* art. The *German* master. *German* beer. (284)

That crisis (the first draft of section 2 refers to the incident as *eine heftige Krisis*—"a severe crisis")[22] was to be accompanied by two more: the worsening health that forced Nietzsche to leave Basel University, and the failed friendship with Lou Salomé, in many ways the catalyst for *Zarathustra*.[23] Each incident marked a weakening of Nietzsche's (putative) ties to his culture, a progressive isolation that made him ripe for *Zarathustra*'s transformative vision. Like a Christian seeker, Nietzsche had endured torments for an ideal.[24]

But surely this reading—the organizing of a life around a single, quasi-religious motive—is incomplete. Despite Nietzsche's ejaculations, for example, the "conversion" was not powerful enough to corral the herd, and the text is studded with the ache of unacknowledged genius. In vain does Nietzsche seek among Germans "some sign of tact, of *délicatesse* in relation to me" (324); "I only need to speak with one of the 'educated' who come to the Upper Engadine for the summer, and I am convinced that I do *not* live" (217). Indeed, ten years after his first important work, "nobody in Germany has felt bound in conscience to defend my name against the absurd silence under which it lies buried" (324). Occasionally the annoyance flared into outright rancor. In a passage excised from the final draft, Nietzsche found far different consequences in his liberating vision:

> At that time, what is most deeply constant in me moved against me with ruthless enmity. No more reverence for my solitude. In the midst of the ecstasies of Zarathustra, struck in the face by handsful of rage and poison . . . I touch on the most uncanny [*unheimlichste*] experience of my life, my only *bad* experience, which invaded my life to incalculably destructive effect. In all those moments when I suffered the enormity of my destiny, there burst upon me something of the utmost indecency [*etwas Äusserste von Indecenz*]. (*MS* 72.1–6, my trans.)[25]

The highest experience that was to transform humanity became a pretext for persecution; indeed the very stridency of Nietzsche's claims for *Zarathustra* may well have compensated for his thorough anonymity. But there are other, more poignant compensations. Nietzsche's adult life was an incessant quest for the quack cures to be had at Europe's spas and sanatoria; in *Ecce Homo* he disguises his desperation as the search for a diet and climate proper to philosophy. Less than a year before his collapse, he cheers himself up with claims that he has never had a fever, has sound digestion (he often vomited phlegm for days), and adequate eyesight, despite his near blindness ("with every increase in vitality my ability to see has also increased again," 223). Not only has he prodigious power (*der furchbarste Mensch, KG* 364), but great health (298). On the eve of his collapse in Turin, he is dynamite; he is Dionysus; he is destiny (326, 335). All of this suggests that the crisis *Zarathustra* addresses was unresolved, that *Ecce Homo* cannot be unified through the conversion paradigm. There remains a destructive surplus.

THE SELF AS OTHER

The strongest evidence for the text's irresolution, its multiplicity, lies in its abundant dyads. For example, in order to justify the demands he will make of humanity, Nietzsche must announce his identity:

> Really one should know it, for I have not left myself "without testimony" [*nicht unbezeugt gelassen*]. But the disproportion between the greatness of my task and the *smallness* of my contemporaries has found expression in the fact that one has neither heard nor even seen me. I live on my own credit; it is perhaps a mere prejudice that I live. (217; *KG* 255)

He must state who he is, yet he does not live. He writes to an audience that has neither read nor understood him, one he considers too feeble for comprehension, yet upon which he relies for the success of his great undertaking. His philosophical canon, to be paraded before the reader one final time, he introduces with the double negative of a *litotes*—"not . . . 'without testimony.' " And there is the curious monetary metaphor that Derrida has made so much of: he lives on his own credit, this pinched unknown, who more than anything else demands, *"do not mistake me for someone else"* (217).[26] He approaches his audience only to shun it, pleads for community while confirming his solitude. His desire secludes him.

Most of the numerous oppositions in the text seem to echo these dyads of distance/intimacy, and isolation/union. Nietzsche claims, for example, to possess a "perfectly uncanny [*unheimliche*] sensitivity" to dirt, an ability to smell the very " 'entrails' of every soul," and to burrow down to "the abundant *hidden* dirt at the bottom of many a character" (233; *KG* 273). Such intimacy, however, merely increases his "reserve," causing "no little difficulties in [his] contacts with other men" (233). Writing, too, is a blend of intimacy and distance, a "spiritual pregnancy" to be protected from the "outside stimuli" of other books. "Should I permit an *alien* thought to scale the wall secretly?" (242). His very body is both intimate and alien, the corpse of his father possessing his mother's animation (222), a sense exemplified in the distance and depth of *Zarathustra*. His prophetic work was "the highest book there is, the book that is truly characterized by the air of the heights—the whole fact of man lies *beneath* it at a tremendous [*un-geheuer*] distance—it is also the *deepest*, born out of the innermost wealth of truth, an inexhaustible well to which no pail descends without coming up again filled with gold and goodness" (219; *KG* 257). But such capacious reserve is paradoxical, for if Nietzsche's task was to prepare humanity's "*great noon*," its liberation from priestcraft and cowardice, he could not avoid his own isolation. Zarathustra's vision is essentially millennial—a great health in a world "whose boundaries nobody has surveyed yet," a world bursting with the "beautiful, strange, questionable, terrible, and divine," open to all humanity throughout an indefinite future (299). In *The Gay Science*, the work immediately preceding *Zarathustra*, Nietzsche put the matter even more forcefully. The *Übermensch* will appropriate all time and all humanity—the grief of the invalid and the old man, of the martyr and the mourner, the nobility of all intellects and heroes:

> if one could burden one's soul with all this—the oldest, the newest, losses, hopes, conquests, and the victories of humanity: if one could finally contain all this in one soul and crowd it into a single feeling—this would surely have to result in a happiness that humanity has not known so far.... This godlike feeling would then be called humaneness.[27]

One senses that Nietzsche experienced this bracing unity at Sils-Maria; and yet the center could not hold, for genius begets isolation. "One comes to men, one greets friends—more desolation, no eye offers a greeting" (*EH* 303). For this "*solitude* become man" (343) there was simply no bridging the vast distance between heroism and the herd.

Nietzsche's travail is not belated romantic agony but the working through of a philosophical problem. If the self is a unity, one ought to be able to find unity in its attributes. Nietzsche attempts as much in his assertions of great health and wit, and in his treatment of his *oeuvre* as the elaboration of a single great theme. But he was too honest, too driven to admit superficial closure; hence he riddles his text with oppositions that resist unity. If he is an epoch in history, he is also a corpse, dispersed by the attacks of his tormentors—a multiplicity of subjects. But if all this is true, if "Friedrich Nietzsche" is no more than a "mere prejudice," how are we to account for his insistence on the personal pronoun, the sense of hard-won integrity and vitality that pervades the text, even in translation? What are we to make of the feeling that we are being addressed not by a diffuse author, but by an authority?

One answer may lie in a complex of words weaving through the text like an Ariadne's thread—the words *ungeheuer, heimlich, unheimlich*, and their cognates. The latter pair, as readers of Freud's essay "The 'Uncanny' " know, are intimately related—*heimlich* meaning hidden, secret, homely, familiar, trustworthy; *unheimlich* meaning unfamiliar, wonderful, fearful, terrible, or uncanny. *Ungeheuer* is often translated enormous, prodigious, monstrous, or fearful—uncanny; that is, something *unheimlich* may also be experienced as *ungeheuer*—spectacularly at odds with nature. The *unheimlich* may also be concealed, buried, or withheld, "so that others do not get to know of or about it."[28] In certain instances, as Freud demonstrates, the *heimlich* may well be *unheimlich*—concealed even from oneself. Nietzsche, the consummate German stylist, was aware of these filiations. Reflecting on the effect of climate, for example, he commends dry air and clear skies for their stimulation of "great, even tremendous [*ungeheuer*] quantities of strength." His own sensitivity allows him to "take readings from [him]self as from a very subtle and reliable instrument," and to "reflect with horror on the *dismal* [*unheimliche*] fact" that most of his life was spent in the wrong places (241; *KG* 280–81). Here the uncanny act of reading himself is associated with heroic weather. Similarly heroic was the labor needed for Nietzsche's moral message, the "revaluation of all values." He had to cultivate the most contrary capacities, he tells us—"more . . . than have ever dwelt together in a single individual . . . a tremendous variety [*eine ungeheure Vielheit*] that is nevertheless the opposite of chaos—this was the precondition, the long, secret work and artistry [*geheime Arbeit und Kunsterschaft*] of my instinct" (254; *KG* 292). As psychologist, Nietzsche has an "uncanny sensitivity" (*unheimliche Reizbarkeit*) to the inner corruptions of others, an ability to "get a hold of every secret [*jedes Geheimnis betaste*]: the abundant *hidden* dirt at the bottom of many a character" (*der viele verborgene Schmutz auf dem Grunde mancher Natur*) (233; *KG* 273). And yet he is no bogeyman, no "moral monster" (*kein Moral-Ungeheuer*) (217; *KG* 255), no monstrous beast (*Popanz*), not one of "those frightful hermaphrodites of sickness and will to power" (*keiner jener schauerlichen Zwitter von Krankheit und Willen zur Macht*) (*KG* 257, my trans.). Rather he announces with "tremendous sureness" (*ungeheueren Sicherheit*) (288; *KG* 325) an epoch in human history, one that is certain to link him with "something tremendous [*etwas ungeheures*]—a crisis without equal on earth" (326; *KG* 363). That he is now unknown, secret, without readers does not concern him; ultimately all will discover that "tremendous up and down of sublime, of superhuman passion" (*eines ungeheuren Auf und Nieder sublimer, von übermenschlicher Leidenschaft*) that marks his greatest truths (265; *KG* 303).

Among Nietzsche's most persistent associations in *Ecce Homo* is that involving the secret or uncanny and writing. The thread begins on the "flysheet," dated October 15, 1888, where Nietzsche "burie[s]" his forty-fourth year, to be preserved in the texts he produced: *The Antichrist, Dionysus Dithyrambs*, and *Twilight of the Idols* (221). The burial, then, was also a pregnancy, the hidden development of genius—a point he makes in the opening riddle. "I am ... already dead as my father, while as my mother I am still living and becoming old" (222). That is, in his susceptibility to illness he bears the corpse of his father; in his literary fecundity he bears the corpus of his mother.[29] As such, his writing is vital and intimate, "an inexhaustible well to which no pail descends without coming up again filled with gold and goodness" (219), "a net that ... brings up from the depths something incomparable" (290). And yet the exacting labor of writing gives birth to an Other, something alien and distant: "Nietzsche" himself had to die so that the work of his forty-fourth year could survive; and although his works are "immortal" (221), as author he does "*not* live" (217). As Gertrude Stein might say, he was a posthumous autobiographer.

The autobiographer captures the ambiguities of life-writing in a telling association of text, woman, and terror. When he is writing, he discloses, he never reads—a practice closely related to gestation:

> Has it been noted that in that profound tension to which pregnancy condemns the spirit, and at bottom the whole organism, chance and any kind of stimulus from the outside have too vehement an effect and strike too deep? One must avoid chance and outside stimuli as much as possible; a kind of walling oneself in belongs among the foremost instinctive precautions of spiritual pregnancy. Should I permit an *alien* thought to scale the wall secretly [*dass ein fremder Gedanke heimlich über die Mauer steigt*]?— And that is what reading would mean. (242; *KG* 282)

Here, in order to protect what is authentically *his* creation, Nietzsche must not only situate it deep within him, but define all other texts as alien—even though (or precisely because) these texts can so easily penetrate. But if woman is associated with the highest creativity, she is equally threatening, a parasite disrupting Nietzsche's labor. Hence, in a passage excised by Elisabeth Förster-Nietzsche, the philosopher heaps scorn upon his female component:

> When I seek my deepest opposite, the incalculable vulgarity of the in-
> stincts, I always find my mother and sister,—to believe that I am related to
> such *canaille* would blaspheme my divinity. The treatment that I have ex-
> perienced from my mother and sister to this very moment, fills me with an
> unnameable horror: here works a perfect Hell-machine, with unfailing cer-
> tainty, from moment to moment, until it can bloodily wound me. (*KG* 266,
> my trans.)

What inhabits him is also a monstrous alien, not a single female principle but a multiple Other. The *heimlich* is *unheimlich*; the spiritual
pregnancy of writing is also a bloody wound. Indeed, with the birth of
Zarathustra even the immortal work, like the indwelling female, becomes an enemy:

> everything great—a work, a deed—is no sooner accomplished than it turns
> *against* the man who did it. By doing it, he has become *weak*; he no longer
> endures his deed, he can no longer face it. Something one was never per-
> mitted to will lies *behind* one, something in which the knot in the destiny of
> humanity is tied—and now one labors *under* it—It almost crushes one.
> (303)

The associations have come full circle; the intimate has become *ungeheuer*, and the expression of one's deepest truths has become destructive text.[30]

THE RETURN OF THE REPRESSED

"I am one thing," Nietzsche begins the review of his works, "my writings are another matter" (259). Acutely aware of the problems of the
subject, Nietzsche was unwilling to consider any simple equivalence
between life and text—nor was he willing to be dissolved into those
texts so abused by his contemporaries. For Nietzsche, as for Derrida,
writing was that dangerous supplement, the alien within, always already present, screening the self from experience.[31] But to a thinker
whose life's work was the revaluation of all values, such alienation was
all the more horrifying. Seeking that unity of experience available only
to the *Übermensch*, he found himself dispersed, undermined by a language he shared with the herd. Autobiography, by this logic, was
impossible.

But here, after putting his entire corpus at risk, Nietzsche rescues
it through a deliberate reversal. In his discussion of the break with
Wagner, the masculine principle of death suddenly emerges to rescue
him from both Basel and Bayreuth. The "*wicked* heritage" of his father,
the corpse he carried within, overcame and delivered him. "Sickness
detached me slowly; it spared me any break, any violent and offensive

step.... My sickness also gave me the right to change all my habits completely; it permitted, it *commanded* me to forget . . . I was delivered from the 'book' " (287). Unable to read or to teach, he could only think and write—wall himself off from the outside and dig deeper: "That nethermost self which had, as it were, been buried and grown silent under the continual pressure of having to listen to other selves (and that is after all what reading means) awakened slowly, shyly, dubiously,—but eventually it spoke again" (287–88). Sickness brought great health—a " 'return to [him]self' " ("*Rückkehr zu mir*") and to his own corpus. This turning—marked by the "crossing" in the post of texts Wagner and Nietzsche sent to each other (288; *KG* 324)—signifies a profound shift in the philosopher's attitude toward writing, the assumption of his prophetic *oeuvre*. Just as he would advocate revaluation, so he used the crisis to revalue his work, his friendship, and his texts. If formerly Nietzsche claimed he was "no monster" (217), now he delights in animal associations: in *Dawn* he is a "sea-animal," basking among the Genoese rocks (290); in *Zarathustra* he is a "female elephant" (295); his thoughts are "divine lizards" (290).[32] Such reversals did not necessarily defuse writing; indeed, as Nietzsche pursued his innermost thoughts, he became increasingly dangerous, an explosive thinker skirting madness. What counted, though, was the desire to enter the corpse of language, and to do so continuously and joyously, to declare himself for himself.

What prevents the self from dissolving into a meaningless play of forces, Paul Ricoeur has said, is the labor of interpretation, the subject's desire to be "reborn in the guise of the interpreter."[33] For Nietzsche, that desire to overcome the dispersions of language is to be found in the rereading of his works, in which his philosophy is the unfolding of a single theme.[34] Already in *The Birth of Tragedy*, despite Wagnerian contamination, he rediscovers "the only parable and parallel in history for my own inmost experience," the symbol of Dionysus (271). There too he now sees the unfolding of what Zarathustra would call the Eternal Return, "a Yes-saying without reservation, even to suffering, even to guilt, even to everything that is questionable and strange in existence" (272). In *Richard Wagner in Bayreuth* he detects "the pre-existent poet of *Zarathustra*, sketched with abysmal profundity" (274), as in *Human, All-Too-Human* he finds a "merciless spirit" invading all the "hideouts [*alle Schlupfwinkel*] of the ideal . . . its secret dungeons and . . . ultimate safety" (283; *KG* 320). In *The Untimely Ones* he plumbs the decadence of scholarship from within, confirming his "prudence": "I was many things and in many places in order to be able to become one thing—to be able to attain one thing. I *had* to be a scholar, too, for some time" (282). Life had groomed him for his messianic role.

But Nietzsche's rereading is even more radical. Collapsing the distinction between signifier and signified, he interprets all his texts as autobiographical *in their entirety*—as expressions of his inmost, Dionysian nature. Regarding *Wagner in Bayreuth*, he has this to say: "in all psychologically decisive places I alone am discussed—and one need not hesitate to put down my name or the word 'Zarathustra' where the text has the word 'Wagner' " (274). In *The Untimely Ones*, Schopenhauer and Wagner, the two harbingers of "a higher concept of culture," are, "in one word, Nietzsche" (277). The name of Voltaire in one of his essays is really an expression of "progress—*toward me*" (283). "With instinctive cunning," he now discloses, he "avoided the little word 'I' " (289) in order to be bathed again in "world historical" glory (288): Nietzsche as Paul Rée, as Montaigne, as Racine, Corneille, and Molière, as Dionysus, and as Antichrist. In thus encompassing his writing, in experiencing both "the fullness and self-assurance of a *rich* life" and "the secret work [*die heimliche Arbeit*] of the instinct of decadence" (223; *KG* 264)—in looking backward and forward—Nietzsche reappropriates himself. But this "highest" and "deepest" insight into his existence is nothing more than the eternal recurrence of the same, the saying Yes to all things (305–6). The act of re-vision, then, is Nietzsche's attempt to reunite life and text. After the works of his forty-fourth year, "*How could I fail to be grateful to my whole life?*" And so the autobiographer tells his life to himself (221).

By revision I mean the act of rewriting in the most literal sense— not only Nietzsche's effort to reconstruct his life as the text of *Ecce Homo*, but the continual rereadings of that text, the adjustments and erasures that produced the final draft.[35] Each addition to the text became a reaffirmation of the whole life, an acknowledgment that this language, with all its strangeness, portrayed "*my* life" (221, emphasis added). By revising his text, by retelling his life to himself, the writer comes to know himself in and through the act of revision, as subject and language meet at the surface of the leaf that marks their constantly dissolving boundary.[36] Conversely, each new phrase is a synecdochic affirmation of the whole, both shaping and being shaped by the text; each textual addition, as Nietzsche's rereading indicates, must disclose the unity of the writer's experience.[37]

For Nietzsche, by definition, this affirmation is a process, a constant becoming in which being takes shape; hence the subtitle of *Ecce Homo*: "How One Becomes What One Is." But as Rodolphe Gasché has observed, the continuous becoming of being in the text, the saying Yes to every moment of life, yields a version of self that is neither portrait nor reflection. If *"nosce te ipsum"* was a "recipe for ruin" (*EH* 254), if the self, like the world, is defined only in the continuous play of forces,[38] then the unity of Nietzsche's autobiography must be found not in a *Gestalt*, a monolithic gathering of attributes, but as *typos* or type—a symbol of the whole capable of being deformed by what it symbolizes— subject to constant change.[39] Like the complex *heimlich-unheimlich* that Nietzsche associated with writing, the word *typos*, according to Liddell's *Greek-English Lexicon*, is richly ambiguous.[40] The word can mean at once a *model* or *pattern* "capable of exact repetition in numerous instances," or the thing stamped, such as the impression of a seal. *Typos* is that which *imparts form*, such as a "die used in striking coins," or that which *receives form*, "a hollow mould or matrix." The word may also refer to texts: to an *inscription*, such as engraved letters; or to the *document* made of those letters; to a rough draft of an official document, or to the complete text. Finally, *typos* may signify the "order and spacing," the "attacks and intervals of a fever," as well as a "rule of life, a religion." As such, the word reduplicates the problem of the subject Nietzsche explored in *Ecce Homo*. Like the *typos*, Nietzsche's "I" is an entity that both gives form to and is stamped by a text that it both engenders and receives, in a process admitting continuous repetition and containing not only the contents of a particular individual, but also the rules for a general life—a life that would overcome the repeated attacks of a personal and cultural malaise. In a sense, *typos* incorporates the self.

A skilled philologist, Nietzsche was aware of this play of meanings, and used it in his autobiography. In *The Untimely Ones*, he "caught hold of two famous and as yet altogether undiagnosed types" (*noch unfestgestellte Typen*), much as Plato used Socrates, to disclose himself (280; *KG* 317–18). The two were "formulas" or "signs" for classes of individuals (280). With "a perfectly uncanny sagacity" (*volkommen unheimlicher Sagacität*, 280), however, the "educators" also revealed what was "the true primary meaning and fundamental substance" of *Nietzsche's* being (quoting *Schopenhauer as Educator*, 281 n)—the models, in turn, becoming signs for the play of Nietzschean forces. It was on walks in the fall of 1886 that Nietzsche recognized Zarathustra himself as a "type" (298), a "contrary type [*Gegensatz-Typus*] that is as little modern as possible—a noble, Yes-saying type [*einem vornehmen, einem jasagenden Typus*]" (310; *KG* 348). For the Eternal Return was intimately bound up with the *typos*: "saying Yes to life even in its strangest and hardest problems; the will to life rejoicing over its own inexhaustibility even in the very sacrifice of its highest types [*seiner höchsten Typen*]—

that is what I called Dionysian" (273; *KG* 310). Just as Zarathustra is folded into Dionysus, so the autobiographer was folded into his texts, in a continuous revision that defined "Nietzsche," too, as a resultant of forces, an inter-pretation. As *typos*, Nietzsche was both writer and exemplar, subject and sign, Dionysus *and* the Crucified.

But just as Dionysus may destroy even his highest types, so the text of *Ecce Homo*—Nietzsche's attempt at unity through revision—leaves a destructive surplus. The text, unpublished during his lifetime (it appeared in 1908), fell into the hands of another editor, that "Hell-machine" Elisabeth Förster-Nietzsche, whom the writer—in a passage his sister excised—had called "the deepest objection to the 'eternal return,' my own *abysmal* thought" (*KG* 266, my trans.). She removed attacks on racialism and anti-Semitism, on her husband, Bernhard Förster, and on other German "*canaille*"; in Nietzsche's terms, she epitomized "the *rancune* of what is great," almost crushing him (303). Förster-Nietzsche, though, was merely the most immediate expression of the uncanny power of writing, that Other inhabiting the self. For once he gave birth to his texts, Nietzsche knew, he must consign them to the herd, that larger pool of interpreters always already in possession of his language.

One senses this in an emblematic revision Nietzsche himself made in "Why I Write Such Good Books," section 3, a sardonic defense of his texts. With droll menace, the original version describes his philosophical corpus:

> I come from another *depth*; similarly, I also come from another *height*; who would know, without me, what high and deep are. Fortunately I also do not want to be an honorable man. I seek my honor in being master of every corruption,—my last desire for honor was to talk about myself with Swabians and other cows. What, above all, spoils readers familiar with my writing is my bravery: everywhere one moves dangerously; not for nothing is one intimate with the beautiful Ariadne[.] One has a special curiosity for the Labyrinth—an acquaintance with Sir Minotaur himself will by no means be declined. (*MS* 36.21–25; my trans.)

Here again are the oppositions of intimacy and distance Nietzsche associates with writing, the burrowing down to splendors, the sense of concealed strength. As in the foreword, Nietzsche reinforces these dyads through *litotes*: "not for nothing" does one desire Ariadne, and even a glance at the Minotaur "will by no means be declined." But there are other dyads here that make the act of *reading* treacherous as well. Both Ariadne and the Minotaur, beauty and terror, reside in the labyrinth of Nietzsche's dangerous texts; hence the nihilist cows yield to the devouring figure of the author, the Minotaur at the center. The message is clear: only by adopting Nietzsche's heroism can the reader hope to survive.

The published revision, however, largely fragments the first draft, reassembling phrases in a manner suggesting less Nietzsche's own menace than the destructive potential of all reading. Here is Kaufmann's translation:

> All "feminism," too—also in men—closes the door: it will never permit entrance into this labyrinth of audacious insights. One must never have spared oneself, one must have acquired hardness as a habit to be cheerful and in good spirits in the midst of nothing but hard truths. When I imagine a perfect reader, he always turns into a monster of courage and curiosity [*so wird immer ein Unthier von Muth und Neugierde daraus*]; moreover, supple, cunning, cautious; a born adventurer and discoverer. (264; *KG* 301)

Gone now are the mythical figures, as is Nietzsche himself, whose heroism is replaced by that of the ideal reader—not only brave, as was Nietzsche, but monstrous. The reader has become Minotaur, a savage animal possessing a "labyrinth" of his own, associated by Derrida with the ear.[41] But the menace of Nietzsche's ideal reader should not be surprising, for he, too, determines what the author would become, in a process Paul de Man called "mutual reflexive substitution."[42] He, too, revises, interprets, dissolves; reinserting into the text that instability Nietzsche sought to control through his own continuous revision. Even the Yes-saying of Dionysus was not immune to the reader's influence, the endless play of difference that allows no closure.

That insight imposes a final paradox upon *Ecce Homo*, one we will see repeatedly in American autobiographies. Nietzsche's autobiographical act began in a moment of crisis. Suppose, he asked in *The Gay Science*, a demon were to enter his "loneliest loneliness," to suggest that his life, with "every pain and every joy and every thought and sigh ...even this spider and this moonlight between the trees" would interminably recur: "Would you not throw yourself down and gnash your teeth and curse the demon who spoke thus? Or have you experienced a tremendous moment when you would have answered him: 'You are a god and never have I heard anything more divine' " (273–74). Confronting his solitude as destiny, Nietzsche attempts to render it "immortal" in the form of an infinitely reproducible text, an autobiography in which he recounts his life to himself. Isolated in his weakness, he seeks communion—not only through an affirmation of "everything ... small or great," but with his readers. Hence he becomes a type, a symbol of overcoming, a Dionysus rendering the chaos of "every pain and every joy" into the "ultimate eternal confirmation and seal" of a great soul (274). But now returns the demon in the guise of *Unthier*—a woman, a sister, an anti-Semite—and again demands his assent: will Nietzsche accept this reader into his labyrinth? Will he consent to this return? To do so is to deliver himself to loneliness and dispersion, to renewed crisis and despair. Yes-saying does not overcome the perversions of such readers. "One day," Nietzsche predicted with unconscious irony, "my name will be associated with the memory of something tremendous [*Ungeheures*]—a crisis without equal on earth" (326). His prophecy of Nazi perversions was all too accurate. But that, too, is the logic of revision, the "crushing" thought of the Eternal Return. There could be no final release from the herd.

In the following pages, I will explore these issues through a range of American life-writings I call "millennial autobiographies." Implicitly or explicitly, each of these texts reduplicates Nietzsche's strategies, attempting an ephemeral unity by confronting its own dispersion. But these autobiographies are distinctive, I believe, in the thoroughness with which they adopt synecdoche, Nietzsche's revisionary trope. This I attempt to demonstrate in Chapter 2, by contrasting John Stuart Mill's *Autobiography* with Walt Whitman's *Specimen Days*. Crisis lies at the core of each work, as it did for Nietzsche: Mill endures a mental collapse; Whitman endures civil war and paralysis. But Whitman's nostalgia for the divine average, the American type, puts him much closer to Nietzsche than does Mill's need for distinction—a need he shared with many of his compatriots. If Whitman's defining trope is synecdoche, Mill's is antithesis.

Chapter 3 traces the roots of Whitman's trope in two early American autobiographers, Thomas Shepard and John Woolman. For Shepard, who migrated from England in 1635, America represented an escape from a demonic and isolating labyrinth. Hence, his *Autobiography* attempts to portray the American experience as corporate, a communal rather than atomic existence. John Woolman also struggled with solitude, fleeing corruption to a paradise within that increasingly threatened his millennialism. Only by means of revision could he project a partial resolution, in the last chapter of the *Journal*. Revision is central to Woolman's contemporary, Benjamin Franklin—the subject of Chapter 4—who not only portrayed himself as national *typos*, but also used his *Autobiography* as a recipe for re-creation. The attentive reader would learn not only the art of virtue, but the virtues of the text. For Franklin, writing was an act of self-affirmation.

With the nineteenth century, though, as Nietzsche knew, the cultural conditions supporting synecdoche waned—particularly in America, where individualism rapidly became ideology. Hence, as white male writers, seeking Mill's exclusiveness, increasingly abandoned millennial autobiography, those at the margins of power often pursued it, in a manner that exposed their vulnerability. There is no better exemplar of these new limits than Frederick Douglass, whose four versions of self, treated in Chapter 5, were poignant, failed pleas for representativeness. Imbued with Franklin's revolutionary millennialism, these texts nevertheless show the fissures and cleavages of *Ecce Homo*, as Douglass strives to incorporate a hostile white readership. The claim to representativeness would become even more attenuated in the twentieth century, as autobiographers at large came to realize the tensions Nietzsche explored. Certainly one of the most idiosyncratic responses to modernity belonged to Gertrude Stein, whose four autobiographies I discuss in Chapter 6. Despite her apparent association with the avant-garde, Stein, as I read her, was temperamentally a conservative who used her life-writing as a shelter from rapid change. Her aversion to audience, her apprehension of death, and her final disclosure as American type all closely relate her to the strategies of *Ecce Homo*. In the final chapter I examine the recent work of Lillian Hellman, Mary McCarthy, Maya Angelou, and W. E. B. Du Bois, to determine whether those strategies perdure.

One word more about methodology. Dominick LaCapra has recently warned against the perils of intention and context in historical interpretation. A lived "text" is seldom as explicit as its written counterpart, which may be affected by "patterns of development or by forms of repetition" that qualify or confute experience. Similarly, there need be no necessary correspondence between historical issues and those in particular texts; rather, the relation between text and context emerges only through considering the ways in which a culture uses texts, and texts use traditional ideas. "The problem becomes that of the way long tradition, specific time, and text repeat one another with variations," how both text and culture exist "in a fully relational network."[43] These cautions seem to apply *a fortiori* to the study of autobiography, a genre that provides a transcript neither of life nor of historical motives, but is an unstable compound of event and artifice, history and textuality. Hence, my discussion of these autobiographies explores two contrasting issues: how the author uses repetition in experience and text to create a "plot" for his or her life, and how that unity repeatedly succumbs to internal and external contradiction. The contest between these textual imperatives creates the autobiographer's complex image.

2 | *The American Voice: Walt Whitman*

Among his "nihilist" contemporaries, few annoyed Nietzsche more than "the flathead John Stuart Mill" (*WP* §30, 21). The English philosopher's defense of selfless "mutual services" (*WP* §926, 489) symbolized, for Nietzsche, the revenge of the herd, choking off nobility through democratic impotence. To such vulgar Utilitarianism, in which "all human intercourse...appears as a kind of payment for something done to us," Nietzsche opposed a Machiavellian *sang froid*, "an aristocratic segregation from the masses," necessary because the noble is, by definition, "unique and does only unique things" (*WP* §926, 489). But as all such philosophical claims are "a kind of...unconscious memoir" (*BGE* 19), so Nietzsche's opposition of the individual to the mass has wider implications—not only for Mill but for an entire category of Americans epitomized by another of Nietzsche's contemporaries, Walt Whitman. Like Nietzsche, both Whitman and Mill wrote autobiographies recording a central crisis, from which they turned to pursue higher ends. Both struggled, like Nietzsche, with overweening influences, and both fashioned a textual self through near obsessive revision. But Nietzsche was wrong in one respect: had he read the *Autobiography*, he might have seen that Mill prized "uniqueness" with a vehemence equal to his own. The synecdochic yearning for the masses was rather a trait to be found among Americans confronting the very problems of self that produced *Ecce Homo*.

In 1826 Mill experienced a mental crisis that Nietzsche himself might have understood. The young Utilitarian idealist and editor, flushed with Jeremy Bentham's schemes for the improvement of mankind, suddenly stopped his activities to confront himself. "Suppose," he asked in his *Autobiography*, "that all your objects in life were realized; that all the changes in institutions and opinions which you are looking forward to, could be completely effected at this very instant: would this be a great joy and happiness to you?"[1] The question, to a Utilitarian, was doubly ironic, for Bentham's creed projected the most sweeping social change through analysis of individual motives—a selfless devotion to humanity based on pleasure and pain. Attempting to apply that calculus to himself, Mill was shocked to find no feeling at all, as if his identity had become wholly fused with abstract social aims. Yet those aims, too, seemed to vanish, and he wondered whether he had ever known true attachment. "There is now no human being," he wrote to John Sterling three years later, "(with whom I can associate on terms of equality) who acknowledges a common object with me, or, with whom I can cooperate even in any practical undertaking without the feeling, that I am only using a man whose purposes are different, as an instrument for the furtherance of my own."[2] It was a paradox so grave and insoluble that it almost drove this conscientious agnostic to faith; his state, he announced many years later, was like that "in which converts to Methodism usually are, when smitten by their first 'conviction of sin'" (*A* 137). Utilitarianism, however, had no such rituals, and Mill was forced to work out his crisis alone.

A generation later Walt Whitman faced a similar crisis. He had begun his literary career by proclaiming the union of artist and society. "Sanity and ensemble," he wrote in the 1855 preface to *Leaves of Grass*—the vital individual in a vital society—"characterize the great master.... The master knows that he is unspeakably great, and that all are unspeakably great."[3] What was more, this identity worked in reverse: America, that great-souled nation, embraced its heroes. "It rejects none, it permits all.... The soul of the largest and wealthiest and proudest nation may well go halfway to meet that of its poets" (458). But the Civil War shattered that unity. Sanity and ensemble were replaced by "a heap of amputated feet, legs, arms, hands";[4] by "butchers' shambles" of the wounded, some with "their legs blown off—some bullets through the breast—some indescribably horrid wounds in the face or head, all mutilated, sickening, torn, gouged out" (*SD* 46–47); by "the dead in this war ... strewing the fields and woods and valleys and battlefields of the south" (114). In *Specimen Days*, his fragmentary autobiography, Whitman recounts his efforts to bind up the wounds, his ministering to more than 80,000 soldiers in the hospitals in and around Washington—ever cheerful, ruddy, sympathetic. In his letters, though, he paints a different picture: these Americans, he confessed over and again, "see[m] not men but a lot of devils & butchers butchering each other." It was a view of his countrymen that made him "almost frightened at the world,"[5] and that literally destroyed his "sanity." For his strenuous benevolence hastened a stroke that would cripple him after the war, claim his populist health as the price of heroism. That, too, he records in *Specimen Days*, amid optimistic catalogs and meditations on nature: "(Ah, the physical shatter and troubled spirit of me the last three years)" (134). The good gray poet, expansive nationalist, was perhaps the greatest casualty of the war.

Despite such broad similarities, however, the two idealists resolve their crises differently—and in that difference lies an American ethos. As his meticulous revisions show, John Stuart Mill wrote to counteract the kind of selflessness Utilitarianism demanded. All his young life he had submitted to an autocratic father, and for much of his mature life, to his muse, Harriet Taylor. Those figures, most commentators agree, surround his mental crisis like the poles of a failed and an achieved ideal. Nevertheless, Mill was more than the sum of his influences: as he portrays these authorities, he attempts to subsume them under an identity of his own. For as Mill's crisis proves—and as his countrymen confirm—there was no middle ground: either one proclaimed individuality, or one yielded to the mass. One could not affirm both and remain sane. Sanity, for Whitman, however, lay precisely in that identification of self and others—again an identity his countrymen confirm. For Whitman's Americans, as for Nietzsche, personal identity was the product of a crisis of doubt followed by the affirmation of an ideal, a movement from isolation to a community that deepened one's individuality. That movement is one Whitman himself traces in *Specimen Days*, as he loses and partially recaptures the epic unity of 1855. In doing so, he defines the paradigmatic revisions of what might be called American "millennial" autobiographers.

JOHN STUART MILL'S *AUTOBIOGRAPHY*

So skillful is Mill in narrating his crisis that one tends to forget it is only an episode in a complex narrative with a triple aim: to record his "unusual" education; to catalog, in an "age of transition," the phases of his opinions; and to acknowledge his debts to others—particularly to Harriet Taylor (5). One forgets, too, that the text itself is communal and evolutionary, having matured through four drafts: an early draft, written by Mill in 1853 and recording his life up to his marriage in 1851; a second revised draft written in 1856; a third transcript made by Mill's stepdaughter after his death; and various rejected fragments, including sketches of his father and wife. Moreover, Harriet Taylor extensively edited the early draft, deleting criticisms of family and friends—2,600 changes in all—and Helen Taylor, to whom Mill bequeathed the second manuscript, added 450 changes of her own (*A* xxiv–xxviii). Finally, one must remember that even so powerful a section as the "crisis" of chapter 5 was written at a great remove. Mill adds illustrative snatches of poetry still alien to him in 1826, and skips repeatedly from his own feelings and thoughts to certain generalizations about art, Utilitarianism, and associational psychology. How can a reader hope to make headway, then, to disentangle "the internal culture of the individual," as Mill puts it, from the mass of intervening influences—if, indeed, there is an individual concealed in the *Autobiography* at all?

One might begin by treating the *process* of writing the entire *Autobiography* as a reflection of the mental crisis.[6] Although Mill informs us that he was "never again...as miserable" (145), the problem of adjusting his individual voice to the numerous perspectives around him remains constant. This he confesses in his initial apology:

> But I have thought that in an age in which education, and its improvement, are the subject of more, if not of profounder study than at any former period of English history, it may be useful that there should be some record of an education which was unusual and remarkable, and which, whatever else it may have done, has proved how much more than is commonly supposed may be taught, and well taught, in those early years which, in the common modes of what is called instruction, are little better than wasted. (5)

The long, tightly controlled sentence jumps from the general to the particular, from all English history to one remarkable boy, and from the vanity of a common education to the extraordinary density of Mill's own. So, too, does the next sentence, which carefully sets off "an age of transition in opinions" against "the successive phases of any mind which was always pressing forward"—the latter phrase itself a deft contrast between any mental specimen and the vigor of Mill's subtly urgent thought, "equally ready to learn and to unlearn either from its own thoughts or from those of others." Even the final acknowledgment of his debts bears a kernel of exclusiveness, since he reserves highest praise not for those of "recognized eminence" or for others less known, but for one "whom the world had no opportunity of knowing" (5). As he announces this conflict in the first paragraph, so Mill sustains it through the various phases of his autobiography; that is to say, at each stage of the composing process, Mill confronts the same "crisis": the disparity between the many influences he must acknowledge and the single voice that ought to emerge. Life, memory, writing, revision—all engage this elemental theme.

A consideration of two moments in the *Autobiography*, chapter 1, "Childhood and Early Education," and the first few pages of the "crisis" in chapter 5, may illustrate this point. In chapter 1 Mill describes his father's educational experiment—commencing when the boy was three with Greek and arithmetic, and progressing, by the chapter's end, to history and political economy—chiefly as a list of formidable texts. In one four-year siege of Latin, for example, he remembers reading "the *Bucolics* of Virgil, and the first six books of the *Aeneid*; all Horace except the *Epodes*; the fables of Phaedrus; the first five books of Livy . . . ; all Sallust; a considerable part of Ovid's *Metamorphoses*; some plays of Terence; two or three books of Lucretius; several of the Orations of Cicero, and of his writings on oratory; also his letters to Atticus" (15). To this he adds his work in Greek—all Homer; some Sophocles, Euripides, and Aristophanes; all Thucydides; parts of Xenophon, Demosthenes, Aeschines, Lysias, Theocritus, Anacreon, Polybius, and Aristotle. The modern reader gasps in astonishment, and Mill likely expected only a slightly milder reaction from late Victorians. Yet his purpose was less to impress than to place himself amid a large and significant "society"—the best history had to offer—organized by his father. Such a utopia, we are to understand, was his true home, a rigorous textual kingdom ruled by a benevolent despot. Much the same may be seen in a passage excised from the final draft, in which Mill summarized his workday at Ford Abbey. From seven until one, the boy studied and tutored his siblings. Then Bentham rose, and "regularly went out for the same invariable walk," always accompanied by James Mill. Later, father would catechize son, "which, when weather permitted, was always done in walking about the grounds." From one until six there were more "regularly allotted" lessons (56–57). Once again, Mill suggests massive textual order, innumerable decisions made for him by his father. Amid his books and stringent studies, even as he records them, he is submerged in those very "influences" he describes in the apology.

But curiously, the prose seems to reflect a certain rebelliousness: not Mill's admission into an intellectual society, but a struggle for mastery between father and son. Mill seeds the first chapter with such words as "compulsory," "constrained," "required," "command," and, above all, forms of the verb "make." Almost all refer in some way to his father. To take but a few examples of the last word: "Aristotle's *Rhetoric* my father made me study with peculiar care . . ." (14); "I remember his giving me Thomson's 'Winter' to read, and afterwards

making me attempt to write something myself on the same subject"
(18); "On Money ... he made me read in a similar manner" (30)—and
this extended passage:

> I well remember how ... he first attempted by questions to make me think
> on the subject, and frame some conception of what constituted the utility
> of the syllogistic logic, and when I had failed in this, to make me under-
> stand it by explanations. I do not believe that the explanations made the
> matter at all clear to me at the time; but they ... remained as a nucleus
> for my observations and reflexions to crystallize upon. (20, 22)

But just as Mill carefully underscores his uniqueness in the opening
apology, so, in chapter 2, he subtly counters his father, who

> impressed upon me from the first that the manner in which the world came
> into existence was a subject on which nothing was known; that the ques-
> tion "Who made me?" cannot be answered, because we have no experience
> from which to answer it; and that any answer only throws the difficulty a
> step further back, since the question immediately presents itself, Who
> made God? (44)

Here Mill subjects his father's overwhelming influence to a futile infinite
regress: as the autocrat's catechism has fashioned the son, so the son
renders him impotent by posing an unanswerable question. So with
this textual "self" his father was constructing over a palpable abyss. To
be made in such a way, Mill seems to be saying, is not really to be made
at all, but unmade—unfit for true social intercourse. Hence, in a rejected passage toward the end of the chapter, he cites his harsh lot, "in
the absence of love and in the presence of fear," shut off from friend-
ships with his peers and unable to perform even simple social tasks
(612). Imbued with an "instinct of closeness," he considers himself isolated, recalcitrant, distinct.

But the prose reflects this relation between father and son on a subtler level, an opposition of verbal voices like the opposition between
master and slave. Consider the following sentence:

> The first intellectual operation in which I arrived at any skill was dissect-
> ing a bad argument and finding in what part the fallacy lay: and though
> whatever success I had in this I owed entirely to the fact that it was an in-
> tellectual exercise in which I was most perseveringly drilled by my father;
> yet it is also true that the school logic, and the mental habits acquired in
> studying it, were among the principal instruments of this drilling. (22)

Every verb in this long sentence expresses state or being—"arrived,"
"acquired," the various forms of the verb "to be," and the numerous

gerunds—while only one phrase stands out: "most perseveringly drilled by my father." Mill composed the sentence in such a way as to highlight the latter phrase. James Mill, on the other hand—a man whose "senses and mental faculties were always on the alert," who "carried decision and energy of character in his whole manner" (39), who "severely took me to task for every violation of his rules" (26)—is almost uniformly surrounded by active verbs.[7] In the text, as in life, the father commands.

What looks like passivity, however, is quite possibly subtle resistance; for the mature Mill is ever aware of the purpose behind this extraordinary dominance: to make him a strong-willed thinker, Utilitarian hero, Bentham's apostle. Paradoxically, then, the only way to extract himself from that training is to appear resolutely passive and isolated, a stance Mill underscores in a concluding vignette. On the verge of entering the world at the age of fourteen, he was taken aside by his father in Hyde Park and cautioned against feeling proud of his learning. He reacts as he was taught, finding it "not at all . . . a personal matter" (37). But the fact was, as he soon informs us, that he was not conversant with society at all, having had "little stimulus" to any activity other than his father's syllabus. Prepared for a role he could barely conceive, Mill responded, but a few years later, with a grand despondency.

Among the paradoxes of Mill's upbringing was his father's insistence on David Hartley, preacher of associational psychology and the inner life. It was Hartley who claimed that the Lockean self, isolated by its own particularity, could nevertheless pass from the " 'gross self interest' of sensation, imagination, and ambition to the 'refined self interest' of sympathy . . . and the moral sense"; Hartley who claimed that the individual remains paramount in all discussions of benevolence and who saw pleasure as the rule of progress.[8] If James Mill's regimen had neglected anything, it was just this aspect of "self interest" and "pleasure," a point Mill himself dramatizes in chapter 4. Intending to describe not "the outside" of his character, but the picture to be had by "penetrating inward" to what the Utilitarians "really were as human beings" (110), he attempts to "speak only of [him]self," of his own motives and prejudices. But he does not remain with himself long, straying inevitably to his "father's teachings" and apologizing for the elder Mill's shortcomings. From thence he turns to Bentham's sect, which found its opinions "constantly attacked on the ground of feeling," and concludes that feeling "had very little place in the thoughts of most of us, myself in particular" (112). Only by tracing this great circle through his associates can Mill return to the point of departure, and of the *Autobiography*—his own inner life. Having achieved a command of eighteenth-century psychology, he found himself incapable of applying it.

That incapacity is clear in chapter 5, where Mill makes a sustained effort to resolve his Oedipal struggle. After recognizing that his "love of mankind and of excellence for their own sake, had worn itself out" (138), he offers a labored, fascinating explanation, throwing together all his childhood conflicts of influence and authority. Intellect, he now realizes, has destroyed feeling, yet it sustains his prose:

> Now I did not doubt that by these means, begun early and applied vigilantly, intense associations of pain and pleasure might be raised up, especially of pain, and might produce desires and aversions capable of lasting undiminished to the end of life. But there must always be something artificial and casual in associations thus generated. . . . For I now saw, or thought I saw, what I had always before received with incredulity—that the habit of analysis has a tendency to wear away the feelings . . . when no other mental habit is cultivated, and the analysing tendency remains without its natural complements and correctives. (140)

Once again, Mill uses verb forms expressing passiveness or state of being—"begun," "applied," "might be raised up," "received," "is cultivated"—even as he attempts to describe his own feelings. Although he is on the verge of rejecting much of his father's influence, he records the event as a dependent, still uncertain of his role. The prose reflects his doubt. "I was not incapable of my usual occupations," he reports; "I went on with them mechanically by the mere force of habit." So "drilled" was he in intellectual decorum, that he "could carry it on when all the spirit had gone out" (142). Clearly, the raw psychology of Hartley would not solve his problem, nor would thought at all, so heavily influenced by his father's regimen.

The problem was that Mill sought a self he could not wholly define. On the one hand were his father's strictures—a psychology that sustained passiveness, a dedication to the public life of party and discussion, to social aims, all subsumed in a mass of texts. On the other hand was Mill's internal revolution, isolating him from those very activities. The problem, he realized, was not his alone, but one inherent in Utilitarianism, which had attempted to bridge the great gap between the isolated, Lockean self and nineteenth-century society by projecting individual psychology upon all England. Mill's solution, announced in the *litotes* "not incapable," was to separate the two through a series of deft negations. After weeping over Marmontel, and perhaps, for the father he has symbolically killed,[9] Mill stumbles onto Carlyle's "anti-self-consciousness theory," and promptly finds a new way to address inwardness:

> I never indeed varied in the conviction that happiness is the test of all rules of conduct, and the end of life. But I now thought that this end was only to be attained by not making it the direct aim.... ask yourself if you are happy, and you cease to be so. The only chance is to treat not happiness but some end external to it, as the object of life. (144, 146)

Hegel calls this adjustment *Aufhebung*, a condition that simultaneously negates and preserves both sides of an opposition. Willing to sacrifice neither self nor society, Mill segregates them.[10] Those ideals of his father—those "external" features—remained "the true object of life"; but through this very renunciation of Hartleian self-consciousness, Mill prepared his inner life for a new analysis. He had begun the chapter with negation—the cloud over him "did not" pass away; a night's sleep had "no effect"; there was "no one" to assist him—and had penetrated to a selfless center of indifference, where "neither selfish nor unselfish pleasures were pleasures to me" (142). Now, discovering Carlyle and Wordsworth, he turns aside those negations through insistent antithesis, through "not ... but" constructions that allow him to feel as well as serve. Wordsworth, he found, had also sensed that "the first freshness of youthful enjoyment of life was not lasting; but ... he had sought for compensation and found it" in the cultivation of feelings (152). What made his poems attractive to Mill "was that they expressed, not outward beauty, but states of feeling," allowed him to find "inward joy" (150). The Everlasting Nay of Utilitarian dejection becomes the everlingering Nay ... But of a new synthesis.

Mill's crisis, then, was a "conversion" only in that it allowed him to separate motives ill-allied. The prose of chapter 5 does not reveal a new, vigorous voice or an outright rejection of old affairs; it does present a cautious inwardness, projected alike from his social activism and his father's influence. That inwardness deepened in Mill's heavily edited treatment of Harriet Taylor. Although his account in chapter 6 has often been called extravagant, it is a remarkable piece of mimetic prose, playing out once again Mill's drama of isolation and union. "To her outer circle," he writes, "she was a beauty and wit ... to the inner, a woman of deep and strong feeling, of penetrating and intuitive intelligence" (192). "Shut out" from a full use of her talents in "the world without," her life "was one of inward meditation, varied by familiar intercourse with a small circle of friends" (194). Soon her penetration affects Mill. The words "admit," "pierce," "pervade," "invest" recur, all portraying Taylor as an energetic double of James Mill, with more than a hint of his phallic aggressiveness. Her mind could "pierc[e] to the very heart and marrow of a matter, always seizing the essential idea" (195); and she could "invest" others with her own intensity, much in the manner of the elder Mill (194). But whereas John had been the passive instrument of his father's energy, he is now an active supplicant. By entering into Taylor's circle, Mill achieves a new interiority, an intimate society based on the principle of feeling. This, then, allows him to address social issues with renewed assurance: his is now no longer "the work of one mind, but the fusion of two" (199).

One can understand Mill's fulsome praise for Taylor in light of the intensity of his conflict: she allowed him to embrace both inwardness and influence, self and society, in the same act—and to call that act the work of a single mind. Nevertheless, there remain flaws in that union. While steadfastly maintaining their interest in "the common good," and welcoming all "socialistic experiments by select individuals," the Mills nevertheless dread "the ignorance and especially the selfishness and brutality of the mass" (241, 238). They thought England's duty was "to unite the greatest individual liberty of action with . . . an equal participation of all in the benefits of combined labour"—a fusion of self and society (238). But since that moment of synthesis was far off, the Mills themselves hesitated. The world had not yet emerged from that very paralysis Mill thought he had overcome; and, not unlike Nietzsche, he predicts the reception of his work with resonant irony. In time some new doctrine would ossify into a monolithic creed, impressing itself "upon the new generations without the mental processes that have led to it. . . . It is then that the teachings of the *Liberty* will have their greatest value. And it is to be feared that they will retain that value a long time" (259–60). Projected on society as dogma, even the resolutely independent ideals of *On Liberty* may well acquire the pernicious gravity of a James Mill, turning energetic citizens into passive subjects. If Mill's experience proved nothing else, it proved this: there could be no lasting reconciliation between inwardness and the multitude.

The final chapter of the *Autobiography*, one not included in the early draft, and hence a "revision" in the extended sense, attempted to resolve this conflict by embracing a principled solitude. The social ideals Mill had developed with Harriet Taylor now become instruments of isolation, as he not only refuses to condescend to his constitutents, but insults them as well (275). He becomes an exclusive member of Parliament, "reserv[ing]" himself for the most "advanced" causes others avoided, calling himself one of only three men in London who really understood the working class (278). The speeches Mill wants us to note, far ahead of the most "advanced liberal opinion," concern capital punishment and the seizure of goods at sea—removal of life and property or exclusion of social groups. The rights of workmen and women and Jamaicans: these are the outcasts for which the widower wants credit. Espousing "our" principles, he manages to commemorate Taylor; but the acts are his own.

Many of Mill's revisions, despite his paeans to his wife, reinforce this hard-won independence. Although he submitted the entire manuscript for her perusal, as a widower he had the last word. Indeed, he abandoned his original design, to divide the work in two—life before and after Taylor—for one in which his own mental crisis occupies the center (xxiv). To this end, Mill's cutting of nasty portraits and significant detail allows his own muted voice to emerge. His excision of the "pugnacious" John Roebuck eliminates a strong adversary; his excision of Mrs. Austin, who "made herself agreeable to young men" (186), removes an unfavorable comparison to his own conduct with Taylor. Even his excision of the Ford Abbey passage quoted above forces the reader back upon Newington Green and Mill's exclusive relationship with his father. The manuscript additions often reinforce this intention. One late assessment of James Mill seems to be a final reflection on the son's own importance. The father was "anything but Bentham's mere follower or disciple":

> He had not all Bentham's high qualities, but neither had Bentham all his. ...[James Mill] did not revolutionize—or rather create—one of the great departments of human thought. But, leaving out of the reckoning all that portion of his labours in which he benefitted by what Bentham had done, and counting only what he achieved in a province in which Bentham had done nothing, that of analytic psychology, he will be known to posterity as one of the greatest names in that most important branch of speculation. (213)

The passage, more authoritative than other such criticisms in the *Autobiography*, is suggestive of Mill's own significance. At last the fifty-five-year-old autobiographer sees his father's labors in the shadow of the great as reflections of his own.

Nowhere is this self-assertion greater than in Mill's revisions of his wife's portrait. Mill reduced this centerpiece of his life by half before inserting it into the text, at the chronological—not the emotional—center. Many of the excised passages are more laudatory and self-effacing than anything that remained:

> Had our acquaintance commenced later; had her judgment of me been first
> formed in maturer years, it would, probably, have been far less favourable;
> but I, at whatever period of life I had known her, must always have felt her
> to be the most admirable person I had ever known, and must have made
> her approbation the guiding light and her sympathy the chief object of my
> life, though to appreciate the greatness and variety of her preeminence
> could only have been possible after long and intimate knowledge, to any
> one not on the same exalted level as herself. (617)

The excised passages are full of this reverent prose, giving Taylor an almost biblical potency, with her "passion of justice," "boundless generosity and a lovingness ever ready to pour itself forth upon any or all
human beings" (618). Also cut are most of her views on feminism
(which Mill later included as a footnote, though claiming that his opinions antedated their friendship), her poetic nature, and her eminent
practicality. Perhaps most telling is the frame Mill gives to each portrait. The original is portentous and exclusive:

> My first introduction to the lady whose friendship has been the honour and
> blessing of my existence, and who after many years of confidential inti-
> macy, deigned to be my wife, dates from as early as 1830. (617)

> All society and personal intercourse became burthensome to me except
> with those in whom I recognized, along with more or less sympathy of
> opinion, at least a strong taste for [Taylor's] elevated and poetic feeling, if
> not the feeling itself. (623–24)

Here Taylor dwarfs Mill, as if she were holding his miniature. In contrast, chapter 6 begins and ends almost casually:

> It was at the period of my mental progress which I have now reached that
> I formed the friendship which has been the honour and chief blessing of my
> existence. (193)

> At the present period, however, this influence was only one among many
> which were helping to shape the character of my future development: and
> even after it became, I may truly say, the presiding principle of my mental
> progress, it did not alter the path, but only made me move forward more
> boldly and at the same time more cautiously in the same course. (199)

His wife now exists in time, an influence rather than an idol. By the end
of the revision she has become a collaborator—a collaborator, it may
be observed, who helped to make Mill famous.

But if Mill's revisions emphasize his independence, the final section, devoted to Parliament, suggests his limitations. Here was a
national projection of his defining struggle—the massive political influences in Commons confronting his single voice; and often, as he enun-

ciates his positions, he does so in the very language of the mental crisis, first recorded sixteen years before. Whereas in 1826 inwardness had been crushed by massive training, now Mill defends inwardness from the masses. He would not consent to run on the usual terms, neither campaigning extensively nor seeking funds. He would not speak on issues that others handled better, reserving himself "for work which no others were likely to do" (275). He would make no deals, consider no "interests" (284), sacrifice no principles. It is somewhat startling, then, to find this unequivocal stance expressed in such equivocal terms. This was not the first time Mill had considered running for office, "but there seemed no probability that the idea would ever take any practical shape" (272), so opposed was he to fund-raising. "I do not say that, so long as there is scarcely a chance for an independent candidate to come into Parliament without complying with this vicious practice," Mill adds. "But, to justify it, he ought to be very certain that he can be of more use to his country as a member of Parliament" than as a private citizen. Hence, Mill decided "not to seek election"; "but the conditions of the question were considerably altered" when he was spontaneously approached to run (273). Once again, the massed negations and "not . . . but" constructions suggest a crisis of conscience, attended this time not by incapacity but by resolution. After the Hyde Park affair, for example, in which Mill helped to subdue workmen bent on battling the police, Mill "not only spoke strongly" against the banning of public meetings, "but formed one of a number of advanced Liberals" who helped to defeat it (279). But his advocacy did not mean, Mill cautions, that he supported other Reform principles—an intransigency for which he was roundly criticized in the press. "I do not know what they expected from me; but [the critics] had reason to be thankful to me if they knew from what I had in all probability preserved them" (279). His presence of mind meant more to him than politics; it was proof of his influence.

And yet influence, as Mill's analysis of *On Liberty* showed, could be as dangerous in Parliament as it had been when exercised upon a young boy. Not the least reason was that it exposed Mill, once again, to a mass of texts he could not hope to master—"letters on private grievances and on every imaginable subject that related to any kind of public affairs, however remote from my knowledge or pursuits" (286). When to this "oppressive burthen" (286) was added the morally crippling means by which parliamentary influence was maintained—the pandering for money, votes, and constituents—it became clear to Mill that he had only two choices, both of which he made. The first was to act radically on principle, in order to preserve inwardness. Thus he argues that his extreme position on the Irish Land Bill was beneficial, since "to propose something which would be called extreme was the true way not to impede but to facilitate a more moderate experiment" (280). The English middle classes desired a "middle course," and Mill's radical proposal strengthened other schemes by making them appear more moderate (280). The radical individualist was also a national benefactor. The second choice was to act like politicians everywhere: Mill took a ghostwriter. Deferring to his daughter's influence, he allowed her to write "a great proportion of all my letters (including many which found their way into the newspapers)...not merely from her willingness to help in disposing of a mass of letters...but...because I thought the letters she wrote superior to mine" (286). The praise was more than a transference of his veneration for his wife; it was a political necessity: Helen Taylor wrote not only "prepared speeches" but his "published writings" as well (287). Thus, at the height of his independence, the point in his *Autobiography* where he is most impressively solitary, Mill once again conflates opposites, allowing the Other, by means of writing, to repossess him. "Whoever...may think of me and of the work I have done," he concludes, "must never forget that it is the product not of one intellect and conscience but of three" (265). The self remains the sum of its influences.

Mill's final *Aufhebung* does not invalidate his will to solitude; rather it underscores the difficult constraints under which he wrote—fiercer, in many ways, than Nietzsche's. But his predicament was by no means universal, even in the nineteenth century, whose ideals of individuality he did so much to fashion. One need only examine Walt Whitman's *Specimen Days* to observe another, perhaps older sensibility, one that saw identity in Zarathustra's terms as a fusion of the many and the one.

WHITMAN'S "SONG OF MYSELF" AND
SPECIMEN DAYS

Although it has become common to call "Song of Myself" autobiographical, Whitman's first masterpiece is more accurately the exploration of a trope, one central to his notion of identity. As he contemplates his spear of summer grass he is at once an attentive observer and an imaginative participant, one whose agile mind can construct its own cosmos, but who needs the responses of others to give it life. His catalogs and exhortations are not intended to record life, even the life of a poet's mind, in the manner of Wordsworth's *Prelude*, but to suggest a democratic literature in which Whitman would play a prominent part. The key to that literature was the trope he explores *ad infinitum* in "Song of Myself"—synecdoche.

According to Whitman in this poem, the self takes its place in a system of which it is both originator and participant. On the one hand is the mind's imaginative sympathy, its ability to project itself into all conditions, all circumstances. Such sympathy allows him to record scenes but not necessarily to embody them; he remains an observer, conscious of his solitude:

> Apart from the pulling and hauling stands what I am,
> Stands amused, complacent, compassionating, idle, unitary,
> Looks down, is erect, bends an arm on an impalpable certain rest,
> Looks with its sidecurved head curious what will come next,
> Both in and out of the game, and watching and wondering at it.[11]

Equally prominent and opposed to the mind's resourcefulness is the diversity of what it must consider. Whitman never forgets, and never lets us forget, that the poet, too, is a phenomenon of nature, and that the diversity he records reflects the structure of the world:

> I remember.... I resume the overstaid fraction,
> The grave of rock multiplies what has been confided to it.... or to
>   any graves,
> The corpses rise.... the gashes heal.... the fastenings roll away.
> I troop forth replenished with supreme power, one of an average
>   unending procession,
> ....
> The blossoms we wear in our hats are the growth of two thousand
>   years.
>
> (38.966–70, p. 60)

Whitman's expansive catalogs notwithstanding, there is no ready meeting of the two extremes; indeed, it is the work of the poem to unite them through an insistent movement from observation to fusion. Hence, Whitman presents two narrative modes. As the "compassionating, idle, unitary" self, he gives cinematic portraits of American scenes:

> The bride unrumples her white dress, the minutehand of the clock
>   moves slowly,
> The opium eater reclines with rigid head and just-opened lips,

The prostitute draggles her shawl, her bonnet bobs on her tipsy
    and pimpled neck,
The crowd laugh at her blackguard oaths, the men jeer and wink to
    each other,
(Miserable! I do not laugh at your oaths nor jeer at you).
(15.303–7, pp. 18–19)

So fine is the detail in such catalogs that one almost overlooks their essential remoteness. Section 15, from which this passage is drawn, begins abruptly with the singing of a "pure contralto" and marches through fifty-nine diverse scenes, unconnected by any sustained logic. The centrifugal force here might well destroy the strongest unity, and it is for this reason that Whitman must insist time and again:

And these one and all tend inward to me, and I tend outward to
    them.
And such as it is to be one of these more or less I am.
(15.327–28, p. 20)

Hence the presence of those countervailing catalogs in which the poet asserts his unity with the mass:

I am of old and young, of the foolish as much as the wise
Regardless of others, ever regardful of others,
Maternal as well as paternal, a child as well as a man,
Stuffed with the stuff that is coarse, and stuffed with the stuff that
    is fine,
One of the great nation.
(16.330–34, p. 20)

Such diversity allows Whitman to approach that union of souls he announced in the 1855 preface—the great nation and the heroic poet. As democratic *typos*, the writer catalogs and creates America.

But announcement, even in visionary poetry, is not realization, and Whitman knows that without one element more, his catalogs would not cohere. That element is the reader, whom Whitman insistently addresses as if to draw him into the dialectic. "This hour I tell things in confidence," he writes early in the poem. "I might not tell everybody but I will tell you" (19.387–88, p. 24). Indeed, he apostrophizes many of his images: the stallion he uses and resigns; the sea, with which he is "integral . . . of one phase and all phases" (22.458, p. 28); the "voluptuous, coolbreath'd earth" to which he returns like

a lover (21.438, p. 27). But those approaches are subsidiary and meaningless without the reader's assent, the ratification of another consciousness. "It is you talking just as much as myself....I act as the
tongue of you," he insists. "It was tied in your mouth....in mine it
begins to be loosened" (47.1248, p. 77). Or again:

> Long enough have you dream'd contemptible dreams,
> Now I wash the gum from your eyes.
> You must habit yourself to the dazzle of the light and of every mo-
> ment of your life.
>
> (46.1229–31, p. 76)

Through such exhortations Whitman completes the complex trope the
poem seeks to establish. His synecdoche works simultaneously in two
directions: the individual affirms himself as part of the mass, and he acknowledges the world's diversity in himself.

As such, Whitman's self remains suspended in that series of substi-
tutions Paul de Man discerned in Rousseau's *Pygmalion*. Bound by the
language in which he proclaims his cosmos, Whitman can be neither
wholly originary nor wholly submerged, neither apart nor absorbed.
Moreover, the aesthetic nature of Whitman's America, that self-
portrait through an infinite sensorium, suggests the same instability
that Pygmalion found in Galathea—"the discrepancy between [a] spec-
ular nature, as an act of the self in which the self is bound to be reflected
and [a] formal nature which has to be free to differ from the self as radically as can be imagined."[12] The result might well be sustained anxiety, the consciousness that self cannot escape its textual engendering,
were it not for Whitman's intrusive bombast, his literal claim to possess the Other, to "dilate" with his own "tremendous breath" (40.1014,
p. 63). The reader, he insists, must be similarly inspired: as America is
an imaginative construct, citizenship must arise through reciprocal
acts of the imagination. But suppose this *typos* collapsed—through indifference, through exhaustion, through civil war: what would come of
the figural self? For the next three decades, Whitman would assemble
the answer to that essential question.

Specimen Days, Whitman's authentic autobiography, bore the same
meticulous, almost obsessive reworking as *Leaves of Grass*. Portions of
the volume, assembled ten years before his death, had appeared previously in *Memoranda During the War*, itself part of *Two Rivulets*; in dispatches to the *New York Times*, the *Weekly Graphic*, and other

periodicals; in occasional pieces he wrote for public ceremonies: Whitman tore out ungathered sheets from these publications and interleaved them with his autographs. The result was a work of almost continuous revision, a thorough reworking of his literary remains. But the large, loose structure of *Specimen Days*—for which he apologized in a note to the printer—was a revision in a deeper sense. After announcing, and continuously refining, the ideal self of the poetry, Whitman attempted to recount his actual life on the same terms. The unity of *Specimen Days* is thus less a matter of "diary-scraps and memoranda ...illustrat[ing] one phase of humanity" (1) than of Whitman's seeking an American sense to his experience. The autobiography is an epic struggle to regain a shattered synthesis, to adjust life to a poetic ideal.[13]

Much like Mill, Whitman organizes his life around central crises— two inner sections detailing the war and his paralysis, enclosed by two outer sections recounting his antecedents and Western travels.[14] The outer sections confirm synecdoche; the inner sections overturn it. He begins his account far back, fixing the moment of his American identity in 1640, with the migration of John Whitman to Weymouth, Massachusetts, and alluding to one Abijah Whitman, "who goes over into the 1500s" and was reputed to have touched America. This is an account of origins, of the utmost reach of the self. Hence Whitman depicts both ancestry and nation as coterminous with nature. As he visits the Whitman homestead in Huntington, Long Island, he notes, amid the remains of gardens and outbuildings, "a stately grove of tall, vigorous black-walnuts, beautiful, Apollo-like, the sons and grandsons, no doubt, of black-walnuts during or before 1776" (6). But behind the landscape's political character stand those grand poetic catalogs of Whitman's textual identity, the account of his youth, for example, with its ranging activity:

> Here, and all along the island and its shores, I spent intervals many years, all seasons, sometimes riding, sometimes boating, but generally afoot... absorbing fields, shores, marine incidents, characters, the bay-men, farmers, pilots...always liked the bare sea-beach, south side, and have some of my happiest hours on it to this day. (12)

Similarly, his record of New York, with its "volume, variety, rapidity, and picturesqueness," the "changing panorama...of white-sail'd schooners, sloops, skiff" (16), evokes the expansive self of the "Song." To be sure, these are conscious echoes of his poetic effusions, but their placement is significant. Whitman's youth, with its wide reading, itinerant hawking, and loafing on Broadway trams, has the broad, vigorous unity of epic poetry. The life he portrays suggests an American ideal.

In the gaslight before the Metropolitan Hotel, however, as he reads of the attack on Fort Sumter, that expansiveness is sharply challenged. Whitman has a complex, puzzled reaction to the Civil War, at once buoyant and anxious, tender and increasingly horrified. Time and again he speaks, in his laureate's voice, of the grand heroism; the grand response of the Union, as one man, to the call; the grand stoicism of wounded soldiers. But such valor had now to contend with other voices, echoes of anguish and division. Characteristically, Whitman blames the early Union defeats on plutocrats, the "shoulder-straps" dining in "Willard's sumptuous parlors and bar-rooms." And here, after Bull Run, is the first intimation of Whitman's own crisis: "The dream of humanity, the vaunted Union we thought so strong, so impregnable," he wrote in July 1861, "lo! it seems already smash'd like a china plate. One bitter, bitter hour—perhaps America will never again know such an hour" (29). Eighteen months later, in a letter to Emerson, he expressed a similar dread:

> I desire and intend to write a little book out of this phase of America, her masculine young manhood, its conduct under the most trying of and highest of all exigency...America, already brought to Hospital in her fair youth—brought and deposited here in this great, whited sepulchre of Washington itself—(this union Capital without the first bit of cohesion—this collect of proofs how low and swift a good stock can deteriorate).[15]

The depradation he feared was that of party hacks, mercenaries secure in their gilded chambers while the "helpless worn and wounded youth" died. But more than his populism was at stake; as his letters and dispatches indicate, Whitman was fighting for a trope.

A demonic, horrifying image that Whitman inserts into the hospital memoranda explains his own protracted battle. In a skirmish near Atlanta, he relates, a strong young rebel soldier is shot in the head "so that the brains partially exuded." Though left for dead, he lived on for three days, the wound causing constant spasms in his legs. "He dug with his heel in the ground during that time a hole big enough to put in a couple of ordinary knapsacks. He just lay there in the open air, and with little intermission kept his heel going night and day" (76). The same spasmodic response characterizes many of Whitman's war scenes. Desperately he attempts to assimilate his experience, and desperately the images dissociate. An early casualty is sympathetic nature, which, in the fierce fighting, retreats to an inscrutable remove:

Amid the woods, that scene of flitting souls—amid the crack and crash and yelling of sounds—the impalpable perfume of the woods—and yet the pungent, stifling smoke—the radiance of the moon, looking from heaven at intervals so placid....And there, upon the roads, the fields, and in those woods, that contest, never one more desperate in any age or land...fierce and savage demons fighting there. (47)

As Whitman observes the scene, he can no longer wrench nature into imaginative union with men: the Civil War had caused a cosmic division, "strange analogies, different combinations, a different sunlight, or absence of it" (94). Hence the prose dissociates, and decay is the only unity remaining in nature—the rotting bodies of wounded soldiers, crumbling into "mother earth, unburied and unknown" (49). Even when the soldiers march in Washington, the fierce heat prostrates them; and as Whitman records these scenes, he can find but one description: "Convulsiveness" (112).

Convulsive, too, are the hospital scenes, with their gently decaying boys. In these vignettes, the bulk of his war memoranda, Whitman comes closest to recapturing the declamatory unity of "Song of Myself," in the panorama of casualties, North and South, with whom he shares his "magnetism." As several critics have noted, the hospitals were Whitman's consummation, the best experience of his life. In the wards he could be openly affectionate with men, unite families by writing letters for the wounded, dispense hundreds of little gifts like some spirit of democracy. "I got the boys," he later wrote to James Redpath, "the boys, thousands of them—I gave myself for them—myself. I got the boys; then I got Leaves of Grass."[16] But through this torrent of contact the center could not hold, for his rhetoric had yet no real place for the vivid presence of death. He had written, in "Song of Myself," of "Formless stacks of bodies and bodies by themselves...dabs of flesh upon the masts" (35.937, p. 58), but the imagery was abstract, part of a complex whole, noble and necessary. Even the somber imagery of "Out of the Cradle Endlessly Rocking" had a desperate dignity. In the wards, however, death isolated, and Whitman found no reconciliation:

The poor young man is struggling painfully for breath, his great dark eyes with a glaze already upon them, and the choking faint but audible in his throat....He will die here in an hour or two, without the presence of kith or kin. Meantime the ordinary chat and business of the ward a little way off goes on indifferently. Some of the inmates are laughing and joking, others are playing checkers or cards, others are reading, &c. (64)

The poet's large sympathy cannot amalgamate this world. As he steps out one Sunday for air, he is inspired by a glorious winter day, warm, glowing, and perfumed; as he returns to the "gloomy" ward, he is confronted by the "corpse of a poor soldier, just dead, of typhoid fever" (110). Occasionally his observations take a chilling, ironic turn. In the Patent Office, which served as a hospital during severe fighting, he noted the "strange, solemn" disposition of casualties among the "high and ponderous glass cases, crowded with models in miniature of every kind of utensil, machine, or invention, it ever enter'd into the mind of man to conceive" (40)—the perfectly enclosed world of imagination, indifferent, like nature, to the dead. Even as he touched thousands of the great nation, he could not deny his essential failure. "(I sometimes put myself in fancy in the cot, with typhoid, or under the knife)," he confided to a friend, "the living soul's, the body's tragedies, bursting the petty bonds of art."[17] But death overran fancy, and reduced Whitman, too, to an isolated observer. His text, like Nietzsche's, concealed a corpse.

The poet, however, was able to cast a kind of shrill unity over the Civil War, in an ironic catalog doubly painful when placed beside the visions of his "Song." What united the nation, gave meaning to its suffering, were "the dead in this war":

> there they lie, strewing the fields and woods and valleys and battle-fields of the south—Virginia, the Peninsula—Malvern hill and Fair Oaks—the banks of the Chicahominy—the terraces of Fredericksburgh—Antietam bridge—the grisly ravines of Manassas—the bloody promenade of the Wilderness—the varieties of the *strayed* dead ... Gettysburgh, the West, Southwest, Vicksburgh—Chattanooga—the trenches of Petersburgh—the numberless battles, camps, hospitals everywhere—the crop reap'd by the mighty reapers, typhoid, dysentery, inflammations—and blackest and loathsomest of all, the dead and living burial-pits, the prison-pens of Andersonville, Salisbury, Belle-Isle ... the dead, the dead, the dead—*our* dead—or South or North, ours all, (all, all, all, finally dear to me). (114)

With his imaginative vigor, Whitman seeks them out, "in bushes, low gullies, or on the sides of hills," in rivers and on sea bottoms, "in every future grain of wheat and ear of corn"—reconstituting nature from the carnage. The catalog is at once poignant and impotent, a formulaic confession of his bitterness. Although Whitman could still imagine unity, he could not prove it through experience, and although the war deepened and broadened his sympathies, it also struck him down. Indeed, the manuscript itself breaks sharply off, as the paralytic recruits himself to write.

Whitman's paralysis serves a double function: it confirms his isolation, and prepares him for a slow, painful return. As he hobbles about the

Stafford farm minutely cataloging birds, trees, and changes of the weather, he attempts on an inch of ivory what he could not accomplish across Southern battlefields. Epiphanies, briefer and more open to doubt, remain his goal, but he is exploratory now, more willing to wait than to exclaim. Above all he is alone: after the thousands of wounded crowding his war scenes, he nurses himself in solitude, occasionally "wrestling" with a young tree or allowing himself to be raked with a coarse brush. It is a restorative pause, this revision, preparation for a final American apotheosis.

Perhaps the most telling comment on this third section is one Whitman appended to the very end of *Specimen Days*. His plan for the Timber Creek notes was "a Nature-poem that should carry one's experiences a few hours, commencing at noon-flush, and so through the after-part of the day" (293)—a version, that is, of his "integral" use of nature in the "Song." In assembling the section he did manage to achieve a loose chronological unity, segregating his musings by season in a manner roughly analogous, some readers suggest, to *Walden*.[18] But even this unity is betrayed by an almost querulous tone, as if Whitman himself recognizes the futility of the original design. "Away then," he exclaims in his most hortatory manner, "to loosen, to unstring the divine bow, so tense, so long. Away, from curtain, carpet, sofa, book— from 'society' ... and the whole cast-iron civilizee life.... Away, thou soul ... for one day and night at least" (121–22). "What is happiness, anyhow?" he asks the following fall. "Is this one of its hours, or the like of it? ... I am not sure" (134). He is a man absorbing a great shock, taking what little pleasure he can amid the ruins of a trope. As he slowly regains his health, he talks increasingly of his restoring exchange with nature: the sap that seems to flow from seedlings into his frame, the luxuriant mudbaths he takes naked in Timber Creek, the "identity" he seems to get from "each and every thing" around him (152). But even this Romantic union is quietist and passive, far removed from the tumultuous embrace of "Song of Myself." Just as often he pauses, hesitant in Nature: "(what was the yellow or light-brown bird, large as a young hen, with short neck and long-stretch'd legs I just saw, in flapping and awkward flight over there through the trees?)" (129). Or again: "I linger long to a delicious song-epilogue (is it the hermit-thrush?) from some bushy recess off there in the swamp, repeated leisurely and pensively over and over again" (128). If Whitman is to be restored, it will be through this mild serendipity. He has no present need for heroism.

Nor has he much use for the great world. In "Song of Myself" natural and national events composed a single identity; here they are rigorously separated. Occasionally, as Whitman heals, he takes short trips to cities, where his old populist delight in the masses returns. But it is a delight he leaves behind. "Not a human being, and hardly the evidence of one," he remarks one summer. "What a contrast from New York's or Philadelphia's streets!" (164). Natural and human diversity now inhabit separate realms. On election day of the nation's centennial year he muses at Timber Creek:

> The forenoon leaden and cloudy, not cold or wet, but indicating both. As I hobble down here and sit by the silent pond, how different from the excitement amid which, in the cities, millions of people are now waiting news of yesterday's Presidential election, or receiving and discussing the result—in this secluded place uncared-for, unknown. (135)

The few "civilizee" intrusions he does allow are often sullen and haunting. The fisherman's buoys he sees from the Camden ferry look "so pretty . . . like corpse candles" (188), and a tramp woman he meets with John Burroughs has the "eyes, voice and manner . . . of a corpse, animated by electricity" (169). Abruptly, after a lyrical passage on "The Oaks and I," he inserts "Three Young Men's Deaths," a soldier, a fireman, and a suffering farmhand, with their familiar impotence and pathos. Even the fragmentary tributes to William Cullen Bryant and Tom Paine are eulogies—the latter an account, by one long dead, of the patriot's "sickness and death" (140). Clearly, the easy commerce between the great-souled nation and its Poet has been disrupted in this long middle section of *Specimen Days*, the brave *typos* all but dispersed.

Whitman begins to emerge from isolation in a strained but striking entry entitled "Hours for the Soul," which most nearly approaches the original design for these nature notes. "Now, indeed, if never before," he exclaims, "the heavens declared the glory of God":

> It was to the full the sky of the Bible, of Arabia, of the prophets, and of the oldest poems. There, in abstraction and stillness . . . the copiousness, the removedness, vitality, loose-clear-crowdedness, of that stellar concave spreading overhead, softly absorb'd into me, rising so free, interminably high, stretching east, west, north, south,—and I though but a point in the centre below, embodying all. (174)

The only dimension missing from this paean—the quality distinguishing autobiography from poetry—is lived experience. That is the thrust of the final section. In 1879 Whitman received an invitation from the Old Settlers of Kansas Committee to grace the Quarter-Centennial Celebration in Lawrence, and used the occasion to make his first grand tour of America. Now sufficiently healed, the "half-paralytic" visited regions he had hitherto only imagined. He pronounced St. Louis a sound, prosperous city, praised Kansans, and found silver in the streets of Denver. Most important, the trip offered a physical parallel to the large unities he had declared in the "Song." "Not long ago," he now boasts, "I was down New York bay, on a steamer, watching the sunset over the dark green heights of Navesink." But an intervening week or two found him watching "the shadowy outlines of the Spanish peaks." The contrast returns him to sanity: "In the more than two thousand miles between, though of infinite and paradoxical variety, a curious and absolute fusion is doubtless steadily annealing, compacting, identifying all" (223). Now the nation, with its mountain sinews, is once again great-souled, a mighty man: "As the anatomists say a man is only a spine, topp'd, fotted, breasted and radiated, so the whole Western world is ... but an expansion" of the Rocky Mountains (213). He looks out on the prairies and sees the "ten million democratic farms in the future" (214); observes the Mississippi River and imagines "it *is* the Union" (222); contemplates General Grant "circumambiating the world," lounging with czars and mikados—fresh from the farm, the million armed men, the fifty pitched battles and the presidency—and proclaims "the capacities of that American individuality common to us all" (226). Synecdoche, once again, is Whitman's vital trope.

But the trope now bears a vital difference. The unity Whitman had fashioned in "Song of Myself" was, like Nietzsche's *Zarathustra*, a monumental pose. "In him all opposites are blended," Nietzsche wrote of his creation; "what is sweetest, most frivolous, and most terrible wells forth from one fount with immortal assurance" (*EH* 305). "I am the credulous man of qualities, ages, races," sang Whitman, "I advance from the people in their own spirit, / Here is what sings unrestricted faith."[19] But just as Nietzsche's vision succumbed to the internal stresses of language represented by the monstrous Other, so did Whitman's trope succumb to a kind of *automachia*, a self–civil war; and like Nietzsche, he struggled to embrace that demon.[20]

CONVERSION AND THE AMERICAN SELF

How is one to explain this radical difference between Whitman's expansive and Mill's exclusive identity, a difference made all the more striking by their common assumptions? Like Nietzsche, both regard autobiography as a process of close, continuous revision in which the self emerges through a series of crises. Both struggle to adjust their inner lives to collective ideals, and both regard their mature identities as the product of complex influences. Yet Whitman's proclamation of a collective "self" would have mystified Mill, whose life's work enshrined originality, and Mill's systematic isolation would have shocked Whitman, who truly lived his populist ideals. The explanation, then, must be found in divergent uses of a common mode, an autobiographical convention both writers shared—the conversion narrative.

Mill's reference to Methodist conviction of sin suggests the importance of conversion narratives, even in an increasingly secular age.[21] The genre, in England, arose in the late sixteenth and early seventeenth centuries, partly in response to the Reformation, to popular biographies, and to the demand for personal religious experience.[22] As such, the autobiographies were a curious amalgam. In one sense they demonstrated the universality of Christian life. Protestants, with the rigor of Ignatius Loyola, mapped out minute stages of preparation, conviction, and assurance: an individual was expected to have glimpsed salvation in childhood and youth, only to lapse continuously into false ease or outright depravity. In maturity, typically after hearing a shrewd sermon, he felt grave doubts about his soul. Then began the long struggle with sin, or "conviction," often attended by visions, hallucinations, and impulses to atheism or suicide. At last the sufferer recalls the Word—opens the Bible like Augustine, or remembers Christ's compassion—and the crisis abates. The seeker continues to study and strive, but with the confidence that he is saved. Whether the accounts were mere testimonies, recording the bare outline of grace, or labyrinthine explorations, such as James Fraser's eight-fold progress, the autobiographies reflected—or seemed to reflect—a settled conviction about identity. "As a Chyrurgion, when he makes a dissection in the body, discovers...the inward parts," wrote Thomas Watson in 1669, "so a Christian anatomizeth himself."[23] The individual was a specimen of the mass—a notion inherited from medieval thought, to which "individual" meant "inseparable," a "member of some group, kind, or species." By definition, the self stood for the multitude.[24]

Concealed within the common trial, however, was an impulse to exclusiveness. At some point, it must be remembered, every autobiographer was expected to endure near insupportable doubt, often expressed through a desire for isolation. An American Quaker, David Ferris, during "a day of the deepest affliction and distress that [he] had known," wondered "what land [he] should flee to" before a divine voice arrested him. Thomas Shepard, who experienced his conversion in England, "went to no Christian and was ashamed to speak" of his atheism, and had "strong temptations to run [his] head against walls." Moreover, that sense of isolation did not depart with grace. The American Quaker Richard Jordan often felt "as if death and hell triumphed,"

and endured "the miseries [of] those souls ... which are forever separated from God"; and the Puritan Richard Rogers constantly laments
the "wandringes and ... unsetling of ... minde" that prevented his
"unity" with others.[25] Even Puritan *topoi* lent themselves to exclusiveness. "I sing my SELF; my *Civil-Warrs* within," wrote George
Goodwin:

> The *Victories* I howrely lose and win;
> The dayly *Duel*, the continuall Strife,
> The *Warr* that ends not, till I end my life.
> And yet, not Mine alone, not onely Mine,
> But every-One's that under th'honor'd Signe
> Of Christ his Standard, shal his Name enroule
> With holy Vowes of Body and of Soule.[26]

As Sacvan Bercovitch observes, the emphasis on personal struggle, on
inner experience—on SELF—often overshadows the common enterprise.[27] An individual who recorded, charted, agonized over every turn
of spiritual fortune could not help but see himself more narrowly than
any anatomist. The very act of introspection separated him from the
whole.

This tension between the communal and the isolated self was mag-
nified by certain developments in eighteenth-century thought. Locke's
insistence on the privacy of the mind's responses seemed to remove individual experience from the external world, and writers like Pope and
Swift were quick to respond through images of the divided mind, at
once observing and mocking social norms.[28] Increasingly, as Stephen
Cox observes, eighteenth-century English moralists sought a way to
deny this private self, "this anxiety ... about the absence of a community of understanding based on objective knowledge." Hence Shaftesbury's insistence on those sympathetic feelings uniting humanity,
and Adam Smith's contention, in *Moral Sentiments*, that the self
achieves identity only through its imaginative response to other
selves.[29] But Locke's psychology, in the hands of interpreters, cut two
ways. It was equally possible to affirm, as did David Hume, in *A Treatise
on Human Nature*, that the very diversity of experience precluded
personal identity. With devastating literalism Hume supposed identity
to mean "sameness"; personal identity would then demand an invariable mental attitude. But so capricious did the English mind seem
that Hume boldly affirmed, "[mankind] are nothing but a bundle or
collection of different perceptions, which succeed each other with an
inconceivable rapidity, and are in a perpetual flux and movement."[30]

"Diversity," long associated with the mass of humanity, had entered the mind itself, paradoxically stripping it of all social bonds. Inwardness had become exile.

The Romantic movement was, in part, a response to that isolation. Blake, Wordsworth, Keats, and Byron all asserted the mind's ability to transcend its limits, to merge with a community, a concept, a cause. "Among the multitudes" in London, Wordsworth thought, even "more than elsewhere / Is possible, the unity of man":

> One spirit over ignorance and vice
> Predominant, in good and evil hearts;
> One sense for moral judgments, as one eye
> For the sun's light. The soul when smitten thus
> By a sublime *idea*, whencesoe'er
> Vouchsafed for union or communion, feeds
> On the pure bliss, and takes her rest with God.[31]

Keats speaks of his passion for otherness, his impulse to peck with the bird at his window and his sense that "the identity of every one" pressed in upon and annihilated him.[32] Byron stalks the Alps, seeking to lose himself in the sublime, and Blake insists that the "true Man" is not to be found in an individual mind, but in "universal Poetic Genius," responsible for the similarities in "Religeons [*sic*] of all Nations."[33] Identity lay in community.

But ecstasy, as the Puritans had discovered, was but one half of self; and just as these writers avowed their selflessness, they confirmed their preoccupation. Of Wordsworth one critic writes: "It was not immediate awareness of others, as with Burns or Keats, which determined his social conscience or poetic world, but a tendency to turn them into versions of himself or fit them as Forms within his scheme of the world."[34] Blake's Four Zoas, as Stephen Cox shows, though expressive of universal attributes, are often characterized by "mutual displays of self-absorption," reflecting the poet's deeply ambiguous sense of genius.[35] Even Keats, whose compassion surpasses understanding, expresses his "camelion" nature in terms of annihilation and loss: "not one word I ever utter can be taken for granted as an opinion growing out of my identical nature—how can it, when I have no nature?"[36] But Keats's solution only underscores the vast distance between the one and the many. "Neither the music of the shepherd," Byron writes from the Alps, "the crashing of the Avalanche, nor the torrent, the mountain, the Glacier, the Forest, nor the Cloud have . . . enabled me to lose my own wretched identity." His desire "to withdraw *myself* from *myself* (oh that cursed selfishness!)" was as treacherous and paradoxical as the Puritan's self–civil war.[37]

I stress the Romantics because they captured what Mill took to be his problem and the problem of his culture. The Romantic dilemma—really one with the Puritan dilemma and the disputes of the moral philosophers—was, in Patricia Ball's words, that "the chameleon never fixed for a moment"; "the egotistical consciousness [was] at once dominant and trying to revoke its power."[38] There was no stasis, no reconciliation: either the self was involved in larger aims, or it was absorbed in contemplation. It was, in Nietzsche's terms, "uncanny." That, indeed, was the leading criticism of Mill's age. "We call it a Society," Carlyle wrote in *Past and Present*, "and go about professing openly the totalest separation, isolation. Our life is not a mutual helpfulness; but rather...a mutual hostility."[39] Yet that mutual hostility, Mill himself saw in *On Liberty*, was the source of all social advance. Everyone, he complains, "lives as under the eye of a hostile and dreaded censorship," for which the sole antidote is genius, eccentricity, individuality. "Eccentricity has always abounded when and where strength of character has abounded; and the amount of eccentricity in a society has generally been proportional to the amount of genius ... it contained." Without that impetus, England would become as uniform and stultified as the East; indeed, he adds with imperialistic disdain, it will "become another China."[40]

English geniuses like Wordsworth, Carlyle, and Mill who sought release from this paradox took refuge in a single trope: antithesis. Only antithesis could manage the peculiar many-sidedness that led Mill to favor either Utilitarianism or genius. Thus Wordsworth in the "Immortality Ode," which Mill admired in the *Autobiography*, stresses his origin:

> Not in entire forgetfulness,
> And not in utter nakedness,
> But trailing clouds of glory do we come
> From God who is our home.

The self, isolated, nearly naked, recalls its plenitude, the "thousand valleys far and wide," the "Tree, of many, one," and the "visionary gleam." But "Not for these" does Wordsworth offer praise:

> But for these obstinate questionings
> Of sense and outward things,
> Fallings from us, vanishings;

Blank misgivings of a Creature
Moving about in worlds not realised.[41]

The exiled poet regains fullness only through dialectical movement, a complex denial that ends in fleeting transcendence. Mill found much the same experience in Carlyle's *Sartor Resartus*. The despairing Teufelsdröckh inhabits one side of the dialectic:

> A feeble unit in the middle of a threatening Infinitude, I seemed to have nothing given me but eyes, whereby to discern my own wretchedness. Invisible yet impenetrable walls, as of Enchantment, divided me from all the living.

Again the sufferer is isolated, sensing only through antithesis the great world beyond. But Teufelsdröckh expresses deliverance in the same terms:

> Truly, the din of many-voiced Life, which, in this solitude, with the mind's organ, I could hear, was no longer a maddening discord, but a melting one; like inarticulate cries, and sobbings of a dumb creature, which in the ear of Heaven are prayers. The poor Earth, with her poor joys, was now my needy Mother, not my cruel Stepdame.[42]

Peace is less a union than a negation: he emerges with the whole only by denying experience, by limiting the chameleon self. Yet even Carlyle has his hero, that autonomous self opposing all claims of the whole. Genius, like the multitude, refused to be subdued.

Confronted with the irreducible dispersion of self, then, Mill, like his English models, fashioned an antithetical image, a palimpsest of authority and influence beneath which shone figures of resistance and individualism. But the case was different in America—at least in antebellum America—precisely because of its stubborn anachronism. American Puritans distinguished themselves from English counterparts through their insistence that New England was New Jerusalem, the site of the Millennium. This made the polity not merely a social contract but the refuge of saints, and the American not an isolated self but an exemplary soul. Conversely, it made all conversion narratives representative, types not only of a class of readers, but of a nation. In Puritan literature America is given heroic status, God's agent marching through history to redeem the world. "Rejoyce . . . all yee his Churches the World throughout," exclaims Edward Johnson:

> for the Lambe is preparing his Bride, and oh! yee the antient Beloved of Christ, when he of old led by the hand from Egypt to Canaan, through that

great and terrible Wildernesse, looke here, behold him whom you have peirced, preparing to peirce your hearts with his *Wonder-working Providence.*[43]

Hence the act of writing conversion narratives, and of being admitted into the church, is synonymous with the trials of America in world history: just as the autobiographer suffers afflictions for Christ, so Christ leads America through the wilderness to glory. To achieve the Millennium, as countless Puritan testimonies illustrate, is to see local events as aspects of cosmic drama; to be saved is to sense one's world-historical mission. The consequences of that stance for secular autobiographers will be traced in the pages ahead; here it is enough to note the consequence for personal identity. Just as America had a special mission, so Americans—New England saints or New York poets—had a missionary role. The more fully realized were their lives, the more fully they saw themselves as emblematic. To live the life of an American was to become all Americans, for American life was a saving ideal. The writer's anguish involved the loss of that millennial vision; his deliverance, captured in revisions, sought to restore it. What may be called an American ritual of identity, that is to say, answered the Puritan dialectic by projecting a *typos*, a national soul. The individual, as Whitman contended, was as superb as a nation.

Whitman began his most searching piece of literary criticism by invoking John Stuart Mill. If one were asked, he wrote in *Democratic Vistas*, to define the difference between America, Europe, and the Orient, one could do no better than turn to *On Liberty*, where Mill cites two Western attributes—"a large variety of character—and . . . full play for human nature to expand itself in numberless and even conflicting directions" (362). But where the Englishman seeks to liberate the individual, protect him from custom, the American seeks to liberate the mass. "The tendencies of our day, in the States," Whitman continues,

are toward those vast and sweeping movements, influences, moral and physical, of humanity, now and always current over the planet, on the scale of the impulses of the elements. Then it is also good to reduce the whole matter to the consideration of a single self, a man, a woman, on permanent grounds. (393)

In America, finally, there was no difference between "ensemble-Individuality" and "special Personalism" (396), for it was "the individuality of one nation" (413) that would lead the world. Americans were great in proportion as they were universal, and American literature, Whitman foresaw, would be that "mightiest original non-subordinated SOUL" (413)—oceanic, variegated, infinite. Nowhere is that impulse to plenitude more fully realized than in American conversion narratives, whose revisions trace the path through the many, toward the one.

3 | The Corporate Ideal: Thomas Shepard and John Woolman

In Book III of *Thus Spoke Zarathustra*, Nietzsche repeats the challenge first whispered by moonlight in *The Gay Science*, two years earlier. Confronting a dwarf instead of a demon, Zarathustra describes a gateway bearing the legend "Moment," from which two "terrible" lanes extend infinitely before and behind. Is the moment not synecdochic, he asks—"this slow spider that creeps along in the moonlight, and this moonlight itself, and I and you at this gateway whispering . . . of eternal things" (Z 179)? Do they not symbolize the eternal recurrence of the same? But the recurrence—marked by Nietzsche's echo of the 1882 passage—now liberates in a different manner: for one of the few times in the text, Zarathustra discloses a private memory. A dog howls nearby:

> Had I ever heard a dog howling in that way? My thoughts ran back. Yes! When I was a child, in my most distant childhood: . . .
> —So that it moved me to pity. For the full moon . . . silent as death, . . . had just stopped still. (Z 179)

Zarathustra's acknowledgment of eternal recurrence releases a welter of verbal echoes—repetitions of phrases, memories, feelings, sounds—associated, like Nietzsche's revisions of *Ecce Homo*, with the anxiety of death. But unlike the author's revisions, those of Zarathustra are designed not to overcome but to prolong the moment of anxiety and the crisis that gave rise to it. The scene changes, and Zarathustra sees a shepherd "convulsed" by a snake that has crawled into his throat. The shepherd survives by biting off the snake's head, whence, like one who has assented to the Eternal Return, he is "transformed" into a being "surrounded with light" (180). The meaning of the riddle, most commentators agree, reiterates the moment by moonlight: only by enduring agonies can one hope to master eternal recurrence.

Nietzsche would no doubt brand as decadent anyone who dared associate Zarathustra with Christian pietists; but in fact, "Of the Vision and the Riddle" bears quite closely on the concerns of spiritual autobiographers. Like Zarathustra, early American pietists—Puritan and Quaker alike—recorded their lives as prolonged, often convulsive crises, dominated by the repetition of a single question. Like Zarathustra, pietists sought escape from crisis in synecdochic affirmation, mingling memory and symbol; and like Zarathustra, American pietists found both their greatest challenge and their greatest solace in a cyclical cosmology—an "eternity" evoked through revision. The autobiographies of Thomas Shepard and John Woolman typify these concerns.

SHEPARD'S *AUTOBIOGRAPHY*

Toward the close of his *Autobiography*, Thomas Shepard attempted, for the last time, to come to terms with the recurrent tragedy of his life. Once again, a son had been born to him, and once again his wife—the second—had died in childbirth. The Puritan minister, who was himself quite ill, steeled himself to accept God's latest judgment; but piety could not mask his pain:

> This affliction was very heavy to me, for in it the Lord seemed to withdraw his tender care for me and mine which he graciously manifested by my dear wife; also refused to hear prayer when I did think he would have harkened and let me see his beauty in the land of the living in restoring her to health again. (70)

The mourner imagines himself an Eli, punished for his negligence by the "rooting out" of his family; yet the biblical rationale does not comfort: the loss, he murmurs, was "very great." But Shepard does find comfort in a figure of a different kind. Looking beyond his own misfortunes, he sees signs of wonder in the New World:

> The Lord hath set me and my children aside from the flames of the fires in Yorkshire and Northumberland whence if we had not been delivered I had been in great afflictions and temptations....The Lord therefore hath showed his tenderness to me and mine in carrying me to a land of peace, through a place of trial. (70)

Like Abraham, he has led his family to a new Canaan, secure from the ruins of Europe; and although New England's trials would doubtless be severe, its promise seemed assured. When "all England and Europe are in flame," God has brought peace to the New World. It was an unmistakable sign of favor.

Shepard's *Autobiography* is a contest between these two views. Ever doubting his own assurance, he is nevertheless eager to project it upon others—upon his son Thomas, upon the students of Harvard College, upon the entire colony. To Shepard alone, God's providences are often tentative, inconclusive; to the colonists, deliverance from an English Sodom to a New Israel has the figural authority of Scripture. Shepard alone is weak, tormented by doubt; Shepard, the sire of a New England line, is almost brazen in his optimism. The text reflects these oppositions. From the security of Newtown, Shepard portrays his English life as a prolonged crisis of faith. The Atlantic crossing offers salvation; and as he writes sometime after 1637, he casts his spiritual life in sharply contradictory terms. The prose of the English section is tentative and private; it circles back on itself in a rhetoric of despair. The prose of the American section is more resolute and public, adopting the fervent tone of Shepard's great sermons. For while his former harried life betrayed nothing so much as the vagaries of faith, life in New England proclaimed "the kingdom of God on earth."[1] Here, Shepard could behold the marvels of God's providence.

In the introduction to his edition of the *Autobiography*, Michael McGiffert deftly captures Shepard's spiritual life.[2] Sainthood, to this most conscientious of ministers, was "rather a process than a settled condition," a dynamic relation of assurance and anxiety, "making despair do the office of delight" (25, 20). Such a process structured life as a cycle of challenges. This is particularly true of the earlier, Old World portion of his account, where God's numerous providences seem only to heighten Shepard's suffering. As a boy he languished in the "little blind town" of Adthorp, "much neglected" by his uncle and put to menial "country work," while the plague raged in his native Towcester (38). Only his mother's death delivers him—into the hands of a cruel stepmother, who sends him off to "an exceeding curst and cruel" village school. His father's death forces yet another return home, and another siege of neglect. It must have seemed to the autobiographer as if God had preserved him in order to refine his torments. When Shepard's brother finally intervenes, and sets him on a course that would end at Cambridge, the pattern of tempered promise only intensifies. The youth, encouraged by his tutor, pores over Latin and Greek, takes careful notes during sermons, and frets when his intense devotion momentarily lapses. Yet at Cambridge, duly sponsored by a fellow of Emmanuel College and destined for the ministry, he lapses more seriously. Now his life is characterized by "much neglect of God and private prayer," by "foolish" pride, by a conduct "most vile" (40). And lest his readers consider such remarks the work of an overactive conscience, Shepard gives further proof of his depravity, averring that he fell in with "loose company": "And I drank so much one day that I was dead drunk, and that upon a Saturday night . . . and knew not where I was until I awakened late on that Sabbath and sick of my beastly carriage" (41). At the very height of his devotion, Shepard rediscovers the blindness of his childhood, as if he were fated to relive the scene. Anxiety, death, and crisis structure his experience.

This, of course, is the classic pattern of Puritan conviction of sin— a dialectical pursuit of grace through depravity. What is striking about Shepard's conversion at Cambridge, though, is how little it truly settles. The meticulously numbered stages of despair, identification with Christ, and renewed understanding of the Word confirm him in the ministry but do not alter the old pattern of blindness and deliverance. Thus, the new Master of Arts, who rejoiced that God had not left him in that "profane, ignorant town of Towcester . . . that sink and Sodom" (40), finds himself dispatched to the town of Earle's Colne, where he could find only one man "that had any godliness" in him (48). No sooner does he begin to win souls in this new Sodom than he is harried by Archbishop Laud himself, who blithely insists that if Shepard can find no work in the provinces, he may starve at the University. Now he flees to Buttercrambe, in Yorkshire: miraculously saved from drowning as he travels, he finds himself once again delivered to "a profane house" in a "vile wicked town," immersed once again in depravity (52). And although he departs months later with a "holy" wife, he finds holiness impossible in "this dark country"; "for I began to grow secretly proud and full of sensuality . . . and my spirit grew fierce in some things and secretly mindless of the souls of the people" (55). Once again, Shepard's spiritual path had returned him to Towcester.

In a word, the English experience, from the vantage of Newtown, is a diabolic recurrence of "renewed conversions" in Sodom. Shepard is explicit about both aspects. As if indelibly marked by "that sink and Sodom" of his birthplace, he discovers it at every turn: at Cambridge, where the most affecting sermon he hears is on Genesis 18.32, "I will not destroy it for ten's sake"; in Earle's Colne, where he can find only one godly man; in Buttercrambe, where he finds none at all; and before Laud, "a man fitted of God to be a scourge to his people" (49). Conversely, Shepard is eager to record instances of "rebirth." "And the Lord made me then to profess that I looked now upon my life as a new life given unto me," he recalls of his near drowning (52).

When he rejects the barbarity of the North and determines on New England, he imagines himself "as one come out from the dead" (56). And as he struggles to leave England's orbit, continually driven back by contrary seas, each brush with death strengthens his need "to live like one come and risen from the dead" (60). Such resolutions were by no means extraordinary; Puritans had long made the world a theater for grace. But England was a chaotic world, and even as Shepard records these providences, he underscores their futility. Despair outweighs favor—repeatedly, in the twice-recorded death of his father and the numerous cruelties of his stepmother; in the blind towns he inhabits and in Laud's continuous harassment. So insistent are these setbacks that they literally drive Shepard into hiding, as if he were forced back time and again upon the lonely fields of Cambridge, where he once retired to contemplate his sins. England offered no haven for the saint.

Perhaps the most decisive measure of Shepard's despair is the degree to which he suffers in solitude. The pattern of isolation begun in Towcester— the paradigmatic isolation of conviction of sin—follows Shepard throughout England. No sooner does he establish some measure of piety in one locale than he is forced off to another, to renew the painful process. At Earle's Colne he wins many souls to Christ; then "Satan ... began to rage, and the commisaries, registers, and others" drive him away (48). He turns up at Buttercrambe, marries, and procures "friends and respect of all in the family" (53), only to be driven off by the Anglican Bishop Neile. He migrates to Newcastle, preaching "up and down in the country," and circulating among the likes of John Cotton, Thomas Hooker, Samuel Stone, and Thomas Weld, only to see them depart for America. And as he determines to follow, he must endure the indignities of a fugitive, hiding in safe houses around London. "Truly," he writes, "I found this time of my life wherein I was so tossed up and down and had no place of settling ... the most uncomfortable and fruitless time to my own soul especially that ever I had in my life" (57). Paradoxically, the protracted flight from England only intensifies Shepard's solitude. In the late autumn of 1634, along with "diverse godly Christians," he hired a leaky ship and set out for America in a storm; the vessel was driven back on land, nearly wrecked, and the passengers dispersed throughout Yarmouth. For Shepard, who watched his young son Thomas die as a result of the ordeal, the storm was a final confirmation of despair. Unable to risk attending the funeral, he mourns in solitude, fearing that the Lord "would take away my wife also, if not myself long after" (61). At no time in his life was he so profoundly alone.

But the storm episode projects a possible end to Shepard's sufferings by invoking precisely that rhetoric that would dominate the American portion of the text. Here, as elsewhere in the *Autobiography*, Shepard is quick to record God's remarkable providence and to offer thanks for his deliverance; but the tone and the intensity of his praise, the vividness of his symbolism as he inches away from England, are wholly without precedent. One need only compare this episode with the earlier deliverance from drowning to appreciate the change. As he flees to Yorkshire from Earle's Colne, Shepard is caught in a storm that floods the town of Ferry-brig. So great is his fear, the waters surging about him, that his head is "dizzied," and had God not guided his horse, he must have surely drowned. As he reaches a bridge across the swollen river, his horse finally slips; yet Shepard clinging to him all the while, both manage to reach dry land. It was a "wonderful preservation," he declares, as if he had been given new life; but it forecasts further trials. "And truly about this time," Shepard writes, "the Lord that had dealt only gently with me before began to afflict me and to let me taste how good it was to be under his tutoring" (52). His deliverance is deeply compromised. The wreck of the *Hope of Ipswich* allowed Shepard to expand these themes; indeed, the preservation of the crew was as miraculous a providence as a minister could ever hope to record. As they set sail a storm arose, driving the ship upon the coast and pitching a crewman overboard. The poor man, carried far out to sea, was picked up an hour later and presumed dead; but like a divine signal, the man revived, and was "pretty well able to walk" some time later. His services were to be sorely needed, for the ship was now threatening to break up. Only the timely cutting down of the mast and the providential strength of a lone anchor dragging along the shallow sands preserved the ship; whereupon Shepard declared his thanks:

> This is one of those living mercies the Lord hath shown me, a mercy to myself, to my wife and child then living, and to my second son Thomas who was in this storm but in the womb of his dear mother who might then have perished and been cut off from all hope of means and mercy, and unto my dear friends then with me, *viz.*, brother Champney, Frost, Goffe, and diverse others, most dear saints, and also to all with me. (60)

Rebirth now is a corporate rebirth, a deliverance of a saintly community. Even yards off the coast of England, Shepard glimpsed an alternative to Sodom.

The main difference between the two passages, however, lies in their figural associations. Shepard, preserved from the raging stream, is cast upon the darkness of Buttercrambe. Wet and hungry, he seeks shelter with his new patron, only to find "diverse of them at dice and tables" (52), impervious to his great deliverance. To the exhausted minister, the scene must have offered yet another variant of Sodom; "far from all friends . . . in a profane house" and "a vile wicked town," he was a Lot confronting atheists. "This one *fellow* came in to sojourn," read the haunting passage from Genesis 19, "and he will needs be a judge: now will we deal worse with thee" (v. 9). In the heart of England, even providence was catastrophic. By contrast, Shepard's depiction of the ocean storm is profoundly hopeful. With uncommon subtlety, he depicts his flight in terms of Jonah's. Like Jonah, he is a bearer of the Word, stealthily fleeing, troubled by the betrayal of his duty. Here, too, a man is cast into the sea—a "type," as Shepard acknowledges, of the passengers themselves; and here, as in Jonah, the man survives. But in Shepard's account, the terms of the story are reversed. The biblical crew cast the prophet overboard: here the crew rescues the sailor; Jonah evades God's command in the desert: Shepard goes to serve God in the wilderness. Jonah suffers alone; Shepard suffers with the chosen. Indeed, the incident has the high drama of Revelation, with "thousands" massing along the walls of Yarmouth, witnessing these "New England men" saved by the slender thread of an anchor cable. Guilt and solitude have become the means toward a corporate grace, as Shepard's sense of recurrent loss, like the storm itself, gradually subsides.

As if to underscore the change, Shepard introduces a surrogate who will be born, baptized, and delivered on the sea. As his first son Thomas dies after the storm, so his second Thomas survives in his mother's womb—immersed, as it were, in a parallel sea. And it is at this point that Shepard expands his litany of providences to include the surviving son, a strategy he will pursue exclusively in the preface to the *Autobiography*. Hence, although the chill waters were as yet insufficient to wash away Shepard's "filth and sinfulness," he nevertheless discovers grace in his son's preservation. Back in London, and in hiding, his wife, "great with child," tumbles down a flight of stairs, without harm; and on the second, successful voyage to New England, the poor woman, child in arms, is "pitched against an iron bolt," again without damage. Clearly Shepard was witnessing regeneration—a literal rebirth—in the child, whom he refused to taint by risking baptism in England. Young Thomas had received his baptism upon the Atlantic; the ceremony in Newtown, in the fall of 1635, only sealed his deliverance.

Sacvan Bercovitch has shown how autobiographers of the Great Migration tended to associate conversion with the Atlantic crossing;

although they duly recorded the conversion experience, the decisive event occurred as they approached the New World.[3] This is doubly true of Shepard, who rejoices that his newly baptized son has been preserved from England's ruin. But Shepard's is an American conversion in a more profound sense, for as he suffers and triumphs now with a party of saints, he sheds the chilling isolation he had endured in England. His establishment in New England has prophetic significance: on this side of the Atlantic, he reunites with Samuel Stone and moves into houses vacated by Thomas Hooker's party, as if the Lord had prepared him a table in the wilderness. At the moment he founds the Second church in Newtown, the prose shifts dramatically:

> No sooner were we thus set down and entered into church fellowship but the Lord exercised us and the whole country with the opinions of Familists, begun by Mistress Hutchinson ... by means of which division by these opinions the ancient and received truth came to be darkened, God's name to be blasphemed, the churches' glory diminished, many godly grieved, many wretches hardened, deceiving and being deceived, growing worse and worse. (65)

The magisterial intensity of the passage, with its rolling periods, recalls Shepard's more protracted denunciations in *The Parable of the Ten Virgins*, his massive attack upon the Antinomians. But the change in pronoun is even more telling: the American phase of his autobiography Shepard conceives not as a record, primarily, of personal but of colonial providences. The actor in his account is less the minister who witnesses and records than the spirit of the "commonwealth" seeking divine assurance. Hence, when Shepard records the deliverance from "Pequot furies" (66), it is with the preamble that "I cannot omit the goodness of God as to myself, so to all the country" (65); and even as he relates events in which he had a large hand, such as the founding of Harvard College, he turns them into communal providences:

> Thus the Lord having delivered the country from war with Indians and Familists (who arose and fell together), he was pleased to direct the hearts of the magistrates ... to think of erecting a school or college, and that speedily, to be a nursery of knowledge in these deserts and supply for posterity. (68)

No longer is deliverance a private affair; henceforth Shepard measures grace by the fortunes of New England.

Once again, a comparison may help to illuminate Shepard's method. When he undergoes his crisis of faith at Emmanuel College, Shepard envisions the torments reserved for him by God:

And because I did question whether Christ did not cast out devils from Beelzebub, etc., I did think and fear I had, and now the terrors of God began to break in like floods of fire into my soul. . . . and I did see God like a consuming fire and an everlasting burning, and myself like a poor prisoner leading to that fire, and the thought of eternal reprobation and torment did amaze my spirits. (43)

As Daniel Shea observes,[4] this incident has its counterpart in the "English" massacre of the Pequots, whose wigwams "were set on fire . . . some [Indians] burning, some bleeding to death by the sword, some resisting till they were cut off . . . until the Lord had utterly consumed the whole company" (*A* 67–68). Shepard externalizes the crisis, as if the recurrence of his vision in history had confirmed New England in grace. What Shea does not mention is how thoroughly the autobiographer had come to identify soul and country. His private rendering of the Nathaniel Eaton affair, for example, preserves the earlier sense of a solitary, guilt-ridden soul. Eaton, first master of Harvard College and Shepard's protégé, starved his students, made off with trust funds, and was brought to trial for the savage beating of an assistant— all overlooked by the trusting minister. In his *Journal*, Shepard dissects his "heavy" sin incurred in supporting Eaton; for the "pride" of not denouncing him immediately, Shepard feared, he would suffer "Eli's punishment," for "the Lord may and doth make sometimes some one godly man a terror and dreadful example of outward miseries that all others may fear" (93). The incident is yet another instance of Shepard's gross imperfection, his need for constant instruction. In the *Autobiography*, by contrast, the affair is shameful because he had jeopardized the entire colony, for the school was a mercy not only to Shepard and his family but also to "the country, such an opportunity of doing good to many by doing good to students" (69). Shepard is no longer a shameful example, but a hindrance to God's own plan for the "many."

The *Autobiography*, then, is a reworking of life for political ends. The same dichotomies that informed the self–civil war—the stark contrasts between sin and grace, anxiety and hope, solitude and communion—became Shepard's revisionary tropes. England is dark, tempestuous, and damning; New England is vivid, heroic, and saintly. Shepard suffers mightily in England; in New England his suffering abates. His prose, too, reflects the difference—a language of private terror framed by the Cambridge conversion yielding to the eschatological voice of the New World minister. Dividing the two is the Atlantic storm, the climax of the English crisis, with its simultaneous tragedy and hope. His English past Shepard buries with his son in

Yorkshire; salvation, announced by the storm's special providences, awaits baptism in America.

Consequently, grace now derives from Shepard's imaginative response to the Migration. "Look upon the face of the whole earth," he had charged his congregants during the Antinomian controversy, "there you may see the kingdoms of men, [and] the kingdom of Satan, sin, and death, which the apostle saith (Rom. v.) reigneth over all men; here is only the kingdom of heaven upon earth, viz., in the visible church" (*V* 17). Shepard may well have intended England for that kingdom of darkness—the word "dark" occurs repeatedly in the earlier portion of the *Autobiography*; but though he denies that his contemporaries have brought about the Millennium, there is no mistaking his intent:

> a man may be under the kingdom of Satan and darkness upon earth, (Col. i.13), which is a kind of hell; and why not as well under the kingdom of God on earth, which is a kind of heaven? especially, I say, now under the gospel, wherein the Lord hath begun to fulfill that which was but only promised under the Old Testament to be fulfilled in the fourth and last monarchy (Dan. ii.44) in the time of the New; in the state of Christ's visible church, which should, by little and little, beat down all other kingdoms of the world. (*V* 17)

God's deliverance of New England, "when all England and Europe" were in flames, seemed to confirm the biblical promise to "break in pieces and consume" all earthly kingdoms and establish another "which shall never be destroyed" (Dan. ii.44). The fulfillment of that promise was church unity, the fellowship of saints become " 'perfect in one' . . . as those that are thirsty for a time, are refreshed with some drops, or waters running in their channels; at last they come to the wellhead, where they partake of all together" (*V* 528). The parallel with New England's saints was precise and compelling, for the purified church was to be an earthly rendering of that end-time state. "Heaven hath been and is found here by God's hidden ones," Shepard insisted, "even such things which eye hath not seen nor ear heard" (19). But if all were perfect in one, then Shepard himself need make no distinction, in this account of his American life, between "I" and "we"—a distinction he attempts to dissolve in the preface to his *Autobiography*.

The events Shepard recounts in the first few pages of the Newtown manuscript are literally revisions of those he had recorded later in the text; they represent the minister's final reflections on the meaning of God's providences. Here, once again, appear Thomas's miraculous escapes—his preservation *in utero* when his mother fell down a flight of stairs; the accident at sea, in which the child narrowly missed being crushed against a ship's bolt—as well as new providences: young Thomas's surviving serious infections and temporary blindness. As if to emphasize this twice-told quality of the fragment, Shepard underscores doubles: the surviving Thomas was the second of that name, preserved from "the dangers of the sea in thy mother's womb"—a sea within a sea (33). The family twice sets sail; the boy survives two illnesses; and, Shepard notes, this favored child of New England was twice spared serious injury. The doubling, of course, involves Shepard, too, as he pleads with God that the healing of young Thomas "would withal heal me of my sins" (35). And as the Lord restores the boy, "suddenly and strangely ... almost ... miraculously" (37), Shepard reaffirms the miraculous sense of his life in a telling emblem:

T. {My Birth and Life} S. (37)

Just as the characters outside the braces embrace birth and life, so this emblem, introducing the father's autobiography, proclaims the entire contents, ultimately, as common property: all three Thomases were present throughout these events. As a history of providences, it could not be otherwise.

But the emblem functions in a more profound sense as well—not only to indicate the recurring character of Shepard's experience, but to suggest its limitations. Like the flysheet in *Ecce Homo*, describing the "posthumous" nature of Nietzsche's texts, Shepard's emblem designates both enclosure *and* exclusion. At the moment when Nietzsche looks backward and forward, reflecting on his life, he is forced to confront his own death—those "immortal" texts that cannot contain the living body. At the moment when Shepard wishes to involve his son in his own recurrences, he must confront the essential bracketing of his text—the inability of his language alone to compel his son's faith. Like Nietzsche, he is a *Döppelganger*. In that regard, one may read the *Autobiography* as less an account of Shepard's struggles with English depravity than as a record of his struggles with Scripture—that sacred text always already in excess of human nature. As *imitatio Christi*, Shepard's life constantly falls short—his English preaching a failure, his every grace marked by punishment. Indeed, rather than inspire, Scripture often haunts him. Drunk at Cambridge, he "hid in the cornfields" where the Lord afflicted him like a latter-day Adam, "with much sadness of heart" (41; cf. Gen. 3.8). "Wrastling" like Jacob with the "spirit of God" (40), he "did break loose"—without a blessing (cf. Gen. 32.24). In America he feared those obscure sins that caused God to "root out" his family like Eli's sons (70). Even the episode aboard the *Hope of Ipswich* had its destructive surplus. "It was very late in the year and very dangerous to go to sea," Shepard records, "but we could not go back when we had gone so far" (57). Thus had God once chastised the centurion who discounted Paul's claim that too "much time was spent" in their "dangerous" voyage toward Rome—the centurion preferring to believe "the master and the owner of the ship" rather than the Apostle (Acts 27.9, 11). Was it not fitting, then, that young Thomas should die as a sign of the father's "fear, pride, carnal content, [and] immoderate love of creatures" (61)? The biblical text was an intimate and inscrutable sign, a promise equally of grace and exile. Hence, in this corporate life, where the text of the father contains the text of the son, Shepard is careful to shadow "T. {My Birth and Life} S." with death. In the "second son Thomas," the father was convinced, "the Lord gave me the first son I lost on sea . . . again" (34), just as the mother, "who did lose her life by being careful to preserve thine" (36), lived on in the child. Like Nietzsche, young Thomas was the living corpse of his forebears.

The saint's life, then, allowed no closure, no final assurance of grace.[5] So, too, with Shepard's millennialism. Out of England, it was true, God's mercies acquired new meaning. An outline for the *Autobiography*, dated "Anno 1639," contains a list of English providences, including rescue from "Egypt, that profane and wicked town where I was born," and conversion in Cambridge, surrounded by "the best ministers in the world" (72, 73). Nowhere in this draft does Shepard suggest the millennial inclusiveness of his American life, in which flight from Egypt, emergence from Sodom, and preservation at sea become types of New England's triumph, signs that God would glorify his children. And yet the death in America of his pious wife remained to trouble this design. "Thus God hath visited and scourged me for my sins," he confesses at the end of the *Autobiography*, "but I have ever found it a difficult thing to profit even but a little by the sorest and sharpest afflictions" (71). Once again, his life revealed eternal recurrences, the perdurance of sin as well as grace. Perhaps, too, Joanna's death was a sign of the fragility of the writer's self.

AMERICAN MILLENNIALISM

Shepard's adoption of a corporate voice late in the *Autobiography* involved a complex set of associations, centered on his millennial expectations. In England such expectations had been building since shortly after Shepard's birth, with the publication of Thomas Brightman's *A Revelation of the Apocalyps* (1611), which dated Armageddon from

Elizabeth's accession in 1558, and predicted the fall of the Turk in 1696, when England's saints would inaugurate the peace of Christ.[6] The year Shepard left Emmanuel College, Joseph Mede published his *Clavis Apocalyptica*, an enlarged edition of which appeared in 1632, unleashing a torrent of millennial fervor that mounted as the civil war drew on. Those Puritans who abandoned England retained this perspective. "Doe you not now see the fruits of your labours, O all yee servants of the Lord?" proclaimed William Bradford in *Of Plymouth Plantation*. "You have not only had a seede time, but many of you have seen the joyefull Harvest. Should you not rejoyse? yea, and say hallelu-iah, salvation and glorie, and honour, and power, be to the lord our God; for true, and righteous are his Judgements. Rev. 19.1, 2." John Winthrop, whose *Arbella* sermon set the tone for later American chiliasts, argued in *Reasons to be considered for justifeinge the undertakers of the intended Plantation in New England* (1629) that the "churches of Europe are brought to desolation & our sinnes, for which the Lord beginnes allready to frowne upon us & to cutte us short."[7] The English persecutions were a sign that God was preparing the American desert for his saints. And Shepard himself, who was guarded in the sermons published in *Ten Virgins*, was almost ecstatic when he considered John Eliot's work among the Indians—a sign, he assumed, of the conversion of the Jews:

> If Mr. *Brightmans* interpretation of *Daniels* prophesie be true, that *Anno* 1650. Europe will hear some of the best tidings that ever came into the world, viz. rumors from the Easterne Jews, which shall trouble the Turkish tyrant and shake his Pillars when they are coming to repossesse their own land . . . I shall hope then that these Westerne *Indians* will soon come in, and that these beginnings are but preparatives for a brighter day then we yet see among them, wherein East & West shall sing the song of the Lambe.[8]

Such hopes, Shepard insisted, followed inevitably from those "Churches of Saints" filling New England. If the dawn of Christ's coming was at hand, could broad day be far behind?

The speculations of Brightman, Shepard, Winthrop, and others rested not only upon a historical reading of the Book of Revelation but also upon an imaginative use of biblical exegesis. Traditional, "papist" exegesis, from Aquinas on, involved a four-fold reading. The primary sense, the *sensus historicus* or *literalis*, examined the text literally, taking account of events in the Old Testament as ancient Israel presumably experienced them. Next, the literal text became a means of moral instruction, symbolic, in this *sensus tropologicus*, of "the progress of the individual soul toward salvation." The third, or *sensus allegoricus*, permitted yet another application, whereby events in the life of Christ represented the progress of the entire church. And finally, the *sensus anagogicus* allowed the exegete to explore last things, using the bare words of the text to project eschatological figures. As Mason Lowance notes, the single word "Jerusalem" yielded a spiritual history of mankind: it was the capital of ancient Israel—the fulfillment of God's promises to the Jews; allegorically it represented the holy church; typologically, the Christian soul; and anagogically, that heavenly Jerusalem foretold in Revelation 21.[9] The text was all-inclusive.

Protestant exegetes rejected this complex machinery, but did not discard its intent; although they insisted on finding only two levels in Scripture—literal and spiritual—they simply collapsed moral, allegorical, and anagogical readings into the latter sense. Thus the English John Owen, in his preface to James Durham's *Clavis Cantici: or, an Exposition of the Song of Solomon* (1669), declared that "the whole is the one holy Declaration of that Mystically Spiritual Commmunion [*sic*], that is between the great Bridegroom and his Spouse, the Lord Christ and his Church, and every believing Soul that belongs thereunto."[10] What American exegetes did was to fuse these readings. Convinced that they were inaugurating Christ's rule on earth, they identified literal and anagogic, moral and allegorical senses. Were they not actually a new Israel, wandering toward New Zion in the wilderness? Then they were literally fulfilling events in the Old Testament—living antitypes to figures in both Exodus and Revelation. Were they not establishing purified churches, filled with Christ's elect? Then there could be no distinction between the spiritual progress of the soul and that of the entire church. The Scriptures themselves proved the two identical. Thus John Cotton, who, like Durham, found Solomon, soul, and church in Canticles, also found there a record of church history from David to the Last Judgment. "Who is this that cometh out of the Wildernesse?" Solomon asks. And Cotton answers: "The words of the Text are the Prayer of the whole Church . . . when as all things shall be accomplished which the Prophets or Apostles have foretold . . . [as well as] an argument of a sincere and chaste heart." That "gracious power . . . to make a wildernesse, a garden of God" was the very power Cotton witnessed in Boston.[11] Under such circumstances, church and soul were one.

Other emphases reinforced this identification of individual and community. The course of millennial history, as both Ernest Tuveson and James Davidson note, was predicated on that of the individual's struggle for grace; as the elect soul undergoes stages of "calling . . . renovation, . . . regeneration, imperfect glorification, final perfection beyond this life,"[12] so the churches' history, outlined in the apocalyptic accounts of Mede and others, embraced pagan darkness, the calling of Constantine, the Reformation, and the Thirty Years' War. Only in America, though, was this progress so clearly fulfilled, allowing personal and eschatological events truly to merge. That sense was reinforced by New England's peculiar Covenant theology, which associated individual and national grace. Like the individual Covenant of Grace, Perry Miller notes, the national Covenant could bestow grace upon an entire people, "supernaturally directed by an especial communication from God."[13] Puritan spokesmen like Richard Mather were quick to note the consequences of this attitude. The churches of New England formed a single soul:

> the forme [of Church-Covenant] is a uniting, or combining, or knitting of those Saints together, into one visible body by the band of this holy Covenant. Some union or band there must be amongst them, whereby they come to stand in a new relation to God, and one towards another . . . even as soule and body are not a man, unlesse they be united.[14]

The New England Puritans' insistence on the literal truth of such ideas made possible a radically new identity. The colonists, in the words of Jesper Rosenmeier, "firmly believe[d] that their lives were divine synecdoches, minute but vital parts in the great arch of grace spanning from Abraham to New Jerusalem."[15] The saints were universal souls.

But millennialism had yet another function, one that would become increasingly important as the New England way paled. In times of crisis, it served as consolation, an escape from history. Just as the saint experienced grace in the teeth of profound despair, so watchful ministers often sensed the Advent in calamitous "Signs of the Times."[16] They had scriptural warrant for doing so. In St. John's vision, the final battle with Antichrist was announced by cataclysm—"lightnings, and voices, and thunderings, and an earthquake, and great hail" (Rev. 11.19)—natural disasters and the persecution of the saints. Christ's faithful would be slain, Babylon would fall, and seven plagues would overwhelm the earth, as the faithful looked on and praised the righteous judgments of God. Only by such cleansing could the world embrace the Heavenly City. This link between disaster and salvation— what Karl Mannheim calls "wish fulfillment"[17]—became a powerful, often revolutionary tool. Repeatedly during the Middle Ages, as Norman Cohn has demonstrated, impoverished peasants responded to war, famine, disease, or depression with outbursts of millennial enthusiasm. Much the same dynamics have been observed among English Victorians, American Plains Indians, and Melanesian primitives.[18] Such movements thrive, writes the psychiatrist George Rosen, "in a situation dominated by insecurity, anxiety, and the need for human warmth," a response to profound dislocation. Other investigators link any severe or protracted crisis—including social isolation—to millennialism. As pressures mount, individuals may seek relief in ideal or fantastic communities offering a "total redemption" from their "abysmal despair." "We are dealing with the prospective of a battle, a hopeless battle," writes Henri Desroche. "The principle of Hope implied in messianism-millenarianism is indeed that: *spes contra spem*, a hope of the hopeless. A cry from the depths of despair." Psychologically, then, millennialism is often an escape from intense pain through the promise of imminent redemption.[19]

Clearly, Shepard's hopes for America were conditioned by his disappointments in England, by the "flames" that drove him toward rebirth overseas. But the threat of catastrophe had important domestic functions as well. Later ministers readily adapted this millennial dialectic to the jeremiad, that castigation of New England's sins in the service of future glory. "When glorious Promises are near unto their birth," declared Increase Mather in 1674, "we may conclude that a day of trouble is near."[20] Was not New England rife with "Spiritual Pride" and "Oppression," with a "loose, carnal, ungirt Conversation," and neglect among the young (22, 23)? "What is like to come on us?" he cried. "Alas! we have changed our Interest.... [our] Religion, which did distinguish us from other English Plantations" (23). Nevertheless, there was cause for hope. The crisis foretold the "day break of...eminent Mercy to the Church," for the "darkest time of all" precedes the day (13). By these signs, Mather assured his listeners, God was preparing the way for that American *"New Jerusalem* to come down from Heaven" (26).

Indeed, as Sacvan Bercovitch, William McLoughlin, and others have demonstrated, Mather's impulse to link social crisis and ecstatic hope is an important cultural trait.[21] Throughout the eighteenth century, when the city on the hill had long since succumbed to social tensions, ministers continued to see signs of the times. "When we might be greatly dejected, and despair of success," wrote Moses Lowman in 1738, "where opposition to the true religion is so powerful and violent as hardly to leave a reasonable prospect of bearing up against it," then does "prophecy...keep up the hearts of good men."[22] The New Light Presbyterian Aaron Burr, responding to the crisis of the French and Indian War, decried not only the British losses in New York and Pennsylvania, but the "mournful growth of Infidelity, Profaneness, and all kind of abominable Immoralities"—all of which made him fear "that

God will purify his *Churches* in the *Furnace.*" Yet for the very reason that corruption had advanced "to the *last Extremity*," Burr took heart:

> Instead . . . of desponding, under the present *gloomy Appearance* of Things, let us be awakened to greater *Fervency* in Prayer, and look forward with more *Earnest* Expectations, for the *Dawn* of that *glorious Day*, when *the whole Earth shall be filled with the Knowledge of the Lord*.

And toward the end of the century, Jonathan Parsons echoed Burr. "When the enemies of the church have got to the height," he assured his readers, when the church nearly despairs over its "incurable" wounds, only then will God restore it to health.[23] The greatest flaws disclosed salvation.

The Millennium, then, was more than a social promise, a fervent, fading dream of the Great Migration. For individuals, it could be a mode of compensation, a way to sustain faith, a response to crisis. Perhaps the greatest Puritan exemplar of these strategies is Cotton Mather, who, as Bercovitch persuasively argues, projected American triumph out of his own profound disappointments. His enthusiasm reached no greater heights than in the years following the Salem witch trials and the new colonial charter, when it became increasingly evident that his influence was waning. All the more reason for grand claims. "The Devil was never more let *Loose* than in our Days," he proclaims in *Wonders of the Invisible World*. But such "prodigious *Wrath*" merely proves that "the *Thousand Years* of Prosperity for the Church of God, UNDER THE WHOLE HEAVEN . . . is not very *Far Off*."[24] Two years earlier, he had made the same argument:

> A Contrary and a Terrible Appearance of Things in the World, is no certain Sign, that our Blessed *State of Peace*, is far Distant . . . Though we see nothing but *Swords* and *Spears* in all hands, and nothing but Uproars, Horroures and Slaughters, in every Country; this do's not infallibly argue, There shall be nothing but wars in our Dayes. It is foretold . . . in Dan. 12.1: "There shall be a Time of Trouble, such as never was—and at that Time the People shall be Delivered." So then, the Blacker you see the Troubles of the Age to grow, the . . . surer maybe the Peace which we are hoping for.[25]

Only then would Mather discern that "Good News for the *Israel* of God, and particularly for his *New English Israel*," the "*Thousand Years*" promised in Scripture.[26]

That "Crisis" raging through the world merely "prove[d]" the imminence of the Millennium. As Bercovitch argues, this tendency to substitute "an apocalypse of the mind for a disappointed historical expectation" became characteristic of a class of American isolates, writers alienated by their culture who substituted "epic-autobiographies" for their personal failures. And just as the epic autobiographer escaped failure through prophecy, so he fled isolation, foreseeing a grand American union tied to the nation's "special appointment," presenting himself "not as an exceptional being, not even as an individual, but *as the community*, as a circle encompassing the country's wonders, principles, and practices."[27] In a sense, it was this radical trope that sustained American faith in the Kingdom of Heaven, a faith that stimulated such diverse movements as the First Great Awakening, the American Revolution, Abolitionism, and the Social Gospel—even as the faithful desired to escape historical change. Where the individual could imagine himself the embodiment of national dreams, he could act, by the logic of millennial thought, with divine assurance. Like Nietzsche proclaiming Zarathustra, he became a "noble, Yes-saying type" of the Eternal Return (*EH* 310).

WOOLMAN'S *JOURNAL*

Like Cotton Mather, John Woolman pursued an apocalypse of the mind. Woolman wrote his *Journal*[28] in a period of declension, when William Penn's "holy Experiment" had collapsed in the face of colonial politics, and like Mather, he turned inward to recapture that lost millennial vision. But Woolman's response was perhaps more complex and subtle, for the Quaker Kingdom of God was less a geographical locale than an inner conviction. George Fox had preached that Christ could so infuse the soul as to restore it to Edenic purity, that converts could "live in accordance with the injunction of the Sermon on the Mount, not in a future Kingdom of Heaven but here and now in this world of flesh and blood."[29] The Quaker sensibility, with its mystic cast, demanded a life lived as if Christ had already returned, as if, as H. R. Niebuhr writes, "the kingdom had [come] to those of whom the spirit of Christ had taken possession."[30] To live piously was, in a sense, to have mastered Zarathustra's riddle of eternal recurrence. But inward perfection is ever subject to social pressure, and as Woolman confronted the paradoxes of Friends paying war taxes or holding slaves, he became increasingly distressed that his own soul was at stake. Torn between the desire to remove himself from such corruption—to nurture the inner light alone—and the desire to reform, he made his way painfully toward a persona that embraced both: a *typos* who suffered and atoned for the nation. His struggle is an allegory of the spectral nature of autobiography, the degree to which one's text bears the shadow of a destructive Other.

"As I went from School one seventh Day," Woolman begins his *Journal*,[31]

> [while] my companions went to play . . . I went forward out of sight, and seting down I read the 22nd chapter of ye Revelations He shewed me a River of Water clear as Chrystal proceeding out of the Throne of God & of the lamb, &c: and in Reading it my mind was drawn to seek after that pure Habitation which I then believd God had prepard for His Servants. (B 1–2, M 23)

This earliest memory, preceded only by the briefest account of his birth, is resonantly emblematic: on the Sabbath, mundane type of the Millennium, Woolman retires from earthly company, and, alone beside an earthly stream, imagines the Kingdom of Heaven. Both the retirement and the delicate transition from Northampton to New Jerusalem are critical to Woolman's experience of grace—to be invoked with increasing desperation as he discovers the corruption around him. When, several pages later, he attempts to describe the change that acceptance of the inner light had wrought, he cites Revelation 2.17: Only those whose passions are "fully regulated" (B 20) and who fully acknowledge "the sound of that voice" (B 19) can know "this white stone, and new name" (B 20, M 29). The allusion to Christ's promise, to bestow "hidden manna, and give . . . a white stone . . . [with] a new name written," is a charged one, for it occurs during St. John's warning to the church in Pergamos, in whose midst were those who held "the doctrine of Balaam . . . to eat things sacrificed unto idols, and to commit fornication" (v. 14). The purest conduct, Woolman implies, may be deeply compromised by social ills; all the more reason to withdraw, to doubt the world, to preserve the purity of the self.

But the world inexorably threatened Quaker saints, and in 1755, Woolman returned to his millennial rhetoric with renewed urgency. Now the Philadelphia Friends were being asked to support the British war against the French by paying taxes for provisions and gunpowder and, as Benjamin Franklin notes in his autobiography, were surreptitiously complying by raising funds for a peculiarly explosive kind of "grain." In an epistle to Friends "on the continent of America," Woolman once again urged inner peace. Since God was "beginning to fulfill" his millennial promises, Woolman wrote, "let us constantly endeavour to have our minds sufficiently disentangled from the surfeiting cares of this life" (A 33, M 49). Only then could Friends rightly enjoy Christ's tender love "throughout the Earth, as to one individual" (A 32):

By which Operation that Spiritual Kingdom is set up which is to subdue and break in pieces all Kingdoms that opose it ... [and by which] the peac[a]ble Kingdom will gradually be extended from Sea to Sea and from the River to the ends of the Earth, to the Completion of those profesies already begun, That Nation shall not lift up Sword against Nation nor learn war any more Isaa: 2:4 Zech: 9:10. (A 33, M 48–49)

The allusions to Daniel's prophecy of the Millennium and to the peaceable kingdom of Zechariah and Isaiah—powerful in themselves—are deeply paradoxical, for that very year saw the accelerating collapse of Quaker political power. As these pacifist saints prepared to leave the Assembly in an act of conscience, they could not but wonder whether this paradise within had been gained at the price of social chaos.

Like Cotton Mather, who thrived on the millennial promise of catastrophe, Woolman saw this crisis in apocalyptic terms. What awaited the taxpayers, he firmly believed, was the same fate that befell the merchants in Babylon. In Revelation 18, John had mocked these grandees, who were made desolate of their "merchandise of gold, and silver, and precious stones, and of pearls, and fine linen ... and beasts, and sheep, and horses, and chariots, and slaves, and souls of men" (v. 12–13). This was the obverse of Woolman's millennial hope—the chilling fear that the merchant mystics in the Society of Friends would bring on destruction. It was this very fear that impelled Woolman himself gradually to withdraw from trade. After several years as an apprentice to a dry goods merchant in Mount Holly, Woolman became uneasy at the great "cumber in the way of trading in these parts," and longed to be "weaned from the desire of outward greatness" (B 36, M 35). Accordingly, he took up sewing, devoting his leisure to the work of the traveling ministry. Twelve years later—significantly, in the very year that Friends left the Pennsylvania Assembly—Woolman again became alarmed at his commerce. The shop had so prospered that he was selling clothing and trimmings of all sorts, "and the road to large business appeared open"; again he felt "cumbered," and again he responded by reducing his affairs, relying on his slender tailor's trade and the produce of an apple orchard (B 83, M 53). Then, too, this horror of commerce impelled his relentless challenges of Quaker grandees, North and South, whose "Love of ease and gain" (B 110, M 63) were behind all the corruptions he discovered. In his mind, the abuse of "Spirituous Liquors" and "the Custom of wearing too Costly apparrel" (B 86, M 54), the keeping of slaves and the dyeing of clothes, the triangular trade in rum and molasses and the use of silver utensils were all bound up in the same savage complex, whose very existence threatened the kingdom within. "It appeared to me," he wrote after touring Maryland in 1757, "that through the prevailing of the Spirit of this world the minds of many were brought to an inward desolation" (B 112, M 64). When the Millennium so acutely depended on the inner peace of Friends, such desolation was troubling indeed: for Woolman, as for Nietzsche, the intimate threatened to become uncanny.

The outward harmony Woolman sought was largely inspired by Quaker worship, itself a reflection of the inner light. In meeting, Friends would gather in silence, in bare unadorned halls, and await divine inspiration—the voice, transmitted by saints, that would bind them in communal love. For a gifted speaker like Woolman, that sense of unity was critical. "Here I found a Tender Seed," he writes of one Maryland meeting, "and as I was preserved in the ministry to keep low with the Truth, The same truth in their hearts answer it, That it was a time of Mutual refreshment from the presence of the Lord" (B 111, M 63). In Newport he rejoiced that "the hearts of the sincere were nearly united together" (B 220, M 115), and on Nantucket, where there was much dissension, he prized those moments when "the Heavenly wing was...spread over us, to our mutual Comfort" (B 213, M 113). And yet this confrontation of the communal and the intimate often produced intense anxiety. One could never anticipate when the "divine opening" might disappear, fairly extinguishing the inner light. So distressed was the young Woolman by one such failure that he "was afflicted in mind some weeks without any Light or Comfort, even to that degree that I could take satisfaction in nothing" (B 26, M 31). Years later, after renouncing dyed clothing, he felt the same constraint, "shut up in the Ministry" among those who "carried shy" of him (B 236, M 121). But to accept social convention often produced the same results. Fearing the ostracism of Friends annoyed by his scruples, Woolman was overwhelmed by an "inward Distress occasioned by the Striving of a Spirit...against the Operation of the Heavenly principle," and was once again cast into "a mourning condition" (B 229, M 119). The unpredictability of these episodes made inwardness as ambiguous as it was vital, a preserve to be warily defended from the treacherous world.

This mingled anxiety and love became acute in Woolman's visits to the oppressed. On a mission to the Delaware Indians, for example, he attended the meetings of a Moravian missionary, David Zeisberger. Dispensing with interpreters, and sitting in silence with an Indian woman, he felt "great awfulness coming over us [and] rejoyced in a sence of Gods Love manifested to our poor Souls" (B 271, M 132). Yet on the way, Woolman happens upon "representations" (B 253, M 126) of Indian battle scenes that present his longing in a different light.

Himself alone in the wilderness during Pontiac's war, and haunted by accounts of hideous torture inflicted on the "English," Woolman becomes absorbed in these texts,

> Thinking on the Toyls and fatiegues of warriors traveling over Mountains and Deserts: Thinking on their Miseries & distresses when wounded far from home by their Enemies, and of their bruises and great weariness in chaseing one another over the Rocks and mountains . . . And of the hatred which mutually grows up in the minds of the Children of those Nations engaged in war with each other. (B 253–54, M 126)

His own hardships in the wilderness—his own solitude—have caused him to "desire to Cherish the Spirit of Love & peace amongst these people" (B 259, M 126). Conversely, the "histories," reflecting the miseries of the proud, become emblems of his own failings, and of the "unquiet state of mind" that moved him to make the journey. Like the warriors, he, too, is in danger of growing fiercely isolated, driven by evils he may combat, but not subdue. The mingled yearning and horror of the histories reiterate his own sharply divided text.

Much the same occurs during his missions to slaveholding Friends. During the 1757 trip through Maryland, Woolman is struck by the report of a "Minonist," or Menonite, who, visiting a slaveholding acquaintance, chose to sleep in the fields. "As I lay by the Fire that night," Woolman quotes this traveler, "I thought that . . . if I had been as poor as one of [the] Slaves . . . I should have recieved [*sic*] from [their master's] hand no kinder Usage than they" (B 138, M 74). Woolman himself had decided to pay his slaveholding hosts, as if in atonement for their sins, yet the "afflictions" he endured drew him more decisively to the slaves. It was this sense of communion in despair that stimulated those shrewd observations that would become current in abolitionist attacks a century later: the slaveholders destroyed black families, beat and whipped slaves, worked them mercilessly, allowed them little food or clothing. These journeys, then—the dominant activity in the *Journal*—symbolize Woolman's attempt to restore that evanescent unity in Christ, even as he withdrew from the greater world. Like a later mystic poet, he might have said, "I suffered, I was there."

Significantly, Woolman's vision of a cleansed society reflected his Quaker sense of community in solitude. It was the desire for luxury, impelling men to seek great estates in the world, that led to oppression; only "attend to that Holy Spirit which sets right bounds to our desires" (B 88, M 55), and the great men could stimulate a reformation. "But for want of Steadily regarding this principle of Divine Love," the principle one found in quiet meditation at meeting, a "Selfish Spirit" had caused "Confusions in the World" (B 89, M 55). The solution for America was a mass withdrawal, like Woolman's withdrawal from business; and yet, increasingly, as he surveyed the world's confusions, Woolman himself felt tainted. The reformation he attempted to lead with Samuel Fothergill, Anthony Benezet, and others left impurities, and as Woolman struggled with his conscience, he was troubled, like Zarathustra, by apocalyptic dreams. In 1742 he recalled a childhood dream in which a great sun withered a "beautiful green tree" in an Edenic setting; then appeared from the north a mysterious being called a "sun worm," moving with all the fierce resolution of an exterminating angel (B 5, M 24). In 1754, during the war crisis, he dreamed of great, blood-red "streams" covering the landscape, amid which appeared "a great Multitude of men in a military posture," as if massed for Armageddon (B 69, M 47). And near the end of his life, in 1770, he dreamed of a fearfully vicious, slave-eating creature, "part Fox and part Cat," like some chimera from Revelation (A 223, M 161). Tormented by the conviction that Friends themselves were inviting these judgments, Woolman made one final appeal, and then, in a sense, himself withdrew.

In 1757 Woolman, with other Friends, reviewed the so-called Pennsylvania queries on slavery to be sent to members of the Society. With the political tact he loathed, Pennsylvania Friends had submitted drafts of the queries to their slaveholding Virginia brethren for comment and amendment. The slaveholders made one small but crucial change that troubled Woolman: instead of demanding whether Friends were "concerned in the importation of Negroes or buying them after imported," the Virginians favored asking if any were buying slaves "to trade in"—thereby implying that trade, rather than ownership, was offensive. Woolman pleaded with the meeting to restore the original language, arguing that owning slaves was like owning contraband, which the Society denounced (B 117–19, M 66–67). But he was outvoted: the Society did subsequently outlaw slave trading, but not slaveholding. In the *Journal* Woolman professes to take comfort in this "one step further," and resigns reformation to God; but in the following chapter he returns to the issue from a different angle. If truth were universal, then he might look to models outside the Society—figures like Thomas à Kempis, who refused to "joyn with the Superstitions in that Church" (B 140, M 75), or John Huss, who "contended against the errors [that] crept in to the Church," and declared before the Council of Constance: "This I most humbly require and desire you all ...that I be not compelled to the thing which my Conscience doth repung [*sic*] or strive against" (B 140–41, M 76). These righteous isolates appeared to Woolman "to have laboured by a pious Example as well as by preaching and writing, to promote Virtue and an inward Spiritual Religion" (B 142, M 76). Woolman, in short, seems to have been seeking a way to incorporate piety and protest, communion and singularity. Increasingly, his ardent desire for purity led him to a testimony that conveyed both: he became an American Ezekiel, a *typos* atoning for the community's sins—a prophet crying in the wilderness.

The tendency had been with him in his youth. One Christmas, he writes in chapter 1, he had been troubled by the merrymaking at a public house but feared his presumption should he denounce it. "The Exercise was heavy," he records, but reading "what the Almighty said to Ezekiel respecting his duty as a watchman" (B 31, M 32), he was decided: he went to the tavern owner and quietly remonstrated with him. What the Almighty told Ezekiel would return to Woolman with increasing force as he matured:

> When I say unto the wicked, Thou shalt surely die; and thou givest him not warning, nor speakest to warn the wicked from his wicked way . . . the same wicked *man* shall die in his iniquity; but his blood I will require at thine hand.
> Yet if thou warn the wicked, and he turn not from his wickedness, nor from his wicked way, he shall die in his iniquity; but thou hast delivered thy soul. (3.18, 19)

Here was a way for Woolman to incorporate his struggle for purity and his desire for communion: by testifying against evil he would at least, he imagined, preserve his own soul. Hence, he remonstrates with slaveholders, publishes "Some Considerations on the Keeping of Negroes," testifies in meetings. But there was another aspect to Ezekiel's prophetic mission to which Woolman would turn after the crisis of 1757: Ezekiel was commanded not only to remonstrate, but symbolically to assume Israel's sins. For 430 days, the prophet records, he lay on his side before a crude model of Jerusalem, bearing Israel's "inquity"; he cut off and burned his hair as a symbol of imminent destruction; he baked bread mingled with his own dung to announce the terrors of the siege (Ezek. 4, 5). "I *am* your sign," he declared to Israel; "like as I have done, so shall it be done unto [you]" (12.11). To Woolman, such a stance was a troubled, almost desperate attempt to retain his ties with a corrupt community. To be sure, Friends had chosen similar roles in the past: George Fox had crisscrossed England denouncing evil; the American Benjamin Lay had once spurted pig's blood over amazed slaveholding congregants; and all knew the lamentable case of James Nayler, who rode into Bristol, shouting hosannas, on an ass. But Woolman's "singularity," as he called it, was designed to atone, to offer a sign whereby the community would know itself. Paradoxically, his public testimony drove him ever deeper into isolation.

In 1761 Woolman declared against the use of dyed clothing, a superfluous luxury that supported the evils of world trade. Wearing homespun, among the brown-clad Friends, was considered the worst sort of affectation. "In attending meetings this singularity was a tryal upon me," Woolman confides, "and more especially at this time, as being in use among some, who were fond of following the changible modes of dress" (B 236, M 121). But the inner light demanded it, and Woolman steeled himself to the curious glances. During Pontiac's uprising he felt compelled to venture into Indian territory, even as he heard stories of whites disembowelled or slowly burned to death; if the "English" must defend themselves, he alone would turn hostage, as a testimony for pacifism. And in a later visit to the South, he felt the need to travel on foot, to "Set an example of Lowliness before the Eyes of . . . [slave] Masters, and be more out of the way of Temptation to unprofitable familiarities" (B 299, M 145). As he does so, Woolman evokes images of solitary righteousness. "It is observable in the History of the Reformation from Popery," he writes during the journey, "that it had a gradual progress from age, to age" (B 305, M 147):

> and . . . through the Darkness of the times, and the Corruption of manners & Customs, some upright men may have had little more for their Days work than to attend to the Righteous Principal in their minds, as it related to their own conduct in life, without pointing out to others the whole extant [sic] of that which the same Principal would lead succeeding ages into. (B 306, M 147)

Woolman's immediate concern is with those few slaveholding Friends who were humane masters, but his implication is clear. With almost Nietzschean resignation he accepts his role as righteous isolate, sole light in a corrupt world.

The manuscripts themselves, extensively revised by both Woolman and the committee of censors that reviewed all "public" documents, reflect these tensions. The *Journal* went through at least two complete and five partial drafts, with the censors revising three of them for publication: the two drafts of chapters 1–10 (MSS A and B) and the "Memorandum" of his English visit Woolman wrote shortly before death (MS S, M 283–87). Although many of Woolman's changes have been lost to his careful erasures, what remains often indicates his struggle to reconcile private yearnings with public duties. Three times in the revised manuscript B he alters his phrasing, as if in search of fragile community. In discussing the crisis of 1755, he excises the comment

"There appeared a variety of sentiments amongst us" for the less divisive "Friends thus met were not all of one mind" (B 148, M 84). He uses an identical strategy toward slaveholders, rejecting the phrase "their Sentiments in all circumstances may not exactly agree" for one evoking a distant unity: "in their different growths they may not all have attained to the same clearness in Some points relating to our testimony" (B 175, M 97). And in a compelling metaphor for his own isolation, he turns the dangers of smallpox into a meditation on conscience. How many needless activities invite infection, Woolman wonders, how many meetings are held in the "narrowness" of party or pride? Nevertheless, as he calls up images of divine punishment for social excess, he cannot fully embrace solitude:

> While Religious Societies many professing Truth are declining from that Ardent Love, & Heavenly mindedness, which was amongst the Primitive followers of Jesus Christ— While I and thee as individuals feel ourselves short of that perfection in Virtue, which our Heavenly Father hath made possible for us to attain to, It is a time for Countries, Societies & individuals us to attend deligently [sic] to the intent of every Chastisement, & Consider the most deep & inward design of them. (B 186, M 105–6)

The revision literally absorbs the individual, just as Woolman hoped to promote a righteous community; and yet even these sentiments must compete with images of annihilation and loss. Such changes merely underscore his stubborn solitude.

But the revisions also underscore the degree to which Woolman's text was never wholly a record of his own experience. Indeed, the censors, charged with enforcing those communal values, were often nervous about Woolman's "singularity." They toned down several of his more ardent criticisms of Friends, eliminating, for example, a reference to a Quaker shipmaster whom Woolman linked to the slave trade (S 350, M 163). They treated gingerly his decision against dyed clothing, altering the language as if to withhold their assent: "I being then willing in case I get safe home, to speak for a hat the Natural Colour of the Fur, and did so, to submit to what I apprehended was required of me and when I returned home I got a hat of the natural colour of the Furr" (B 235–36, M 120). The censors' revision reduces Woolman's testimony from a prophetic act to a mere "apprehension," subtly defending the community against such aberrations. Similarly, they guarded against enthusiasm, excising every one of the apocalyptic dreams, and reduced Woolman's citation of Habbakuk, as if resisting his prophetic identity:

> At this time I had a feeling of the Condition of Habbakuk ~~as thus Expre[st?]~~ as thus Expressed. When I heard my Belly trembled, my lips quivered, ~~my appetite faild & I grew outwardly weak~~. I trembled in my self that I might rest in the day of Trouble, I had many cogitations, & was sorely distrest. (B 198, M 109)

Acting for all readers, the censors blunted many of the journalist's sharper edges, enforcing that self-effacement for which Woolman has become so well known. Like the editor of *Ecce Homo*, they imposed their own reading on the autobiography.

But Woolman, too, knew that the prophetic attitude was unstable. Although he yearned for communion, the very logic of his testimonies drove him toward solitude. Seeking millennial harmony, he ended in anguished doubt—an anxiety that only heightened his chiliasm. Such conflicts reached a climax in the concluding sea narrative, chapter 11 of the *Journal*. Recovering from a "pleurisy" at age fifty, Woolman feels drawn to England and visits the Philadelphia wharf to examine outgoing ships. Once again, however, he has scruples, objecting to ornate scrollwork in the ship's quarters, and releases the weight of his ethical system upon the captain:

> I told the owner, that I had at Several times in my travels, seen great oppressions on this continant [*sic*] at which my heart had been much affected, and brought often into afeeling [*sic*] of the state of the Sufferers. And . . . I have often percieved [*sic*] that a view to get riches, and provide estates for Children, to live conformable to customs which Stand in that Spirit wherein men have regard to the honours of this world,—That in the pursuit of these things, I had Seen many entangled in the Spirit of oppression. (S 353–54, M 164–65)

Despite his anger, he takes passage on the ship—in steerage, where he suffers the ill effects of foul air and cramped quarters, and comes to sympathize with the "poor Sailors" (S 362, M 167) who endure such discomfort. Indeed, for the time he becomes one of them, talking with them during their leisure, praying with them, observing them on deck during a storm. And yet he finds them to be a godless lot, respectful perhaps, but brutalized by drink and hardship, and "so deeply imprest with that almost universal depravity amongst Sailors," that he is reminded "of the degenerate Jews A little before the Captivity, as reported by Jeremiah the prophet There is no hope" (S 370, M 170). Again Woolman is isolated, and as he dwells on his condition, he comes to identify the ship with slavery, with the evils of world trade, and at last with "labour for a reformation" (S 371, M 170), the preparation for the

Kingdom of Heaven. In one of the *Journal*'s most vigorous passages, Woolman captures his despair:

> A great trade to the Coast of Africa for Slaves, of which I now heard frequent conversation among the Sailors!
> A great trade in that which is raised & prepared through grievous oppression!
> A great trade in Superfluity of workmanship, formed to please the pride and vanity of peoples mind!
> Great and extensive is that depravity which prevails amongst the poor Sailors! (S 372, M 171)

Woolman's pliant imagination has turned the craft into a ship of fools—one from which he must stand apart. He could have found no more powerful image of his own anguished commerce with the world.

At stake was nothing less than Woolman's own "reformation." Unaffiliated, divorced from corruption, he was literally enslaved by his own singularity. "There is no hope," the inhabitants of Jerusalem had said, "but we will walk after our own devices, and we will every one do the imagination of his evil heart" (Jer. 18.12). It is the very force of Woolman's perfectionism that sets him apart from his contemporaries—even, it should be noted, from Quaker journalists, who stressed their diffidence, their doubt, their humility. Woolman's uniqueness, however—what Whitman would call "perfect Individualism"—had driven him from a quiet, forceful counselor of errant Friends to an uncomfortably eccentric embarrassment. In London Meeting, it is reported, his "white hat, . . . coarse raw linen shirt, without anything about the neck, his coat, waistcoat and breeches of white coarse woolen cloth with wool buttons on, his coat without cuffs, white yarn stockings, and shoes of uncured leather with bands instead of buckles, so that he was all white," sent a shudder of disgust through the staid English Friends, who promptly thanked him for his visit and wished him to depart.[32] He had lost that experience of community so vital to reformation. Into this breach, Woolman, careful editor of the *Journal*, inserted a final, saving vision, intended not only to reassert community but to cleanse all humanity in the spirit of Quaker millennial hope.

That vision was the last phase of his conversion, the experience of inner light begun when he was an apprentice in Northampton. In youth, he notes in chapter 1, he fell ill and was humbled, only to indulge in vanities when well. As he withdrew from company and sought "a very private life" (B 22 M 30), he became less agitated and began to speak in meeting. But it was not until his pleurisy, near the end of his life, that he experienced true grace. Woolman deliberately shifted this account from its chronological position in the narrative to the end of the English manuscript—the final two chapters written shortly before his death and deposited with William Tuke in London, later to be joined to the American portion in Philadelphia. After his rejection in London Yearly Meeting, after his anguish in the merchant ship, he records an illness in which he was so near death as to forget his name:

> being then desirous to know who I was, I Saw a mass of matter of a dull gloomy colour ... and was informed that this mass was human beings in as great misery as they could be & live, and that I was mixed in them & that henceforth I might not consider myself as a distinct or Separate being. (S 406, M 185)

As a voice announces his death, he sees "the mines, where poor oppressed people were digging rich treasures for those called Christians" (S 407, M 186), and is grieved to hear Christ blasphemed for the sins of professors. But "death," as Woolman comes to understand it, is the death of his own will, and as he regains the power of speech, he finds himself uttering the words of Galatians 2.20: "I am crucified with Christ, nevertheless I live; yet not I, but Christ that liveth in me." At this crucial moment of his assurance Woolman has reworked the major themes of the *Journal*. Still alluding to the "oppressions" of Christians, he emphasizes his union with the mass of humanity; the corporate body of Christ, not the individual, becomes his focus. Although he suffers, he is no longer "singular"; indeed, his suffering is now a sign of grace. That he chose to insert this passage after the emblematic sea-crossing makes this the most persuasive moment of the autobiography. Conversion, community, and social vision coincide.

Had the *Journal* ended here, Woolman might have demonstrated the integrity he desired. Like Nietzsche rediscovering Dionysus in all his works, Woolman would have reconstituted the self, not on the basis of some fragile purity, but on a consciousness of universal sin. Yet the *Journal* trails off in a cloud of contradictory gestures. After the sickness, Woolman reports, "I spake not in Publick Meetings for Worship for near one year," so troubled was he by the oppression of slaves. As in his youth, when divine "openings" failed, he was "shut up from speaking" (S 411, M 187). Purity dominates the final entries as well. Traveling through the dank English fall, Woolman is moved to decry the "dirtiness ... and ... Filth" of "thicksettled [*sic*] towns," teeming with "that which is impure" (S 417):

> Here I have felt a longing in my mind that people might come into cleanness of Spirit, Cleanness of person, Cleanness about their houses. and Garments.

> Some who are great carry delicacy to a great hight themselves. and yet the real cleanliness is not generally promoted—Dies being invented partly to please the Eye. and partly to hide dirt, I have felt in this weak state . . . a Strong desire that the nature of dying Cloath to hide dirt may be more fully considered. (S 417–18, M 190)

Once again, the imperatives of inwardness reassert themselves in a demand for purity, for the avoidance of social contagion. The menace, pervasive and invisible, must be repelled by a rigorous asceticism—precisely the measures that led to Woolman's singularity. For the dye, like all else in his mental universe, was symbolic. A Friend had a dream, Woolman wrote shortly before his death, in which he saw a multitude of people walking "backwards and forward" (S 419, M 191) in a pool of blood. The blood was that of Africans, and it spotted their garments. Impurity, for Woolman, remained akin to murder.

Millennialism, then, for both Woolman and Shepard, was more than a social ideal: it was a refuge for the isolated sinner, a timeless order in which all conflict ceased. That millennialism also offered an autobiographical strategy—a means of securing a fragile textual subject—was of far less importance to authors fighting for their souls. It would remain for a Philadelphia deist to make that textual concern the focus of his autobiography, as the *typos* of "*a rising* people."[33]

4 | *Republican Dionysus: Benjamin Franklin*

Early in 1782 the American minister to France received a curious letter from a Philadelphia admirer. The Quaker, Abel James, entrusted with the papers of a mutual friend, had found among them the manuscript of Franklin's memoirs, twenty-three closely lined sheets written in England eleven years before. The manuscript had almost acquired a life of its own, deposited with Joseph Galloway outside Philadelphia, abandoned when the British troops advanced, recovered in 1778. Franklin must have been flattered and amused by James's Quaker propriety. Comparing the memoir to "our public Friends' Journals," James spoke of Franklin's role as an icon of republican virtue: "I know of no Character living nor many of them put together, who has so much in his Power as Thyself to promote a greater Spirit of Industry & early Attention to Business, Frugality and Temperance with the American Youth" (185). When Franklin showed the letter "and the minutes accompanying it" to his English editor, Benjamin Vaughan, he got a similar response. "All that has happened to you," Vaughan wrote, in lines enshrined in the *Autobiography*, "is also connected with the detail of the manners and situation of *a rising* people; and in this respect I do not think that the writings of Caesar and Tacitus can be more interesting to a true judge of human nature and society" (185–86). In the interior drama of the text's composition, these letters mark a decisive turn— away from the personal narrative of a rising printer toward prescriptions for a young republic. Two years later, when Franklin resumed writing the *Autobiography*, he was fully conscious of his emblematic status: in the fullest sense, his had become a corporate life.

To be sure, Abel James could have understood the manuscript in no other way, for the Quaker journals to which he was accustomed stressed communal values. They were written chiefly by "public Friends," "unofficial emissar[ies]," as Luella Wright calls them, whose lives became "the depositories of all facts, emotions, and experiences that pertained to individuals who had the welfare of the Quaker group at heart." That James transferred this sectarian consciousness to national concerns may reflect the charged atmosphere of the Revolutionary period, when "the individual's voluntarily subordinating himself to the group"[1] became an obsessive concern. But his response also bore on the peculiar manner in which Quaker journals were composed—revised alike by journalist and censors. As the censors enforced group consciousness, then, so James, by soliciting Franklin, acted as censor for the new nation. But Franklin, by his inclusion of the letters in his own text, played the same role. Admitting a reader into the text, he announced that he, too, was submitting to this process of turning private attitudes into public currency. Henceforth, he would write his memoirs with a censor at his elbow.

As such, Franklin's *Autobiography* is a radical response to the problem of the subject. Consciously eschewing the interiority of conversion narratives, he presents himself as an emblem, an American type. Much like Nietzsche's Dionysus, the "representative" of "*transfiguring* virtues," and "the key to culture" (WP §1009, 522; §1033, 533; §1017, 525), the narrator of the *Autobiography* is a symbol of the republic, key to its future glory. "An urge to unity, a reaching out beyond personality" are among the virtues Nietzsche assigns to Dionysus; a "full and powerful soul [who] not only copes with painful, even terrible losses, deprivations, robberies, insults; [but] emerges from such hells with a greater fullness and powerfulness" (WP §1050, 539; §1030, 532). So, too, with Franklin's American, who would emerge from colonial decadence to republican probity. He would, as Benjamin Vauhgan declared, "better the whole race of men" (189).

In providing a handbook for revolution, however, Franklin also dethroned the self. As Roland Barthes argues in "The Death of the Author," the reader's encounter with a text inevitably depersonalizes the writer, releasing the communal significance that always lies behind his work. Thereafter the text is absorbed into a cultural tissue of meanings, a marketplace of anonymous utterances: "writing is the destruction of every voice, of every point of origin. Writing is that neutral, composite, oblique space where our subject slips away, the negative where all identity is lost, starting with the very identity of the body writing."[2] It was this paradox that led Nietzsche to insist on his own typical stance in *Ecce Homo*, for the *typos* transcended mere particularity and the destruction of authorship. By revising his life to reflect world-historical concerns, "Nietzsche" became a resonant symbol. So, too, with Franklin. This printer's life—and Franklin is insistent in his association of life with language—would be a profoundly public document, or rather, the story of how such a public life is achieved. Beginning in poverty, ambitious, but surrounded by a corruption in which he often participates, Franklin moves toward national eminence by "revising" his life as he would a text, by denying or negating all that impedes his progress, and by adopting an increasingly public role. As he does so, the nature of his audience changes—from the intimate "you" of part 1, to the legions of tradesmen who may profit from his virtue, to the visionary community of the early republic—and so, too, does the nature of his prose—from the self-consciously ruminative, to the hortatory, to the documentary. As he leads the reader through these calculated transformations, Franklin expects to be emulated, not only morally but linguistically. He expects the reader to regard life itself as a composing process. That Franklin, like Nietzsche, could be "crushed" in the process was but another consequence of the political life he espoused.

FRANKLIN AND COLONIAL CORRUPTION

Readers of the *Autobiography* often seek the essential Franklin in part 1, narrative of the printer's rise to wealth. The dishevelled entrance into Philadelphia; the initial success with the printer Keimer; the triumphant return to Boston, the boy's pockets bursting with exotic currency; the callow trip to London on Governor Keith's empty recommendation; the return to Philadelphia with the merchant Denham and Franklin's subsequent establishment of a printing shop with borrowed funds—all this is too well known to need comment. Indeed, those who associate Benjamin Franklin with Father Abraham, the garrulous narrator of *The Way to Wealth*, have found the work's communal significance precisely in this rise. Such a reading was the basis for D. H. Lawrence's "snuff-coloured" little Benjamin, avatar of shifty capitalism, or, more affirmatively, for J. A. Leo Lemay's "representative" Franklin, "example of the fulfillment of the American Dream." Occasionally, Franklin's rise is associated with a particular moral program—a purgation of those agrarian vices that he knew would hinder his own progress. By continual contrast with social failures—drunkards, time-servers, shiftless aristocrats, tippling printers—Franklin highlighted his prominence, choosing incidents "so as to illustrate specific weaknesses of character . . . prejudicial and damaging to a young tradesman."[3]

Less often acknowledged, though, is the care, in part 1, with which Franklin immerses himself in vice. If the colonial world was undisciplined and treacherous, it was also a world in which a young Boston rebel thrived. The list of corrupting influences is impressive. In New York and Philadelphia, Franklin lives with John Collins, who drinks, steals his money, and eventually absconds. The governor of Pennsylvania, like Fielding's benevolent Gentleman, befriends young Franklin, sending him all the way to England with great expectations; only in London does he discover the hoax. There he rooms with James Ralph, who had abandoned a wife and child in Philadelphia, and who steals Franklin's name, as well as his money. In London, too, he discovers that Keimer is a "knave," and when he returns to Keimer's shop, he finds himself surrounded by other knaves—lapsed scholars, drunken or incompetent workmen. In short, Franklin moves in a world defined by license, selfishness, and the main chance—a world, it should be stressed, that the shrewd printer bent to his will.

Indeed, in many ways, Franklin makes clear, he participates in the corruption, exhibiting precisely those vices displayed by others. Just as Governor Keith had the cheek to "pla[y] such pitiful Tricks, & impos[e] so grossly on a poor ignorant Boy" (42), so an upstart apprentice once took advantage of his brother's troubles with the Boston authorities to "assert [his] Freedom" from indentures (20). As James Ralph abandoned a family, so Franklin abandoned Deborah Read, and considered himself partially responsible for the young woman's disastrous marriage to an abusive bigamist. As Franklin lost large sums to thieving friends, so he let stand for an unconscionable time his own debt to Samuel Vernon. And as he had brushes with prostitutes, so once he attempted to seduce Ralph's mistress, and confesses that he "had hurried...frequently into Intrigues with low Women that fell in my Way, which were attended with some Expence & great Inconvenience, besides a continual Risque to my Health" (70). Insofar as such youthful actions represent a defiance of social authority, Franklin is trebly guilty. He defies his father's authority by rejecting the chandler's trade and uses his threat to go to sea as leverage to work for his less threatening brother. There he spends Sundays in study instead of prayer, and helps James Franklin twit the Boston magistrates in a series of satirical pieces for the *New England Courant*. Absconding to Philadelphia, he represents himself to a ship's captain as a young wastrel "that had got a naughty Girl with Child, whose Friends would compel me to marry her" (20). At Keimer's shop he supersedes his master by courting powerful officials, and in England he defies the rules of Watt's printing shop, and suffers by having his work sabotaged. And there is the matter of his notorious self-seeking: his sending an asbestos purse to Sir Hans Sloane so that he could advertise the lord's patronage, his demure use of the Junto Club to advance his own career, his determined cultivation of *"Appearances"* of industry (68). Franklin, of course, was far from being the besotted or corrupt wastrel he represents in his gallery of rogues—but he was vulnerable; and it is his vulnerability as much as his success that marks the first installment of his life.

In portraying such widespread vice Franklin was merely typical of his class and of his age. The first half of the eighteenth century, as James Henretta points out, was a period of slowly mounting disorder. Families were no longer able to control an increasingly diverse group of indentured servants, who rebelled much as Franklin did, to become disaffected, often volatile drifters.[4] Many turned to crime, or alcohol, or mob action. In the Boston of Franklin's youth, according to Carl Bridenbaugh, residents suffered through "epidemic[s]" of robberies, endured "Riots & Tumults" as troops and sailors debarked at the wharves, and dolefully observed the "Levity and Wanton Frollicks of the Young People" who tippled in the "Ordinaries" on Sundays. Sexual license, too, was becoming common, as Cotton Mather himself discovered in 1713, when he decried the loose "Houses ... where there [were] young Women of a very debauched Character and extreamly Impudent; unto whom there is a great Resort of young men."[5] It was Mather, in fact, in an important prefiguration of Franklin's strategy in the *Autobiography*, who attempted to reassert control by forming a "Society for the Suppression of Disorders"—a dozen or so members who gathered to quell disturbances and to admonish wayward youth.

Similar conditions obtained in Pennsylvania. The Quaker city suffered from its share of larceny, riot, and promiscuity. William Penn himself had complained in 1697 "that there is no place more overrun with wickedness, Sins so very Scandalous, openly Comitted in defiance of Law and Virtue: the facts so foul, I am forbid by Comon modesty to relate."[6] In one notable siege during 1741, a group of sailors so incensed the populace by stealing the public pumps that a riot erupted, and a few weeks later, the aroused mob turned its anger on local bakers, who refused to accept suspect specie. Franklin, too, in the *Pennsylvania Gazette* and elsewhere, was quick to note instances of social excess. "Last Monday Morning," he wrote in the *Gazette* on December 7, 1732, "a Woman who had been long given to excessive Drinking, was found dead in a Room by her self, upon the Floor," a profligate who had defeated the best efforts of her virtuous husband; "for who ever heard of a Sot reclaim'd?"[7] Two weeks later he was reporting on counterfeiters caught passing twenty-shilling bills, who claimed, with perverse logic, "that it was no Sin, for it would make Money plentier among poor People" (*P* 1:279). Hence one senses more than hyperbole in Franklin's comic survey of Philadelphia's vices. "I shall take no Notice," disingenuously proclaims the Busy-Body,

> who has, (heretofore) rais'd a Fortune by Fraud and Oppression, nor who by Deceit and Hypocrisy: What Woman has been false to her good Husband's Bed; nor what Man has, by barbarous Usage or Neglect, broke the Heart of a faithful Wife, and wasted his Health and Substance in Debauchery: What base Wretch has betray'd his Friend, and sold his Honesty for Gold, nor what yet baser Wretch, first corrupted him and then bought the Bargain. (*P* 1:127–28)

All this was part of Franklin's milieu, and—humorously or not—an issue of lively concern.

Franklin, of course, was no Puritan, troubled by the nagging suspicion that someone in Philadelphia was having fun. But he was a republican, and involved, at the time he wrote the first part of the *Autobiography*, in a lively debate over the fitness of Americans for self-government. The focus of that debate, as Richard Bushman notes, was a single dichotomy: "corruption"—a word that, to Franklin's contemporaries, meant "luxury, vice, ambition, lust, effeminacy, profligacy"—and its opposite, "virtue"—meaning "honor, reason, simplicity, benevolence, public spirit, patriotism."[8] For years the clergy had been attacking American greed; now, when writers like Tom Paine were proclaiming the dawn of a republican golden age, there were those who wanted "some assurance . . . that ambition, pride, avarice, and all the dark train of passions which usually attend them" had disappeared, that Americans truly possessed "that Industry, Frugality, Economy, that Virtue which is necessary" to found a republic. The very imminence of revolution caused many to fear that America "never was, perhaps, in a more corrupt and degenerate State than at this Day." "How have animosities been cherished . . . !" proclaimed aroused ministers. "And How prevalent has been every kind of iniquity!"[9] Colonial readers were familiar with John Trenchard's strictures in *Cato's Letters*, that people were driven by passions, "which being boundless and insatiable, are always terrible when they are not controuled";[10] and what greater spectacle of luxury, greed, and vice than that in the developing colonies? "To increase in numbers, in wealth, elegance and refinements," warned one Revolutionary minister, "and at the same time to increase in luxury, profaneness, impiety, and a disesteem of things sacred, is to go backward and not forward."[11] Even after the Revolution

Franklin was troubled by this charge. "I have not yet indeed thought of a remedy for luxury," he wrote to Benjamin Vaughan in 1784. "I am not sure that in a great state it is capable of a remedy."[12] His hope was that the rude state of the country itself would absorb most tendencies to vice, draining the "rich and luxurious" from the "trading towns" to those uncultivated areas where labor and frugality were at a premium. But this stance, he well knew, only invited other ills, for the frontier could corrupt as well as civilize. He had seen too many sharp deals with the Indians to trust in the spontaneous benevolence of his countrymen.

Benevolence, however—virtue—was universally considered key to political stability. Adverting to classical models, the patriots proclaimed a civil religion based in abstract good. Virtue, declared Phillips Payson in 1778,

> was the life and soul of the state which raised it to all its glory, being always awake to the public defense and good; and in every state it must, under Providence, be the support of government, the guardian of liberty, or no human wisdom or policy can support and preserve them. Civil society cannot be maintained without justice, benevolence and the social virtues.

"Without some portion of this generous principle," wrote Jonathan Mason, Jr., "anarchy and confusion would immediately ensue, the jarring interests of individuals, regarding themselves only, and indifferent to the welfare of others, would still further heighten the distressing scene, and with the assistance of the selfish passions, it would end in the ruin and subversion of the State." It was the current generation, patriots believed, that would determine the course of American virtue. As late as 1787, John Adams was appealing to the republican conscience. "With such affecting scenes before his eyes," he wrote in *A Defence of the Constitutions of Government of the United States of America*, "is there, can there be, a young American indolent and incurious; surrendered up to dissipation and frivolity; vain of imitating the loosest manners of countries, which can never be made much better or much worse? A profligate American youth must be profligate indeed, and richly merits the scorn of all mankind."[13] Such political rhetoric, it should be noted, obliterated the distinction between private acts and national policy; to the patriots, the state was the sum of its individual members, and would succeed or fail through their collective conduct. This was the reason for Vaughan's encomium to Franklin's "Art of Virtue," and the basis for the second part of the *Autobiography*.

THE "ART OF VIRTUE"

The continuation of his memoirs, Franklin confesses in 1784, "might . . . be much better done if I were at home among my Papers, which would aid my Memory" (73). If memory had shaped part 1 to highlight disarray, it would now work to opposite effect. Among his papers, in the safekeeping of Abel James, was an outline for the entire work composed in 1771, listing, in due course, "Marry. Library erected. Manner of conducting the Project. Its plan and Utility. Children. Almanack. the Use I made of it," and so on, through his establishment of a partnership in South Carolina, his reconciliation with his brother James—and finally, "Art of Virtue" (203). In most points, the *Autobiography* steers remarkably close to the outline; but here, at the beginning of part 2, Franklin swerves, moving up the projected "Art of Virtue" to a position following the library scheme, and allowing it to swell to seventeen manuscript pages. Clearly, this displacement was a response to the letters from Vaughan and James, but it also reestablished a crucial balance. If, indeed, there was a crisis of probity in the republic, an exemplary life had to offer some solution, one based on virtue and community rather than vice and faction. Franklin saw his own rejection of Presbyterianism as such an enlightened response; hence his remarks, in part 2, on the narrowness of Calvinist "Dogma." The Presbyterians' chief failing, he thought, was their factionalism, their inability to embrace national concerns. Lured to church one Sunday by a sermon on Philippians 4.8, "*Finally, Brethren, Whatsoever Things are* true, *honest, just, pure, lovely, or of good report, if there be any virtue,* or *any praise, think on these Things*" (77), he expected to hear a discussion of such principles as might mold national purpose. Instead he heard special pleading for Sabbath observance, Bible study, and the support of Presbyterian functions—and resolved to go no more. What was needed, Franklin felt, was the generalized piety he had recorded over fifty years before, addressed to a principle of creative plenitude who abhorred "Treachery and Deceit, Malice, Revenge, [*Intemperance*] and every other hurtful Vice," but loved "Justice and Sincerity . . . Friendship, Benevolence and every Virtue" (*P* 1:105). That "Worship" became the basis for Franklin's "arduous Project of arriving at moral Perfection" (78), the substance of his "Art of Virtue."

One mark of how successfully Franklin's project evaded narrow concerns is the range of interpretations to which his thirteen virtues lend themselves. They have been called an extension of the *Nichomachean Ethics*, of Shaftesbury's *Characteristics of Men, Morals, and Opinions*, a gloss on industrial capitalism. In Franklin's insistence on

"Industry"—"Lose no Time.—Be always employ'd in something use-ful.—Cut off all unnecessary Actions" (79)—Richard Brown discerns "the emergence of an American variant of the modern personality syndrome...to be realized by time-thrift and planning."[14] But most significant, perhaps, in Franklin's array of prudential virtues is how precisely it answers the moral lapses of the first part of the *Autobiography*. To counter the widespread swilling Franklin offered "Temperance. / Eat not to Dulness / Drink not to Elevation." To the inability of wastrels like George Meredith and the Oxford scholar Webb to establish themselves in the world, he offered "Order"—"Let each Part of your Business share its Time"—and "Resolution"—"Resolve to perform what you ought. Perform without fail what you resolve." Resolution would also answer the thieving propensities of Collins, Ralph, and the debtor Franklin, who would further profit from "Frugality": "Make no Expence but to do good to others or yourself: i.e. Waste nothing." And to the breaches of confidence that ruined the Ralphs and wounded Deborah Read, Franklin offered "Sincerity" ("Use no hurtful Deceit"); "Justice" ("Wrong none, by doing Injuries or omitting the Benefits that are your Duty"); and, above all, "Chastity": "Rarely use Venery but for Health or Offspring; Never to Dulness, Weakness, or the Injury of your own or another's Peace or Reputation" (79–80). As Alfred Aldridge observes, this list is largely "personal"; it focuses on individual rather than explicitly social virtues, such as charity or benevolence.[15] But in Franklin's political milieu, there was no clear distinction between the two domains. To cultivate private virtue was to secure civic grace.

Perhaps the most curious aspect of Franklin's scheme is his preoccupation with "a *great and extensive Project*" (89) for proselytizing his civic religion. That project, he relates in part 3, was for "an united Party for Virtue" (91), a Masonic system of "Virtuous and good Men of all Nations...to be govern'd by suitable good and wise Rules, which good and wiss [sic] Men may probably be more unanimous in their Obedience to, than common People are to Common Laws" (91–92). In some respects, the plan was to be a projection of the Junto Club, whereby members would "engage to afford their Advice Assistance and Support to each other in promoting one another's Interest Business and Advancement in Life" (93); but more important, it would institutionalize Franklin's moral organon by requiring all members to undergo his quarterly self-examination. That Franklin saw this as an answer to *political* ills is evidenced by the preamble he inserts summarizing his "Reading History in Library" in 1731. Franklin's "Party" would reverse the tendency of all previous parties in history to promote particular rather than general concerns. No matter how altruistic their principles, these parties were bound to decay, like the Presbyterians, into narrow factionalism, for "each Man has his particular private Interest in View," a condition assuring "That as soon as a Party has gain'd its general Point, each Member becomes intent upon his particular Interest, which thwarting others, breaks that Party into Divisions, and occasions more Confusion" (91). Division, confusion, faction: these were the ills that republicans sought strenuously to avoid, particularly in the 1780s as the country framed its constitution. So Franklin, even as he admitted the improbability of his utopian scheme, underscored the "social dimension" of his virtues.[16] They would promote, he insisted, a "Principle of Benevolence" (91).

The prose, in this second section, reinforces the principle. If benevolence promoted social order, Franklin would waste no opportunity to make his text decorous, orderly, precise. His greater control may be seen through several comparisons. In part 1, Franklin refers, in a prelude to his "Art of Virtue," to journal entries claiming "that tho' certain Actions might not be bad *because* they were forbidden by [the Bible], or good *because* [the Bible] commanded them; yet probably those Actions might be forbidden *because* they were bad for us, or commanded *because* they were beneficial to us, in their own Natures, all the Circumstances of things considered" (59). The parallelism and repetition betray a need to reduce the tangled events of his youth to some general principles, but the prose is loose, almost garrulous. More precise—after a passage devoted to *"Order"* (83)—is his formulation in part 2: "vicious Actions are not hurtful because they are forbidden, but forbidden because they are hurtful, the Nature of Man alone considered" (89). The aphorism reinforces the moral. Perhaps more to the point is Franklin's treatment of his own actions. Early in part 1, he reports another great and extensive project, his apprenticeship to the *Spectator*, "Prose Writing" being "a principal Means of my Advancement" (12). The intently methodical copying of this "excellent" writing—an attempt to reduce his own raw thoughts to order—is reflected in the repetitions throughout the paragraph: "I . . . read it over and over, . . . I took some of the Papers, and . . . try'd to compleat the Papers again, by expressing each hinted Sentiment . . . as fully as it had been express'd before" (13). In his remarks on *Order* in part 2, the repetition and parallelism become almost obsessive:

> This Article . . . cost me *so much* painful Attention & my *Faults*, in it vex'd me *so much, and* I made *so little* Progress in Amendment, & had such frequent Relapses, that I was almost ready to give up the Attempt, *and* content my self with a *faulty* Character in that respect. Like the *Man* who

in buying an *Ax* of a *Smith* ... desired to have the whole of its Surface as *bright* for him if he would *turn* the *Wheel*. He *turn'd* while the *Smith* press'd the broad Face of the *Ax* hard & heavily on the Stone, which made the *Turning* of it very fatiguing. ... says the *Smith, Turn on, turn on*; we shall have it *bright by and by*; as yet, 'tis only *speckled*. Yes, says the Man; *but I think I like a speckled Ax best*. (86–87, emphasis added)

Again, the prose insists on order, in a manner echoing his moral plan. Increasingly, after 1784, Franklin's intentions became embodied in his text.

The broad structure of parts 2, 3, and 4 reinforces this shift. If the first part reflects disorder, in the picaresque rise of the young printer, part 2, with its stress on regimen, announces a new mode. After recording the repetitive exercises, to which he "ow'd the constant Felicity of his Life down to his 79th Year" (87), Franklin, in his eighty-third year, transformed his early, public life into a series of repetitions. *Poor Richard's Almanac*, he notes, soon becomes an annual "Art of Virtue." In his *Gazette*, he had repeated opportunities to print libelous articles, but refused them all. In 1733 he established the first of numerous partnerships. Even his study of languages bears this obsessive cast, in his agreement with a chess-playing friend to match each loss with "Tasks ... to perform ... before our next Meeting" (97). He found similar patterns in his public projects, his scientific experiments, and his dealings with the British. That a man of Franklin's age chose to recall his life as a series of repetitions is not surprising, but the choice had important moral consequences. By structuring life and prose in such resolute fashion, he was reinforcing virtue. For Franklin, as for Nietzsche's Dionysus, repetition confirmed probity.

REMAKING AMERICA

Implicit in Franklin's "Art of Virtue," then, is a problem that preoccupied eighteenth-century political and moral thinkers. Just as an individual dominated by passion fell to ruin, so a state subject to arrant factionalism became corrupt. For the republic to survive, Americans in the Revolutionary period declared, all private interest must yield to the good of the whole. Political division itself was often regarded as vicious, the result, as one spokesman put it, of "false ambition, avarice, or revenge"—a point of urgent concern to a young representative democracy. The antidote to faction was informed self-sacrifice, whereby "each individual gives up all private interest that is not consistent with the general good, the interest of the whole body." Such action, the patriots thought, would do more than any system of checks and balances to enforce the national will. As Gordon Wood observes,

> The very fact that the social basis for such a corporate ideal had long been
> disintegrating, if it ever existed, only accentuated its desirability in Amer-
> ican eyes. Despite, or perhaps because of, the persistence of social inco-
> herence and change in the eighteenth century, Americans creating a new
> society could not conceive of the state in any other terms than organic un-
> ity.... The ideal which republicanism was beautifully designed to express
> was still a harmonious integration of all parts of the community.

But if the state were to remain, as Samuel Adams maintained, "a moral person, having an interest and will of its own," then new habits would have to be instilled among its errant members. According to Samuel Stanhope Smith, this was the purpose of republican laws: to give "ideas & motives a new direction ... till they overcome those of vice & again untill after repeated struggles, & many foils they at length acquire the habitual superiority."[17] This ideal was precisely the point of Franklin's organon. Not only did he attempt to achieve perfection by eliminating those vices that so marred colonial America, but he did so in eloquently symbolic fashion. His account book—emblem of his intersecting moral and monetary drives—becomes a record of progressive effacement, achieved by "scraping out the marks" of his faults, and later, when he transferred the ledger to ivory, by "easily wip[ing them] out with a wet Sponge" (86). What he desired was a "clean Book" (82), a "blankness," as Mitchell Breitwieser observes, that accorded with a harmonious, public persona, free of all possible faction.[18] In so doing, Franklin becomes the very type of a self-sacrificing people.

It was both fortunate and instructive that the narrative of Franklin's public career should have fallen at this point in the *Autobiography*. As if personally embodying that "Benevolence" and "Charity" that would counter factional ills, he retires from business and devotes himself to social reform. As in the past no opportunity to advance his career escaped him, so now no detail of American life was too minor not to warrant improvement. Were conventional fireplaces drafty and inefficient? Enter Franklin with his ingenious stove, for which he refused a patent, contending that *"we should be glad of an Opportunity to serve others by any Invention of ours, and this we should do freely and generously"* (116). Were Philadelphia's streets dust-blown and foul? Enter Franklin with cobblestone and broom to promote schemes for public works. Was a library, a hospital, a garrison, a fire company, a college wanting? Franklin would provide the proposal, the men, and the means. In so doing, he was also establishing those social controls he found wanting in his youth. Thus his revamping of Philadelphia's constabulary had much to do with a drop in that city's crime,[19] and his role in founding the University of Philadelphia insured that Pennsylvania's youth would "pass thro' and execute the several Offices of Civil Life, with Advantage and Reputation to themselves and Country" (*P* 4:108)—unlike the wastrels of his own youth. He remade the city in his image.

Important, too, in Franklin's approach to civic problems, is its apparently limitless scope. Like his Society of the Free and Easy, which would progressively absorb all the worthy youth of all nations, or his scheme for moral perfection, stretching off in a lifetime of quadrennial applications, Franklin's social schemes often exhibited an almost organic principle of development. His Junto Club, for example, sprouted a network of sub-societies founded by the original twelve members, bearing names like "the Vine" and "the Union" (99); his proposal for the Union Fire Company was so successful that it quickly generated others: "And this went on, one new Company being formed after another, till they became so numerous as to include most of the Inhabitants who were men of Property" (103). So, too, the militia formed at Franklin's behest to meet the French threat "amounted at length to upwards of Ten Thousand.... all furnish'd... with Arms; [and] form'd... into Companies and Regiments" (109). Such success, once again, recalls the efforts of Franklin's spiritual forebear, Cotton Mather, whose "Society for the Suppression of Disorders" attacked social ills in a similar manner. But more important, these grand projects complete Franklin's "arduous Program" by substituting masses of Philadelphians for the blank tablets of his moral ledger. As Franklin advances from private to public works, so all Americans may unite in self-effacing public virtue.

But corporate virtue, as I have tried to show, was deeply involved with American millennial identity. Indeed, Franklin's broad perfectionism sets him squarely within the millennial tradition, one that had been undergoing a profound shift during the Englightenment as men sought to remove the Heavenly Kingdom from the realm of theology. To these thinkers, as Carl Becker notes, salvation would be attained "not by some outside, miraculous, catastrophic agency... but by... the progressive improvement made by the efforts of successive generations." In Enlightenment America it was Jonathan Edwards himself who gave spiritual warrant to the doctrine of progress—"a series of reformations in history, and therefore a fulfillment of social as well as spiritual norms." Such was certainly the case with Joseph Priestley, who foresaw, in *An Essay on the First Principles of Government*, a new city on a hill, where men will make their situation in this world abundantly more easy and comfortable; they will probably prolong their existence in it, and will grow daily more happy, each in himself, and more able (and, I believe, more disposed) to communicate happiness to others. Thus, whatever was the beginning of this world, the end will be glorious and paradisaical, beyond what our imaginations can now conceive.

Faith in human capacity and hope in the future marked the doctrine of progress, a faith Franklin distinctly shared.[20]

Franklin's comments on scientific progress, many of them made to Priestley, are well known. Such "rapid Progress," he wrote to his friend in 1780, "occasions my regretting sometimes that I was born so soon. It is impossible to imagine the Height to which may be carried, in a thousand years, the Power of Man over Matter"—an expression of postmillennialism.[21] Many of his comments on American prospects reflect the same sentiment. Had not America become a "Garden of a Wilderness," a land of such abundance that its population doubled every twenty to twenty-five years (*P* 2:303)? The most cursory examination ought to convince any skeptical Briton that America blessed the virtuous: "If there be a Sect . . . in our Nation, that regard Frugality and Industry as religious Duties, and educate their Children therein, more than others commonly do; such Sect must consequently increase more by natural Generation, than any other sect in Britain" (*P* 4:232). By numerous early marriages, he remarks elsewhere, "we are blest with more Children, and from the Mode among us founded in Nature of every Mother suckling and nursing her own Child, more of them are raised. Thence the swift Progress of Population among us unparallel'd in Europe" (*P* 15:184). Like his social programs, Americans themselves would multiply in unlimited affirmation of the nation's "glorious Task assign'd us by Providence": to reform *"all Mankind"* (*P* 24:7). Fecundity, progress, and the American continent—all were involved in what Paul Conner calls Franklin's "Virtuous Order":

Here the ideal society would increase numerically, expand geographically, and rise culturally. While the individual might progress only through time, the New Order would evolve through time and space. Limits there were, but far distant. The immediate obstacles were sloth and inefficiency, both remediable. The New Order was inevitably the order evolving in America.[22]

In such a state, as Franklin's *Autobiography* proved, personal and national reformation could merge in a millennial ideal.

BRITISH CORRUPTION

As Franklin worked through these issues in the *Autobiography*, his attitude toward social corruption underwent an interesting change. If republican virtue was truly purging America and setting it on a path toward the New Eden, then some outlet had to be found for the factionalism and vice that was, if anything, increasing as rapidly as Franklin's projects. His answer was to displace American corruption onto the British. Here, too, he was in good company. The Revolutionary period had brought a torrent of stinging diatribes, accusing England of almost hereditary depravity. "It is grown a vice here to be virtuous," complained the American John Dickinson of England in 1754. "People are grown too polite to have an old-fashioned religion, and are too weak to find out a new, from whence follows the most unbounded licentiousness and utter disregard of virtue, which is the unfailing cause of the destruction of all empires."[23] With every thump upon the pulpit, American ministers decried the fall of Babylon, "the last efforts, and dying struggles" of the English "man of sin."[24] Franklin's version is remarkable for the symmetry and care of his attack. In part 1, for example, Sir William Keith, "a pretty good Writer, & a good Governor for the People" (42), sends Franklin on a fool's errand across the Atlantic, promising to dispatch phantom letters of recommendation and to spend large sums on the young printer. For all this Keith is adjudged fallible but well-intentioned: his prank was merely "a Habit he had acquired.... He was otherwise an ingenious sensible Man.... Several of our best Laws were of his Planning, and pass'd during his Administration" (42). In 1724, British incompetence is a matter for calm, somewhat amused reflection.

Thirty-three years later, however, Franklin is once again sent on a fool's errand, this time by Lord Loudoun, whose strongest feature was "*Indecision*"—the very reverse of American Industry and Resolution. The protracted delay to which Loudoun subjects Franklin and an entire American fleet is an epitome of how Britain had been corrupting America. As his lordship squabbled with the Assembly over proprietary rights, the ship on which Franklin had intended to depart sailed without him, incurring "some Loss" of his sea stores. Dispatched on another "Pacquet" at Loudoun's behest, Franklin again found himself waiting for "Letters, which were always to be ready to-morrow" (159)—again at great personal expense. Almost two months elapsed before Franklin's ship could depart; the rest were detained considerably longer—so much so that one afflicted passenger swore, in a passage Franklin cut from the final draft, to "sue him for Damages, and if he could not recover them, he would cut his Th[roat]" (161). Loudoun had exposed the colonies to attack during the war with the French; he had "distress'd our Trade by a long Embargo on the Exportation of Provisions" (162); he had ruined the "Carolina Fleet" by leaving it exposed to the worm. In short, he was the exemplar of chaos.

Franklin insists on this identification. His long account of the Braddock fiasco is a study in how British incompetence and corruption introduce chaos into the virtuous American order. With his usual skill Franklin had seen an opportunity to defend the colony and reap profits for local farmers by leasing wagons to General Braddock's expeditionary force against the French. The "brave" general, who might have made a fine figure in Europe, lacked the essential American "Humility," and paid for it dearly. Deaf to Franklin's warning that his slender column of regulars would be minced in the wilderness, he marched with all his Pennsylvania property into a devastating ambush, "and then being seiz'd with a Pannick the whole fled with Precipitation. The Waggoners took each a Horse out of his Team, and scamper'd; their Example was immediately follow'd by others, so that all the Waggons, Provisions, Artillery and Stores were left to the Enemy" (140). When to this disaster was added the depradations of the troops on their march—"they had plundered and stript the Inhabitants, totally ruining some poor Families" (141)—it was clear that the British had replaced thieves and drunkards as the chief source of American corruption. Like the undisciplined Americans of his youth, these British were liars, refusing to accept Franklin's claim for personal damages in the Braddock affair; indeed, they accuse the virtuous American himself of theft. "We understand better those Affairs," claims Loudoun, "and know that every one concern'd in supplying the Army finds means in the doing it to fill his own Pockets" (163). If Americans were moderate and tranquil, the British were "proud" and "angry," "haughty in expression" (168), given to treachery, riot, and avarice. They were polluting the Virtuous Order.

Franklin lost no chance to point out this disastrous foreign influence. The reluctance of the Penns to be taxed, he claimed in England, would bring ruin to the colony:

> for that the Money, 100,000£, being printed and given to the King's Use, expended in his Service, & now spread among the People, the Repeal would strike it dead in their Hands to the Ruin of many, & the total Discouragement of future Grants, and the Selfishness of the Proprietors in soliciting such a general Catastrophe, merely from a groundless Fear of their Estate being taxed too highly, was insisted on in the strongest Terms. (169)

Years earlier, in *Plain Truth*, Franklin had used the same strategy to unite the colony. Should naive Pennsylvanians "obstinately refus[e] to fight against the French, proclaiming *'We are not affected, and therefore will lend no Assistance!'* " (P 3:195), the result would be chaos. The French would surely invade Philadelphia:

> The Man that has a Wife and Children, will find them hanging on his Neck, beseeching him with Tears to quit the City, and save his Life, to guide and protect them in that time of general Desolation and Ruin. All will run into Confusion, amidst Cries and Lamentations, and the Hurry and Disorder of Departers, carrying away their Effects. (P 197–98)

Now Franklin again uses the specter of chaos to unite his countrymen, for if the British were the cause of the Revolutionary War, then Americans, having purged themselves of vice, had truly established a Virtuous Order. All savagery and ineptitude had returned to the Old World.

But the utmost measure of British corruption was how treacherous it made writing itself. Here Franklin encountered a severe paradox. He had structured his autobiography on a series of oppositions between virtue and vice, emerging from poverty to prominence on the strength of his ability to compose type. To compose type was also a key to his social role: from the early days of the *New England Courant* to *Plain Truth* and the political pamphlets, Franklin's success depended on his creating consensus through language—a consensus that applied *a fortiori* to the *Autobiography*, where social grace is tied to the submersion of self in language. All readers would agree that the "corrupt" Franklin of part 1 is also the most vivid; as the narrator matures, he increasingly effaces himself until he is little more than abstract virtue. But ironically, abstraction could well increase his vulnerability. In the Braddock affair, for example, Franklin's broadside, promising farmers "light and easy service" in exchange for "a very considerable Sum ... of the King's Money," nearly ruined him (194). Amid British corruption, language ceased to signify—as was evident in the phantom letters of Keith and Loudoun. Franklin's verbal skirmishes with the proprietors only made matters worse. In London, in 1757, he took his colony's case to the Penns, who professed their "Disposition to reasonable Accomodation"; but, Franklin dryly adds, "I suppose each Party had its own Ideas of what should be meant by *reasonable*" (167). When he committed his position to writing, however, he met even greater hostility. Once again, he was forced to await a Briton's pleasure, and was bypassed a year later—another phantom letter—when the Penns sent a message to the Pennsylvania Assembly,

> reciting my Paper, complaining of its want of Formality as a Rudeness on my part, and giving a flimsey Justification of their Conduct, adding that they should be willing to accomodate [*sic*] Matters, if the Assembly would send over *some Person of Candour* to treat with them for that purpose, intimating thereby that I was not such. (168)

But if Franklin's language could be so easily dismissed, the "Character" he had created was equally jeopardized. Like the English of Stephen Dedalus, his text was both familiar and foreign, an imperial incursion at the heart of thought. The dangerous supplement of a borrowed tongue might well prove the greatest threat to a republican identity. Faced with this subtlest of dangers, Franklin adopted the strategy that Nietzsche used when confronting a similar dissolution: he sought refuge in revision.

THE VIRTUES OF REVISION

One notable incident in Franklin's youth captures precisely how he sought salvation. When the apprentice printer sat down to learn how to write, he secured a copy of the *Spectator*, which he made a model for his own prose. From memory, Franklin produced a text, compared his version with the original, and revised, performing the cycle again and again until he had a polished style (13–14). The incident, as Elizabeth Davis notes, constitutes a textual "event," a moment in the *Autobiography* when language generates its own life-story.[25] But Franklin's point is even more emphatic. As he details the careful steps of his self-education, he is demonstrating how, *as a reader*, he incorporated an exemplary text. Like Nietzsche telling his life to himself, Franklin's revision intends to reclaim the text as his own. His spectacular success argues that the reader of the *Autobiography* would do well to conform, composing himself in the same manner. The life of the text itself becomes Franklin's most powerful prescription.

Although it is not surprising to find books prominent in a printer's autobiography, Franklin's insistence on the identity of life and text is striking. "Were it offer'd to my Choice," he confesses at the outset, "I should have no Objection to a Repetition of the same Life from its Beginning, only asking the Advantage Authors have in a second Edition to correct some Faults of the first" (1). This life-text he was narrating, this durable "*Recollection . . . pu[t] . . . down in Writing*" (2), is a tissue of other written records. The "Notes" of an uncle stimulating his curiosity, Franklin traveled to Ecton, in England, where he "search'd the

Register" and found "an Account of [the] Births, Marriages and Buri-als" of his ancestors (3). As for his less distant relations, he must rely on memory, being, at the time of writing, "some Distance from my Papers" (3). There was his uncle Benjamin, who "left behind him two Quarto Volumes, M.S. of his own Poetry" (5), of which Franklin in-tended to provide a specimen. The poem, included in the masterful edition by Lemay and Zall, is highly interesting—an acrostic, weaving Franklin's own name into a text:

B e to thy parents an Obedient Son
E ach Day let Duty constantly be done
N ever give Way to sloth or lust or pride
I f free you'd be from Thousand Ills beside
A bove all Ills be sure Avoide the shelfe
M ans Danger lyes in Satan sin and selfe
I n virtue Learning Wisdome progress Make
N ere shrink at Suffering for thy saviours sake
F raud and all Falshood in thy Dealings Flee
R eligious Always in thy station be
A dore the Maker of thy Inward part
N ow's the Accepted time, give him thy Heart
K eep a Good Conscience 'tis a constant Frind
L ike Judge and Witness This Thy Acts Attend
I n Heart with bended knee Alone Adore
N one but the Three in One Forevermore. (178)

The effect of the poem is a double identification: as Franklin reveals himself in the conventional pieties of the verse, so he merges with his poetic uncle. Author, text, and life become a complex whole.

Franklin's penchant for associating life and text is well known. In an epitaph composed for "B. Franklin / Printer" around 1728, he lik-ened his corpse to "the Cover of an Old Book / Its Contents torn out, / And stript of its Lettering and Gilding," but which, he wittily hoped, would "appear once more, / In a new & more perfect Edition, / Cor-rected and amended / By the Author" (*P* 1:111). Two years before, on his return with Denham from England, he looked to the poets to help him with a "Plan of Conduct" for his life:

Those who write of the art of poetry teach us that if we would write what may be worth the reading, we ought, always, before we begin, to form a regular plan and design of our piece: otherwise, we shall be in danger of in-congruity. I am apt to think it is the same as to life. (*P* 1:99)

But Franklin's literary self-conception—self-creation might be a better term—was not merely one whereby the ambitious printer discovered his métier in books; rather it was a transformation in which fragments of texts, memories, and attitudes were polished to reveal a public persona. The odd volumes of what he thought were his uncle's shorthand transcripts, the fragmentary encomium to his grandfather Peter Folger he reproduces, "if I remember the Words rightly" (5), from Cotton Mather's *Magnalia Christi Americana*, are emblematic of his own use of documents, remarks, and reminiscences to produce a narrative of his life. And just as a "regular Plan" required a supervening consciousness to assemble and revise, so a life dependent upon books required a shrewd critical sense, to shape and discard. Hence the lifelong importance Franklin places on a "Specimen of a Dispute in the Socratic Method" he discovered in "an English Grammar" (15). The Socratic mode of discourse allowed him to adopt an attitude of humble inquiry, assuming the language of his opponent in order to lead him into unforeseen "Difficulties" (6). His opponent, that is to say, became a kind of text that Franklin could extract and revise at will, all the time concealing his own views. Even after he rejects this method of argument, he retains "the habit . . . of modest Diffidence," concealing his own intentions behind a carefully polished pose, contending *"I conceive,* or *I apprehend* a Thing to be so or so, *It appears to me,* or *I should think it so or so, for such & such Reasons"* (16). This pose—the transformation of his private thought into the bright, hard surface of public discourse—will become increasingly important in Franklin's civic life. His role in establishing Philadelphia's first library taught him how exposed were public servants to envy; "I therefore put my self as much as I could out of sight, and stated it as a scheme of *a Number of Friends,* who had requested me to go about . . . to Lovers of Reading" (75). As the English grammar taught him the art of revising his thoughts to accommodate others, so the subscription library schooled him in the virtues of *public* works. Though Franklin wrote the proposal, he allowed his correspondents to shape the enterprise.

That the correspondent—the reader—is crucial to Franklin's self-conception is evident throughout the *Autobiography*. Part 1, readers have often noted, appears to be a fatherly homily to an ambitious young man. "Now imagining it may be equally agreeable to you to know the Circumstances of *my* Life," Franklin begins, alluding to his spectacular success, "I sit down to write them for you" (1). But as governor of New Jersey in 1771, William Franklin was successful in his own right, hardly in need of counsel, and, at forty-four, hardly a young man. Rather, Franklin seems to be writing for the "Posterity" he addresses several lines later, indeed, for all American readers, who may find his narrative "suitable to their own Situations, & therefore fit to be imitated" (1). Hence his character, as Mitchell Breitwieser notes, would "liv[e] on in the person of the emulating reader, and ... gai[n] a wider circulation than it otherwise would have."[26] As he announces his intention to recount the "conducing Means"—the process—by which he achieves eminence, so Franklin's prose emphasizes the reader's own immersion in that process. The fourth sentence in this introductory paragraph (a revision, incidentally, of an earlier draft) is resonantly ungrammatical:

> Having emerg'd from the Poverty & Obscurity in which I was born & bred, to a State of Affluence & some Degree of Reputation in the World, and having gone so far thro' Life with a considerable Share of Felicity, the conducing Means I made Use of, which with the Blessing of God, so well succeeded, my Posterity may like to know, as they may find some of them suitable to their own Situations, & therefore fit to be imitated. (1)

As Campbell Tatham notes, the two dangling participial phrases shift the emphasis from the grammatical subject to "my Posterity," as if "future Americans in general" had taken Franklin's course to affluence and were now eager to understand the "Means," the particular process of their ascent.[27] The very act of reading forces one to assume Franklin's stance.

But if the *Autobiography* is a cultural model for success, then that process, Franklin stresses, is one of revision, of his readers' discovering what passages are "suitable" to their "Situations" and incorporating them as Franklin incorporated the *Spectator*. He makes that process clear in discussing his "ingenious" uncle Thomas, a "Scrivener" and "a considerable Man in the County Affairs ... a chief Mover of all publick spirited Undertaking for the County, or Town of Northampton" (3). His "Life and Character," Franklin continues, addressing his "Posterity" through William, "I remember struck you as something extraordinary from its Similarity to what you knew of mine. Had he died on the same Day, you said, one might have suppos'd a Transmigration" (4). The passage operates on several levels. Since Franklin is exemplary, his "Transmigration" is one of those "Situations" his readers ought to note; and, indeed, they do, recalling the similarities that made the nephew like his uncle. And as Franklin's incarnation is a revision of his uncle's life, so the perceptive reader will revise his own life, incorporating those same traits of ingenuity and public service. Both autobiographer and reader would recollect in order to revise.

The process had a further consequence. Just as the intimate "you" of Franklin's son becomes the universal "you" of posterity, so the exemplary autobiographer is transformed from a man recollecting his life into an object for his readers, a national cynosure. The transformation becomes clear in Benjamin Vaughan's letter, the point of transition from Franklin as rising apprentice to Franklin as moral type. Since the success of the American Revolution "will necessarily turn our attention towards the author of it," Vaughan contends, it is proper for the world to see that Franklin's "virtuous principles . . . have really influenced" (188) affairs. Well knowing his correspondent's modesty, Vaughan suggests that his letter would "at least interest and instruct [him]self" (185), and then grows slightly bolder: "but as the terms I am inclined to use may tend to offend a person of your manners, I shall only tell you how I would address any other person, who was as good and great as yourself, but less diffident. I would say to him, Sir, I *solicit* the history of your life" (185). As he continues, this generalized other Vaughan has created for his instruction becomes the embodiment of all promotional and homiletic literature in precisely the manner that Franklin's son expands to include all American readers. The autobiography would present "a table of the internal circumstances of your country," a "noble rule and example of *self-education*," "a strong lesson to shew the poverty of glory, and the importance of regulating our minds" (185, 186, 188). Hence, readers would observe not merely self-education, but the education of

> *a wise man*; and the wisest man will receive lights and improve his progress, by seeing detailed the conduct of another wise man. And why are weaker men to be deprived of such helps, when we see our race has been blundering on in the dark, almost without a guide in this particular, from the farthest trace of time. (186)

The Franklin that Vaughan creates is explicitly a universal figure, detached in world history as he is objectified in the letter. Vaughan's reading of the text has rendered him public, objective, impersonal.

Franklin used Vaughan's letter to announce a distinct shift in his own narration. Whereas the incidents in part 1 hewed rather closely to historical fact, those in parts 2 and 3 are often *exempla*, pretexts for maxims or homilies. If it was true that moral improvement was like copying "perfect Writing," through which the student's "Hand is mended" (87), then Franklin ought to provide such passages for his readers to "Cop[y]." Thus, when he returns to his printing press in part 3, it is to narrate an incident in which he was asked to print an incendiary pamphlet, and refused, fearing "false Accusations . . . Animosity even to the producing of Duels, and . . . scurrilous Reflections on the

Government of neighbouring States, and even...national Allies" (95)—in short, the very factionalism the young republic needed to avoid. The episode is not merely a private affair, but a public warning:

> These Things I mention as a Caution to young Printers, & that they may be encouraged not to pollute their Presses and disgrace their Profession by such infamous Practices, but refuse steadily; as they may see by my Example, that such a Course of Conduct will not on the whole be injurious to their Interests. (95)

As Elizabeth Davis observes, the passage is yet another instance of how Franklin intends his text "*alone* [to] work as our Spectator, our stylistic model";[28] the exemplary design comes to determine narrative content. Soon Franklin details his Carolina partnership, saved from ruin by a sturdy Dutch widow who so well managed the shop that she erased her husband's losses, established her son in business, and turned Franklin a tidy profit. "I mention this Affair chiefly for the Sake of recommending that Branch of Education for our young Females, as likely to be of more Use to them...than either Music or Dancing," Franklin intones (96). His ease in learning Latin after he had gotten French, Italian, and Spanish—rather than in the usual manner, from Latin to its derivatives—allows him to "offer...to the Consideration of those who superintend the Eduting of our Youth" his own stepwise method (98); and his success in winning over a contentious opponent by borrowing a valuable book allows him to point the maxim: "*He that has once done you a Kindness will be more ready to do you another, than he whom you yourself have obliged*" (100–101). At the age of eighty-two Franklin had certainly earned the right to such reflections, but his organization of the text around them indicates that his life had become material for universal truths. The self he projected was abstract, public—typic.

But how should successful readers respond to such *exempla*? Franklin provides an explicit model in part 1, in the famous account of his entry into Philadelphia. As many readers have noted, it is unlikely that the boy's transit took precisely this course: the progress from bakery to meeting hall, and past Miss Read's disapproving eyes to the wharf is too neatly emblematic of his future involvements in the city.[29] In his hands the episode becomes yet another *exemplum*—one the reader himself is required to complete: "I have been the more particular in this Description...of my first Entry into that City, that you may in your Mind compare such unlikely Beginning with the figure I have since made there" (24). The reader is required to recall Franklin's eminence, to project it into the text, and thereby to revise his estimate of this homeless waif in order to grasp the significance of the passage.

The "three great Puffy Rolls" Franklin shares with a woman, the meeting house in which he falls asleep, the significance of his walk up Market Street and past Miss Read's—all this is consequent only if the reader "completes" Franklin by discerning the finished man. Franklin's ideal reader, that is to say, is an ideal "compositor."

To educate his audience, Franklin presents several partial interpreters in much the same way he presented moral misfits. At the lowest level is Keimer, who took no time to consider or revise, but composed pieces "in the Types directly out of his Head" (26), a clumsy and inefficient method. Franklin himself points the comparison by describing how when he once thought his day's work done, an accident reduced his forms to "Pie"; "I immediately distributed & compos'd it over again before I went to bed" (62). The ability to revise, to reproduce through one's own labor, marks Franklin's success. In part 3, George Whitefield and Samuel Hemphill point the same moral. Despite the revivalist's great influence and personal charm, Franklin dismisses Whitefield as a naive polemicist. At fault were his "Unguarded Expressions," which so incited his numerous enemies that one almost wished he had written nothing at all; then "his Proselites would be left at Liberty to feign for him as great a Variety of Excellencies, as their enthusiastic Admiration might wish him to have possessed" (107). But Whitefield's real fault was not his writing itself, but its haphazard, unsystematic nature. He wrote only "from time to time," and with virtually no eye to revision, so that the "erroneous Opinions," which "might have been afterwards explain'd, or qualify'd by supposing others that might have accompany'd them" (107), were never modified. The result was that, despite the ardent faith of his admirers, Whitefield's good works produced only faction. Franklin is a much more "zealous Partisan" (96) of the plagiarist Hemphill, whose photographic memory allowed him to reproduce eloquent sermons verbatim. But here, too, the result was faction, as his too faithful transcription led to his detection. Like Whitefield, Hemphill shunned revision, and the result was a protracted and damaging "Contest" (96).

Opposed to such disastrous compositors were those civic-minded Philadelphians who joined together under Franklin's plans. Typically, in his self-effacing manner, Franklin would propose an improvement and draw up a prospectus, allowing his eloquence to advance the matter. To attack the problem of fires he "wrote a Paper, (first ... read in Junto but ... afterwards publish'd)" (102), drew up "Articles of Agreement," and allowed Philadelphians to meet, amend, and reproduce the plan all over town. When Franklin, "Calling in the Aid of Religion," proposed a fast "to promote Reformation, & implore the

Blessing of Heaven" in the defense against the French, he drew up a proclamation "in the accustomed Stile, it was translated into German, printed in both Languages and divulg'd thro' the Province" (110, 111). Once his text was diffused, he could count on the various ministers to adapt and alter the message, "Influencing their Congregations to join in the Association" (111). His printing partnerships worked in the same manner, Franklin writing the articles containing "every thing to be done by or expected from each Partner," and allowing his associate to adapt to local conditions. The result was a growth of virtue: most of his partners "did well, being enabled at the End of our Term, Six Years, to purchase the Types of me; and go on working for themselves, by which means several Families were raised" (108). Acquiring his "types" for their own use was what Franklin wanted of Americans—"born adventurer[s] and discoverer[s]" (*EH* 264), like Nietzsche's ideal reader. Through revision, they, too, would become what they were.

Franklin's own revisions underscore this adaptation. As P. M. Zall points out, the seven "errata" of part 1—faults Franklin interprets as printers' errors—are themselves revisions, marginal adjustments he made to the text when he returned to Philadelphia in 1785. In revising his text, the printer was reenacting those corrections he thought necessary in life.[30] Equally interesting is the consistent and escalating pattern by which Franklin alters grammatical subjects. Although he was the guiding spirit behind the early partnership with George Meredith, this step toward commercial virtue convinced him to change the initial draft: "I took Thos Godfrey a Glazier, & his Family, who were to pay a considerable Part of [the rent] to me," became in the revised version "We took in" the family, who paid the rent "to us" (60). When he recounts his initial difficulties in publishing the *Pennsylvania Gazette*, that guardian of colonial virtue, he is again careful to alter "my Paper" to "our Paper," as if in anticipation of the consensus he hoped to promote (63). Later he details how "I We reprinted" an address by the Assembly that won "us" a contract (64)—a prefiguration of his "modest Diffidence."

But the issue of effacement, at this stage of the text, remains a vexed one. "I perceive that I am apt to speak in the singular Number," Franklin confesses. "The Reason may be, that in fact the whole Management of the Business lay upon me. Meredith was no Composotor, a poor Pressman, & seldom Sober" (64). His partner, that is, was unwilling to adapt to the printer's virtuous example, and Franklin, struggling to free himself from vice, felt the association harmful. His struggle to find suitable pronouns confesses as much. Referring to recommendations from the Junto Club, he excises Meredith: "But my

giving this Account ... is to show something of the Interest ~~we~~ I had"
in procuring business (62). Franklin resolves the conflict by turning from
vice to virtue: two members of the Junto Club independently offer to
buy out Meredith on Franklin's behalf. Once again, the text accords
with Franklin's progress:

> I recurr'd to my two ~~kind~~ Friends; and because I would not give an unkind
> Preference to either, I took half what ~~they~~ each had offered & I wanted, of
> one, & half of the other; paid off the Company Debts, ~~discharg'd~~ and went
> on with the Business ~~alone~~ in my own Name, advertising that the Partner-
> ship was dissolved. (66)

Attempting to strike a balance between his two friends, Franklin forms
a truly virtuous partnership—at the same time preserving his independence (although not too strongly insisting upon it). At issue in the
passage is the "kindness" of his upright—and wealthy—friends, as opposed to the unkindness of his original backer, who had the bad grace
to experience a business reversal. By accepting Coleman and Grace's
offers, Franklin resolves the conflict and, typically, internalizes the
moral issue, so that the actions of others become reflections of his own
probity: he himself would be "unkind" were he to impede this spontaneous virtue of his associates. Hence, he allows "each" a role in his salvation, rejecting the less "kind" pronoun "they," and frees himself of
Meredith. But although his independence—this freedom from vice—
was the problem all along, he is finally unwilling to remain "alone"; to
do so would be not only to deny the timely aid of his friends, but to pre-
vent them from participating in his renewed virtue. Hence, he takes out
papers in "my own Name," acknowledging the influence of others. His
amended text allows for virtuous participants.

When Franklin again addresses his moral development in part 2, it
is with considerably less circumspection. Now recounting events "intended for the Publick" (72), he increasingly presents his progress as a
series of corporate triumphs. His description of the "bold and arduous
Project" is a palimpsest of shifting pronouns. "I wish'd to live without
committing any Fault at any time" (78), he begins, renewing his desire
to preserve himself from corrupting influences. But this very self-
absorption convinced him of the impossibility of the task: "While my
Attention was taken up Care was employ'd in guarding against one
Fault, I was often surpriz'd by another." The sentence is overcrowded,
Franklin adding the phrase "Care was employ'd" to the original but
failing to decide on a final form. But if the struggle alerts him to his human limitations, it also allows him to escape solipsism:

> I concluded at length, that the mere speculative Conviction that it was ~~my~~ our Interest to be completely virtuous, was not sufficient to prevent ~~my~~ our Slipping, and that the contrary Habits must be broken and good Ones acquired and established, before we can have any Dependance on a steady uniform Rectitude of Conduct. (78)

Once having acknowledged vice within himself, Franklin can no longer evade it by dissolving a partnership; instead, the realization allows him to view his struggle in universal terms, as a specimen of what all must endure. Hence, when he concludes this passage, he presents himself in the third person, as if he is now no longer a fastidious novice but a representative man. Americans, he implies, will overcome the British in the same manner.

Franklin's awareness of "Posterity" has forced the change. He had announced part 2 by drawing a sharp distinction between the private affairs of part 1, written to gratify the "suppos'd Curiosity of my Son; and others of my Posterity" (72), and the more expansive concerns of part 2. Now, as his "Art of Virtue" becomes a public document, Posterity and public coincide, and Franklin portrays himself through their eyes:

> And it may be well my Posterity should be informed, that to this little Artifice, with the Blessing of God, their Ancestor ow'd ~~the Fortune & the Reputation he acquir'd, with~~ the constant Felicity of his Life down to his 79th Year ~~when~~ in which this is written. What Reverses may attend the Remainder is in the Hand of Providence: But if they arrive the Reflection on past Happiness enjoy'd ought to help his Bearing them with more Resignation. (87–88)

So intent is Franklin on conveying the universal importance of his project that he is unwilling to let a reference to his business life intrude; this was not the place, as in part 1, for commercial rectitude. Hence he strikes out a more extensive reference:

> To Observation of The Precepts of Losing *Lose no Time, be always employ'd in something useful. Cut off all unnecessary Actions*: he ow'd the Time for Study in the Midst of Business, that procur'd him some Degree of Reputation among the Learned; and the Mass of the to the whole, that Mass of the. ...(88)

To the very end of this address, Franklin maintains his exemplary status; even when he does return to the personal pronoun, it is to urge that "~~his~~ my Descendants may follow ~~his~~ the Example & reap the Benefit" (88). As he urged posterity to revise its faults, so his own revisions underscored his public role.

As Franklin explores his *typos*, the first draft expands to accommodate it. The partnership he establishes in South Carolina, for example, itself a specimen of his exemplary influence, is an insertion Franklin made; so too, when he returns to the matter twenty pages later, he provides another insertion, the manuscript miming his business expansion. Whereas with Meredith he shrank from contamination, now he is willing to take on men of less than ideal character. "He was a Man of Learning," Franklin writes of Louis Timothée, "but ignorant in Matters of Account; and tho' he sometimes made me Remittances, I could get no Account from him, nor any Satisfactory State of the State of our Partnership while he lived" (95). But Franklin has been sobered by his own moral lapses, and is willing to trust in the virtue of his example. He was not disappointed: Timothée's widow saved the enterprise, and when he was "encourag'd to engage in others," he found that "most of them did well" (108). Another mark of his influence was his brief "Colonelship" (150) in the militia during the Indian crisis of 1755. In an insertion, Franklin relates one unforeseen consequence of his popularity. As he was about to leave Philadelphia for a trip south, a group of his officers "took it into their heads" to provide a martial escort. Franklin professes to be "chagrin'd at their Appearance," "being naturally averse to the assuming of State on any Occasion," but submits, riding amidst their drawn swords out of the city. The apparent point of the anecdote is to demonstrate why Thomas Penn so feared him: "no such Honour had been paid him when in the Province; nor to any of his Governors; and he said it was only proper to Princes of the Blood Royal" (151); but Franklin's disposition of the episode suggests another purpose. Here once again, swelling the first draft, was an image of his absorption into the populace, who surround him defiantly as if asserting his virtue against British corruption. Franklin expands the English opposition, too—the phrase, "nor to any of his Governors," is an interlineation—as if to emphasize his moral presence. Though he calls it a "silly Affair," he is well aware of its emblematic value, and amends his text to mark his growing influence.

This is not to say that Franklin always intends to lose himself in abstract virtue. Ever the shrewd politician, he is always ready to advance his own claims. After his description of the *"Proposals"* he drew up for the University of Philadelphia—during which he makes clear his central role in the "affair"—he inserts into the manuscript a columnar note calling attention to his modesty:

> In the Introduction to these Proposals, I stated their Publication not as an Act of mine, but of some *publick-spirited Gentleman*; avoiding as much as I

> could, according to my usual Rule, the presenting myself to the Publick as
> the Author of any ~~Project thing~~ Scheme for their Benefit. (117)

The confession, needless to say, is disingenuous. Significantly, however, all trace of such posturing disappears in the fragmentary fourth part of the *Autobiography*, a transcript of Franklin's activities as agent for Pennsylvania. Now literally representing the people in England, he passes easily from personal to colonial perspectives. In a discussion with Lord Granville, he is told that "You Americans" desired too much power, "FOR THE KING IS THE LEGISLATOR OF THE COLONIES" (167). Franklin is troubled by the suggestion:

> I recollected that about 20 Years before, a Clause in a Bill brought into Parliament by the Ministry had propos'd to make the King's Instructions Laws in the Colonies; ~~which~~ but the Clause was thrown out by the Commons, for which we ador'd them as our Friends & Friends of Liberty, till by their Conduct towards us in 1765, it seem'd that they might reserve it for themselves. (167)

If Franklin was a political partisan in America, he was clearly something else overseas. Once again "recollecting"—not personal but colonial—history, he finds himself transformed into an exemplar of injured America.

As James Sappenfield notes, by 1788, after a long residence in Europe, Franklin had literally become the "symbol of America," delighting in his dour fur cap as he courted aristocrats.[31] That symbolism was but the last of numerous transformations, each instructive of how self-seeking may be made virtuous, of how private acts may have public resonance, of how a young nation may sustain a noble mission. In its largest sense, the *Autobiography* was Franklin's Art of Rhetoric; as Mitchell Breitwieser observes, it provided Americans with an essentially *"rhetorical"* model for virtue.[32] But for Franklin, rhetoric and civic virtue coincided. Like an exemplary text, a self-made man was the sum of his successful revisions.

And yet, like Nietzsche's, Franklin's self-fashioning leaves a residue of dissociation, a sign of his textuality. Although the *Autobiography* was to have been a paean to republicanism, for example, the Revolution itself does not appear, cut off by Franklin's dilatory composition. More significant is the fragmentary nature of the text. What Louis Renza calls the "stuttering effect" of Franklin's documentary intrusions is doubly true of the narrative's dispersion: the halting march from St. Asaph's to Passy to Philadelphia, with its attendant loss of outlines, drafts, papers; the fortuitous letters of James and Vaughan; the segmental narration all suggest a series of accidents, rather than the controlled development of the "Art of Virtue." Franklin's polished style tends to hide such discontinuities. In part 3, for example, he breaks off a discussion of his Almanac and newspaper to consider in turn his printing partnership, the wiles of Samuel Hemphill, the study of languages, reconciliation with his brother, the death of a son by smallpox, and the Junto Club (93–100). Two paragraphs, those concerning partnership and his son, are columnar insertions added to the initial draft. But the loose chronological order does not entirely fuse these associations; indeed, Franklin's editorial intrusions highlight the grafting: "I mention this Affair chiefly for the Sake of recommending that Branch of Education for our young Females, as likely to be of more Use to them . . . than either Music or Dancing"; "From these Circumstances I have thought, that there is some Inconsistency in our common Mode of Teaching Languages"; "This I mention for the Sake of Parents, who omit [innoculation] . . . on the Supposition that they should never forgive themselves if a Child died under it" (96, 98, 99). Moreover, the grafts tend to mask the inconclusive play of the text's primary dyad, corruption/virtue. Hemphill's plagiarism—an abuse of language—discounts Timothée's partnership, in which printing promotes virtue; the establishment of Franklin's nephew in business is offset by the careless treatment of his son. Law and violation alternate with apparent indifference, as if no order were possible.

But the death of Francis Folger Franklin to smallpox discloses a far deeper disturbance in the text, a threat to its moral structure. For the father's refusal to innoculate was actually a denial that corruption and virtue could be identical—that one poisons in order to save, saves to poison. Here again the placement of associations is significant. Preceding the death is an experience of moral closure: by caring for his nephew, Franklin atones for his ill-treatment of the father. But these "ample Amends" (99) for youthful defiance are qualified even as they are made: when James was grown, Franklin reports, "I assisted him with an Assortment of new Types, those of his Father being in a Manner worn out" (98–99). An act of filiopietism quickly turns into renewed defiance, as the exemplary brother takes the place of his ineffectual elder. This ambiguity may in part explain the columnar insertion about Francis, with its air of retribution and despair, "my Example showing that Regret may be the same either way" (99). In a larger sense, though, this anguished defiance applies to many of Franklin's dealings with authorities. When, in 1753, he was commissioned to negotiate with Indians at Carlisle, he forbade them rum long enough to conclude a treaty. What had been an instrument of order, though, soon became one of riot, as the Indians drank until they "form'd a Scene the most resembling our Ideas of Hell that could well be imagin'd" (121). Liquor was another poisonous boon, "annihilat[ing]" the seacoast tribes as it secured their land for "Cultivators" who corrupted them. Again, during one contentious session of the Assembly, when his messages were "often tart, and sometimes indecently abusive" (133), Franklin reports that Governor Robert Morris remained cordial. Instead of "cutting Throats" (133), they drank wine and traded ripostes. To the governor's wondering query why he did not sell out the "damn'd Quakers" to the proprietors, Franklin responded, "The Governor . . . has not *black'd* them enough. He had indeed labour'd hard to blacken the Assembly in all his Messages, but they wip'd off his Colouring as fast as he laid it on, and plac'd it in return thick upon his own face," so that Morris soon resigned (134). The Assemblyman dines and insults, blacks and is blacked in a murderous charade, as language turns treacherous.

When that defiance approaches the king himself, however, Franklin's suavity falters for one of the few times in the *Autobiography*. Informed by Lord Granville that the Assembly's actions were treasonous, "for THE KING IS THE LEGISLATOR OF THE COLONIES," Franklin immediately takes refuge in writing, "his Lordship's Conversation having a little alarm'd me as to what might be the Sentiments of the Court concerning us" (167). Again the outcome was ambiguous, the proprietors choosing to ignore Franklin and deal with the Assembly; yet Franklin's failure to impose his *typos* may be as significant as Pennsylvania's temporary victory. Perhaps, amid the political jockeying, he felt the danger in this ultimate act of filial defiance; but the text raises the more disturbing prospect that Franklin's moral categories, intimately associated with writing, are themselves compromised. The possible perversion of all writing is the aporia at the heart of Franklin's politics.

The concern is evident in his preoccupation with faulty translations, the moral implications of which appear in part 1. When the rogue James Ralph, determined to be a poet, applied to young Franklin for aid, the latter agreed to masquerade as the author of his friend's "Version of the 18th Psalm" (38). The facsimile drew immoderate praise from a rival, Charles Osborne, much more than he would have given to Ralph himself; but the prank bears a disturbing message. Writing could well have no intrinsic merit. Its fortunes seemed to depend not on thought, but on the vanities of its audience. That, indeed, is what Franklin discovered when he proposed the library, as Osborne's envy was repeated in neighbors suspicious of anyone who would "raise [his]

Reputation in the smallest degree" (74). Benevolence became avarice in this distorted reading. That most people have difficulty with foreign languages Franklin established in part 3, proposing his own method to remedy the error; but that his crisp English should be so misconstrued was another matter. Hence his distress at the reception of the Albany Plan, which met with equal and opposite distortions: "The [American] Assemblies did not adopt it, as they all thought there was too much *Prerogative* in it; and in England it was judg'd to have too much of the Democratic" (131). Partisan passions had killed a measure that would have avoided a "bloody Contest" (132). Conversely, Franklin refused to defend his *Experiments and Observations* before French critics, fearing "that a Dispute between two Persons writing in different Languages might be lengthened greatly by mis-translations" (154). Again, though, the issue was more than misconstruction; for behind the debate lay Abbé Nolet's paranoid conviction that the *Experiments* had been "fabricated by his Enemies at Paris" (154). Writing—independent of the author's intentions—unleashed the very passions Franklin sought to control: anxiety, ambition, deceit. It may be for this reason that perfection, in his moral account book, was achieved through erasure. Only by becoming a cipher could he hope to compel virtue.

Perhaps John Adams had the last word on Benjamin Franklin:

> While he had the singular felicity to enjoy the entire esteem and affection of all the philosophers of every denomination, he was not less regarded by all the sects and denominations of Christians. The Catholics thought him almost a Catholic. The Church of England claimed him as one of them. The Presbyterians thought him half a Presbyterian, and the Friends believed him a wet Quaker. The dissenting clergymen in England and America were among the most distinguished asserters and propagators of his renown.[33]

When one adds to this list Franklin's secular admirers, the legions of readers charmed by the *Autobiography*, one senses how successful was the printer's transformation—and how vulnerable. He had arisen at a historical moment desperate for consensus, and he had provided America with an enduring model—a model, however, already fragmented by the competing interests it embraced. It was, perhaps, the last time in American history when such an ebullient myth was possible, for even as his grandson proceeded to publish the *Autobiography*, American society was yielding to the very strains Franklin had worked so hard to quell. Imitators he would continue to have, but, like James Gatz, using "The Art of Virtue" as Jay Gatsby's primer, his "Posterity" would come to understand his message as purely economic. To a nation of self-seekers, Franklin's corporate life remained a challenge, and a dream.

5 | *Black Jeremiah: Frederick Douglass*

As with so much else in his life, Franklin's *Autobiography* tapped the impulses of its time. Already in 1790, his eulogists were exploiting that audacious equation between personal and national history. It was Franklin, proclaimed Abbé Fauchet in the name of the French Revolution, who "at one and the same time . . . governed nature in the heavens and in the hearts of men"; Franklin who "preached up human happiness" and "regulated the lightning"; Franklin who was "one of the first founders" of "the city of mankind!"[1] But the millennial identity was an unstable one. At bottom, as Franklin himself stressed, it was nothing more than a trope, a linguistic device—a social artifact, subject to the control of others. So long as public usage and public experience corresponded to private usage and experience—so long, that is, as language and history corresponded to an autobiographer's use of synecdoche—the way remained clear for an identification of self and nation. That identification was never assured. Each of the millennial autobiographers—Shepard, Woolman, Franklin—struggled to achieve a perfection of form that was at once personal, literary, and cultural. The challenge for the writer was two-fold: to make a radical equation between self and society while strenuously pursuing a distinctiveness of epic significance. But in nineteenth-century America that task was rendered infinitely more difficult—by civil war, by cultural pluralism, by self-reliance, and by economic competition. Perhaps nowhere are these tensions more evident than in the four autobiographies Frederick Douglass published between 1845 and 1892. For while Douglass, in his own way, strove to embody the millennial ideals of an America foretold in the Declaration of Independence, he was constrained by the very language he used, the readers he addressed, and the cataclysmic events he had a hand in shaping. His autobiographies bore the double burden of expressing heroism to skeptics—white readers who doubted his humanity, who saw the black as a cipher, a blankness, an Other. Douglass's almost obsessive need to publish his life, then, is a grand, pained plea for unity. His revisions are expansive, scrupulously representative, yet thoroughly ironic: each one betrays its impotence.

"WHAT TO THE SLAVE IS THE FOURTH OF JULY?"

On July 5, 1852, Frederick Douglass delivered an oration in Corinthian Hall, Rochester, New York, entitled "What to the Slave is the Fourth of July?"[2] During the preceding eleven years he had acquired a reputation as one of the nation's foremost public speakers, in an era that prized eloquence, and like hundreds of other orators in that seventy-sixth year of independence, he was participating in a national ritual. Douglass's great address, delivered a day late as a mark of protest, is a fair example of his complex relationship with America's literary norms.

In most respects, the speech is a sublime attack. After a brief apology for his lack of "elaborate preparation" (he had, in fact, worked on the speech constantly for nearly a month, and submitted it to friends for criticism), Douglass informed his predominantly white audience that he had no place in the ceremony. "It is the birthday of your National Independence, and of your political freedom," he said pointedly; it called up biblical associations with "the emancipated people of God ...the signs and ...wonders" of a latter-day chosen people (*P* 2:360). As he recounted the ritual themes—the small army, the mighty oppressor, the prescient statesmen—he salted his prose with ironic associations of his own. The colonists were "weak and scattered," he observed, and "There were then no means of concert and combination, such as exist now" (364)—precisely the contemporary status of the slave. Like the three million slaves of 1852, there were "three millions" of patriots in 1776 (364); and as the patriots "seized upon eternal principles, and set a glorious example in their defence" (365), so Douglass calls his auditors to mark "the first great fact in your nation's history—the very ring-bolt in the chain of your yet undeveloped destiny" (363). Should that "*chain* [be] broken" (364), he warned, all was lost—a telling thrust at his pro-slavery counterparts. A black orator, even a freedman, could use such language only with the sharpest irony.

But Douglass soon turned from the ritually embellished past to the raw "PRESENT" (366). If Washington himself "could not die till he had broken the chains of his slaves" (367), how much more reason for a truly patriotic orator to attack the institution? "Identified with the American bondman, making his wrongs mine," Douglass unleashes his poetic fury:

> America is false to the past, false to the present, and solemnly binds herself to be false to the future. Standing with God and the crushed and bleeding slave on this occasion, I will, in the name of humanity which is outraged, in the name of liberty which is fettered, in the name of the constitution and the Bible, which are disregarded and trampled upon, dare to call in question and to denounce with all the emphasis I can command, everything that serves to perpetuate slavery—the great sin and shame of America! (369)

A representative of slaves, Douglass uses all his evocative powers to suggest the full horror of slavery. "You know what is a swine drover?" he demands. "I will show you a man-drover"—and paints a scene that might have come from *Uncle Tom's Cabin*: the "flesh-jobbe[r], armed with pistol, whip and bowie-knife," the "savage yells and . . . blood-chilling oaths," the young mother plodding in the hot sun, "her briny tears falling on the brow of the babe in her arms," the clank of fetters, and the "scream, that seems to have torn its way to the centre of your soul" as the poor wretch is punished for her tardiness (373). As the images pour forth, Douglass transforms himself from an American orator into an Old Testament prophet:

> In the solitude of my spirit, I see clouds of dust raised on the highways of the South; I see the bleeding footsteps; I hear the doleful wail of fettered humanity, on the way to the slave-markets, where the victims are to be sold like *horses*, *sheep*, and *swine*. . . . There I see the tenderest ties ruthlessly broken, to gratify the lust, caprice and rapacity of the buyers and sellers of men. My soul sickens at the sight. (374)

It is this visionary solitude that allows Douglass to utter God's judgment. Emulate ancient Egypt, he warns, and America will surely be "thrown down by the breath of the Almighty" and buried in "irrecoverable ruin!" (374).

Douglass's savage fluency has a double purpose. Not only does it allow him to propose a revised America, overturning the idyllic images of Independence Day oratory, but it also allows him to claim citizenship. Just as in Baltimore he daily heard the slaves' clanking chains as they were herded at night aboard New Orleans–bound steamers, so now, in terms oddly predictive of Whitman, he evokes his own vision of the American sublime. He sees blacks

> ploughing, planting and reaping, using all kinds of mechanical tools, erecting houses, constructing bridges, building ships, working in metals...engaged in all manner of enterprises common to other men, digging gold in California, capturing the whale in the Pacific, feeding sheep and cattle on the hill-side, living, moving, acting, thinking, planning...and, above all, confessing and worshipping the Christian's God. (370)

With each thrust against the hypocrisy of church and Congress, with every paraphrase of the Gospels and the Declaration of Independence, Douglass purges the Independence Day ceremony of its bloated rhetoric, as if to restore to the abject present an ennobling sense of the past, a sense of true community. Hence in his peroration, he "leave[s] off... with *hope*" (387). The Declaration of Independence, the "genius of American Institutions," and the progress of nations—all will in good time return a purified America to its millennial role: "The far off and almost fabulous Pacific rolls in grandeur at our feet. The Celestial Empire, the mystery of ages, is being solved. The fiat of the Almighty, '*Let there be light*,' has not yet spent its force" (387). The inspired orator can look forth at last to "the year of jubilee" (387).

The oration, then, is a purgative ritual. By attacking Americans for their complaisance in the face of corruption, Douglass hopes to recall them to their world-historical mission. But even as he struggles to situate himself in this corroding society, Douglass ironically reproduces the very arguments of his antagonists, who challenged blacks to "prove that we are men" (370). One has only to glance through the thick volume of Independence Day speeches collected by Frederick Saunders to mark the nation's centennial,[3] to see the ironic parallel. Despite Douglass's continued prominence during the post-Reconstruction period, he is excluded from the volume; indeed, although he appeared on the platform of the Philadelphia Centennial Exhibition on July 4, 1876, he was not allowed to speak.[4] But those who did speak that day virtually reproduced his oratory of fourteen years before. In Pittsburgh, for example, John M. Kirkpatrick evoked "Echoes from Lexington and Bunker Hill." Like Douglass he calls attention to the abolition of slavery, without which America could not be an "ever-advancing civilization" (70), and then turns to the present, in which "injustice and iniquity, and fraud and corruption in high places" marred American life. Expunging such evils, Kirkpatrick warns, is of the first moment, in order to avoid the fate of all past republics—to "perish utterly from off the face of the earth, leaving not a name, not a vestige, not even a wreck behind" (72). Only by remaining true to its founding principle, he urges, can "the Republic...live... and...become greater and stronger and cover the earth with its beauty, and all people with its blessings until the latest syllable of recorded time" (72). For Kirkpatrick, as for Douglass, America's millennial inheritance, purged of vice, was sufficient unto itself. Indeed, in a volume from which Douglass himself was excluded, the promise was all the more resonant.

Douglass, that is to say, was hobbled by a genre created by whites for the expression of national ideals. The "American jeremiad," as Sacvan Bercovitch has argued, was a ritual use of anxiety to perfect America. The latter-day Jeremiah saw the present as a corrupt parenthesis between Revolutionary glory and millennial promise, and structured his speeches in Douglass's precise manner, recalling the Fathers and excoriating contemporaries so as to insure the future. "To be post-Revolutionary," Bercovitch remarks, was "to exemplify (in one's life and in one's generation) the stormy course of its progress";[5] that, surely, was Douglass's impulse in 1852, as it was for a host of contemporary orators. In one sense that unity proved Douglass's point: he was a man among other men, an American fully able to share in the Promise. But in another sense, the unity must have been profoundly troubling; for Douglass, striving with all his passionate intensity to produce the authentic cry of the slave, succeeded only in reproducing the clichés of his oppressors. His most severe attacks on American institutions served, ultimately, to endorse them.

THE COLUMBIAN ORATOR AND THE PROBLEMS OF LANGUAGE

It was by no mere accident that Douglass so faithfully reproduced the jeremiad; in fact, he had virtually been raised on it. The first book he ever owned, for which he scraped together fifty cents as a slave in Baltimore, was *The Columbian Orator*, a textbook of extracts from patriotic speeches, tracts, and plays, published in 1797. "These were choice documents to me," Douglass recalled in his first autobiography. "I read them over and over again with unabated interest. They gave tongue to interesting thoughts of my own soul, which had frequently flashed through my mind and died away for want of utterance."[6] Seven years later, among the slaves of William Freeland's farm, he was still recalling its contents, and discussing its great ideas with his friends. Those ideas were largely the sentiments of Revolutionary America, enunciated by Franklin in his *Autobiography*. Here again, for example, was the preoccupation with national virtue and vice. "Let this sacred maxim receive the deepest impression upon our minds," warned Jonathan Mason in 1780, that if avarice, if extortion, if luxury, and political corruption, are suffered to become popular among us, civil discord, and the ruin of our country will be the speedy consequence of such fatal vices. But ... while industry, frugality and temperance, are held in estimation, and we depend upon public spirit and the love of virtue for our social happiness, peace and affluence will throw their smiles upon the brow of individuals; our commonwealth will flourish; our land will become a land of liberty, and AMERICA an asylum for the oppressed. (300)

Here Douglass found an extract from Cato's speech on Catiline, excoriating the Romans for their love of riches, "sloth and effeminacy": "We make no distinction between the good and the bad; whilst ambition engrosses all the rewards of virtue. Do you wonder, then, that dangerous conspiracies should be formed?" (49). Here, too, the slave boy read an attack by the Briton Galgachus against the Roman army—an attack he would later turn on his own masters. "Does not wantonness enervate them?" the Briton demanded. "Do they not even go to excess in the most unmanly vices? And can you imagine that they who are remarkable for their vices are likewise remarkable for their valour?" (187). To the young Douglass such extracts were no mere classroom oratory; they formed the core of his mature thought. As his best biographers have observed, the importance of *The Columbian Orator* in Douglass's development cannot be overestimated.[7]

But the school book was more than a compendium of set speeches promoting national virtue; like Franklin's *Autobiography*, it made a subliminal argument for the Millennium. The two great moments in the volume are the American and the French Revolutions—the one predicting, and the other confirming the dawn of what Francis Blake, in a speech on July 4, 1796, called "the grand POLITICAL MILLENNIUM" (236). George Washington himself set the tone in his first speech to Congress, by averring that "every step" in the nation's independence "seem[ed] to have been distinguished by some token of providential agency" (36), to which his successors added their own fulsome predictions. "That ... blissful period will soon arrive," foresaw one Independence Day orator,

when man shall be elevated to his primitive character; when illuminated reason and regulated liberty shall once more exhibit him in the image of his Maker; when all the inhabitants of the globe shall be freemen and fellow-citizens, and patriotism itself be lost in universal philanthropy. Then shall the innumerable varieties of the human race unitedly "worship in her sacred temple, whose pillars shall rest on the remotest corners of the earth, and whose arch will be the vault of heaven." (268)

Another prophetic speaker beheld Columbia's name "on the last page of Fate's eventful volume," where "the approaching end of Tyranny and the triumph of Right and Justice are written in indelible characters" (274). It was the golden age, Douglass learned, proclaimed by "our orators and poets" (284); "that on this our native spot of earth, slavish government and slavish hierarchies shall cease; that here, the old prophecies shall be verified; that here shall be the last, universal empire on earth, the empire of reason and virtue . . . " (285):

> O'er all the earth shall freedom's banner wave,
> The tyrant blast, and liberate the slave.
> Plenty and peace shall spread from pole to pole,
> Till earth's grand family possess one soul. (239)

American ideals alone would inaugurate the end of time, "when the four angels, that stand on the four corners of the globe, shall with one accord, lift up their voices to heaven; proclaiming PEACE ON EARTH, AND GOOD WILL TO ALL MEN" (237).

What must have been Douglass's excitement, then, to learn that all this was to be brought about not by statesmen or generals, but by the orator? Only a virtuous land, it was true, could harbor great ideals, but only the greatest orators could insure that a nation was virtuous at all. Like the exemplary Franklin of the *Autobiography*, the task of the Columbian orator was "to rouse to action all the latent energies of man, in the proper and ardent pursuit" of republican glory (31); and as the nation fulfilled its promise, so oratory would recreate "that bright day . . . which we have anticipated" (33). Caleb Bingham, whose own pieces punctuate the extracts he collected, had in mind a specific model for this millennial voice: it was the momentous call of the archangel announcing the Day of Judgment. On that day, as throughout human history, the "voice of mercy" would plead with the obdurate for repentance. "But this is a voice which shall, which must reach every one of the millions of mankind, and not one of them will be able to stop his ears" (98). Here at last was an eloquence to rouse the world:

> Where sleeps the music of his voice divine?
> Where hides the face, that could so sweetly shine?
> Now hear that slighted voice to thunder turn!
> See that mild face with flames of vengeance burn!
> High o'er your heads the storm of ruin roars,
> And, round th'immense, no friend your fate deplores. (171)

The archangel, like the orator, would unite mankind by purging it of vice, through an "all-penetrating call" that assembled the quick and the dead. It was the jeremiad on a cosmic scale—but a scale well within reach of Americans, the greatest orators the world had ever known. Those schoolboys who heard Bingham's call were God's own agents, exposing "those quicksands of vice, which have ever proved the bane of empire." Only they could insure Columbia's great promise, "till the last trump shall announce the catastrophe of nature, and time shall immerge in the ocean of eternity" (34). It was a call that would haunt Douglass for the rest of his life.

Douglass began his antislavery career under peculiar circumstances. Invited to attend a convention of the American Anti-Slavery Society in 1841, he was suddenly called upon by the abolitionist William C. Coffin to give an account of himself. Only three years out of slavery, and still legally a fugitive, he rose to speak "but a few moments" (*N* 117) before the all-white audience about his eventful life. The brief speech, he reports in his second autobiography, *My Bondage and My Freedom*, threw him into confusion, but it had just the opposite effect on his listeners. Whereas Douglass was oppressed by this unexpected summons—in truth, he still "felt [him]self a slave" (*N* 117)—his listeners were galvanized, not so much by the black man's remarks as by what followed them. William Lloyd Garrison rose to speak, "taking me as his text," and unleashed an eloquence that Douglass still found astonishing fourteen years later:

> It was an effort of unequaled power, sweeping down, like a very tornado, every opposing barrier. . . . For a moment, he possessed that almost fabulous inspiration, often referred to but seldom attained, in which a public meeting is transformed, as it were, into a single individuality—the orator wielding a thousand heads and hearts at once, and by the simple majesty of his all controlling thought, converting his hearers into the express image of his own soul.[8]

Undoubtedly, Douglass felt himself a part of that great soul, for he soon signed up as an agent for the Society; but his own participation was no simple matter. He had come to the convention an anonymous laborer, having made a precarious living at the docks and factories of New Bedford, Massachusetts; yet he discovered his voice when he was compelled to narrate his life as a slave. His white audience, that is to say, wanted to see him as an escaped slave, not an industrious freedman, and Douglass himself—who makes this the climactic moment of the

Narrative—found his calling as a representative victim. His audience provided the forum and the form for this self-discovery, and, returning him to slavery, united around him. It was almost a purgative ritual in reverse, the man becoming a "text" for the manipulation of whites, who felt "excited" and ennobled by this representative slave. The inspired community discovered itself by expunging its weakest member.

As he reflected on the episode in *My Bondage*, Douglass could not help but remark the irony. The antislavery movement, under Garrison, relied on shock value—searing rhetoric and tales of whips and chains—and the black agent was expected to provide authenticity. "I was generally introduced as a *'chattel,'* " Douglass recalled, "a *'thing'*—a piece of southern *'property'*—the chairman assuring the audience that *it* could speak" (*BF* 360). When Douglass did attempt to discuss other issues, assert himself as a freedman, he was admonished by white agents simply to "tell [his] story" (361)—to narrate the facts—to give the white audience what it wanted to hear. In effect, Douglass was claiming an identity denied him by white Southerners only by acceding to the equally imperious demands of white Northerners. This was largely true throughout his career, both before and after his break with the Garrisonians. It remained a matter of astonishment to his audience that a black could possess such fluency, that an "unlettered slave" could speak as shrewdly as whites. "Many of the speakers who followed him, and of a lighter complexion, men who boasted that they were ministers, and who had, doubtless the advantage of education . . . might well be desirous of emulating the appropriateness of his elocution and gesticulation, and the grammatical accuracy of his sentences," wrote a correspondent to the *Boston Courier* in 1842. "He is a surprising lecturer," wrote another in 1844. "How a man, only six years out of bondage, and who had never gone to school a day in his life, could speak with such eloquence . . . with such precision of language and power of thought" amazed a third audience. In the 1870s the response had hardly changed. "For ourselves," wrote one listener,

> we were constantly astonished at the massiveness of mind, the wonderful accuracy and felicitous use of language, the admirable elocution, and the evidence of intellectual strength and culture that characterized this oration of a man who lived until past twenty years old as a slave, and has since then been mainly self-taught.[9]

The black Columbian orator faced a formidable irony. The more eloquently he spoke, the more doubt he excited; the more fully he voiced republican ideals, the more his audience pictured him a slave. "Better have a *little* of the plantation manner, of speech," one Garrisonian had warned him (*BF* 362). And yet "the plantation manner" was precisely what Douglass sought to overthrow. His very rhetoric seemed to enslave him.

Unlike slavery, this bind was largely inescapable; it was inherent in the freedman's use of language. As Douglass describes it, slavery was a preliterate existence; he refers somewhat disparagingly to the jumble of African patois on the Lloyd plantation as "broken...speech" from which he could glean nothing "in the way of knowledge" (*BF* 77). Had Douglass remained in the slave quarters, he might have learned to understand the subtleties of that patois, which, as Eugene Genovese points out,[10] was often a subversive code. But he had early befriended "Mas' Daniel," the Lloyd heir—or rather, Daniel had befriended him—and learned many of his "tastes and pursuits" (*BF* 77).[11] This was the origin of his singular fluency—and to the extent that language embodies culture—of his mastery of cultural motifs like the jeremiad. A man who has a language, Frantz Fanon observes, "possesses the world expressed and implied by that language."[12] And yet, for Douglass, the passage to literacy was far from simple and never complete; for at the heart of the slave's preliterate world was an experience that could not possibly be captured by the dominant tongue. Here again was resonant irony. The slave narrator, as Houston Baker observes, had not only "to seize the word"; "his being had to erupt from nothingness." That enabling act of literacy, for which Douglass struggled so hard in Baltimore, allowed him to express his desire for freedom but denied him authentic expression as a slave. All of his recollections were refracted through a language that forbade "ontological certaint[y]," a double bind whose "linguistic codes, literary conventions, and audience expectations" obliterated his "authentic voice."[13] In America, to write faithfully about slavery was to distort the slave beyond recognition.

As slave narrator, then, Douglass was both inside and outside language, a figure to be embraced and excised, a prophet and a pariah. This range of qualities Jacques Derrida has associated with writing itself. In the *Phaedrus*, he argues in "Plato's Pharmacy," written texts are likened to a *pharmakon*, a drug capable both of healing or poisoning. Unlike speech—a legitimate child of thought, both vital and intimate—writing is a dangerous orphan that "scarcely remains a son at all and no longer *recognizes* its origins."[14] Divorced from the "presence" of *logos*, it soon becomes "patricidal" and must be extruded from pure thought in a move very like the banning of the *pharmakos*, the scapegoat Athens offered to the gods:

> The city's body *proper* . . . reconstitutes its unity, closes around the security of its inner courts, gives back to itself the word that links it with itself within the confines of the agora, but violently excluding from its territory the representative of an external threat or aggression. That representative represents the otherness of the evil that comes to affect or infect the inside by unpredictably breaking into it. Yet the representative of the outside is nonetheless *constituted*, regularly granted its place by the community, chosen, kept, fed, etc., in the very heart of the inside. (133)

Writing is then the very source of ambiguity, a function "played out on the boundary line between inside and outside" (133), the fearful embodiment of indeterminacy. Writing "cannot simply be assigned a site within what it situates, cannot be subsumed under concepts whose contours it draws" (103). Like Douglass on Nantucket, it must be sacrificed to be believed.

The slave narrator's life thus shared the fate of his elusive medium; but the slave's was a verbal body doubly bound. Just as slave life became "nothingness" when reduced to writing, so the slave narrator became a blank when he went before whites, a vessel to be filled by sensational tales of beating, rape, and murder. On the lecture platform, as John Sekora notes, the black speaker was literally surrounded by whites, who introduced and followed him, in effect supplying proof for "facts" that could not be believed on the slave's terms alone.[15] In print, where white testimonials appear as lengthy prefaces and appendices, the slave narrator was often reduced to a mere witness to cruelty: he had no inner life to relate, but existed simply to document the excesses of white Southerners. William Wells Brown, for example, whose *Narrative* appeared two years after Douglass's, begins his account with the flogging of his mother, continues with the savage beating of a fellow slave, and moves on to detail the worst abuses of a succession of bad masters, including a rapacious slave trader who compelled him to act as overseer for coffles to New Orleans. So thoroughly does he admit the imposition of others, that Brown depicts the two cardinal moments of his identity, the loss and regaining of his name, as brought about by whites. As a boy his name had been changed to Sandford because his master's nephew went by his name, William; "and this name I was known by, not only upon my master's plantation, but up to the time that I made my escape. I was sold under the name of Sandford." But as a freedman, finding that he needed "two names," he gave a white Quaker "the privilege of naming" him. "If I name thee," was the response, "I shall call thee Wells Brown, after myself."[16] Even as he wrote novels and travelogues, Brown retained this borrowed name, a telling mark of his otherness. The slave narratives of John Thompson, J. W. C.

Pennington, Josiah Henson, and William and Ellen Craft—all Douglass's contemporaries—generally reproduce this strategy.[17] They were written to inform the white world of the evils of slavery, and only incidentally to display the inner life of the slave.

An episode in the Crafts' narrative, *Running a Thousand Miles for Freedom*, particularly illustrates this point. William and Ellen Craft were slaves in Georgia when the "shameful" sale of William's family and the likelihood that he would be separated from his wife convinced the couple to escape. Their plan was the more audacious since they could not write passes for themselves, and had to slip through most of the Deep South. In the manner of George Harris in *Uncle Tom's Cabin*, they resolved on disguise, and taking advantage of Ellen's light skin, dressed her up as a man. To hide her face they applied a poultice and dark glasses, and to disguise her illiteracy, they bound her arm in a sling. Thus literally "defaced," Ellen Craft traveled North as a white invalid, attended by her obedient slave, rarely responding to her white interlocutors, allowing them to interpret her curious silences as assent to their bigotry. "You will excuse me, Sir," remarked one officer, "[but] you are very likely to spoil your boy by saying 'thank you' to him. I assure you, Sir, nothing spoils a slave so soon as saying 'thank you' and 'if you please' to him" (298). "I would not take a nigger to the North under no consideration," vowed another. "I have had a deal to do with niggers in my time, but I never saw one who ever had his heel upon free soil that was worth a d—n" (296). "Cap'en," said a third, "if I was the President of this mighty United States of America, the greatest and freest country under the whole univarse, I would never let no man ... take a nigger into the North and bring him back here ... to taint all quiet niggers with the hellish spirit of running away" (297). Such shrewd irony merely underscored what slaves had always known: that to survive in a white world, one had to assume a vacancy, a blank neutrality. Behind the Crafts' heroism was a complicity in their own suppression.

No contemporary of Douglass better knew the costs of this suppression than Friedrich Nietzsche. Although couched in moral terms, his attacks on the slave mentality capture, from the vantage of an escapee, the despair and timidity of the herd. For Nietzsche, the slave is a creature so weak that he fears independence, finding security instead in the perversions of the mass. Consequently, slaves prize pity, suffering, and truthfulness—"Not to be deceived—and ... not to deceive!" (*WP* §278, 158)—all instruments of cohesion. Truthfulness also fed the illusion that one's inner nature lay exposed by "clear and constant signs," open to the policing of others (*WP* §277, 158). Indeed, community was paramount. The massed slaves considered "the exception, whether it be below or above [them], as something opposed and harmful" (*WP* §280, 159), a parasite to be expunged. Beyond the herd lay "danger and . . . deception"; "mistrust," then, became the principle of order (*WP* §278, 158). Douglass would have had no trouble in recognizing these as attributes of the *white* Christians he generally loathed. But for the rebel, the escaped slave, the costs were equally severe: it was the herd that read Nietzsche as a "moralistic monster," and kept him a "mere prejudice" in his lifetime (*EH* 217), "invaded" and "crushed" him in their *rancune* for the great. But even Nietzsche enjoyed a luxury that Douglass could not abide: the philosopher wrote for those great souls of the future who would see him as their avatar. Douglass wrote to the present—about slaves, for slaves. He had to embody the perversions he would overturn.

DOUGLASS'S *NARRATIVE*

Undoubtedly, Douglass was aware of many of these constraints when he published his *Narrative of the Life of Frederick Douglass* in 1845. By then it was clear that his very fluency was undermining his cause: people doubted his veracity. He refused, in his antislavery lectures, to name names; he gave only vague locations; he would reveal no dates. Whites thought him an eloquent impostor. Indeed, the *Narrative* itself tries to confront the blankness imposed by white audiences; it details his emergence from the terrifying nothingness of slavery to the self-mastery provided by writing, and attempts, through its cadences and rhetorical devices, to underscore that control. And, as it was written to secure his identity as a freed slave, it strove in some measure for representativeness, with the same urgency that Douglass had found in the extracts of *The Columbian Orator*. But for all his eloquence, and the great risk he ran in publishing the book—he was immediately forced to flee to avoid capture—the *Narrative* fails to evade the crippling demands of its white readers. The precipitate flight to England itself suggests how severe those demands could be.

The *Narrative* begins with almost chilling sparseness:

> I was born in Tuckahoe, near Hillsborough, and about twelve miles from Easton, in Talbot county, Maryland. I have no accurate knowledge of my age, never having seen any authentic record containing it. By far the larger part of the slaves know as little of their ages as horses know of theirs. (1)

The attempt to fix the precise locality of his birth quickly breaks down amid the prevailing blankness of slavery, under which a black was granted little more consciousness than a beast. Douglass thus calls attention to the chief motive of the *Narrative*, to overcome that blankness through writing. If he cannot fully recover his childhood, he can at least expose it, in prose as stark as slavery itself. Thus, he reports, he knew no real family: he "never saw [his] mother, to know her as such, more than four or five times" (2), and had not "the slightest intimation of who [his] father was" (3). For these absent individuals were substituted nightmare figures—Mr. Plummer, the overseer, who "always went armed with a cowskin and a heavy cudgel" (5), and Captain Anthony, who took "great pleasure" (6) in whipping slaves. Douglass illustrates the point in a graphic scene of sadism that repeats the scene of the *pharmakos*. Captain Anthony, driven to sexual frenzy by Douglass's young aunt, strips her for courting a neighborhood slave; "and after rolling up his sleeves, he commenced to lay on the heavy cowskin, and soon the warm, red blood (amid heart-rending shrieks from her, and horrid oaths from him) came dripping to the floor" (7). Here was the slave's pre-literate terror—the only words Douglass records from the scene are "d—d b—h," deepening the sense of bestiality—as the young witness saw his family being literally torn apart. And the boy's response was equally telling: afraid that he would be next, he hid himself for hours in a closet, neither witnessing nor fleeing the scene—immersed himself in darkness. As a slave narrator, Douglass's task was to recreate that death-like anguish.

But as he soon acknowledges, the task is an almost impossible one. "Within the circle" of slavery (14), he could only glimpse its profound brutalization. Indeed, it was the slaves' "unmeaning jargon" (13) that first alerted him to his pain, in the "apparently incoherent" work songs that expressed an anguish beyond words. "They would sometimes sing the most pathetic sentiment in the most rapturous tone," Douglass recalled, "and the most rapturous sentiment in the most pathetic tone" (13). There was no getting at these concealed feelings; as a "tale of woe" they eluded young Douglass's comprehension, and once beyond the pale, he recalled less a language of sorrow than of "dehumaniz[ation]" (14). Like the *pharmakos*, he was neither inside nor outside, an experience repeated when he recalled other plantation scenes. An unwitting slave who admitted to Colonel Lloyd that he was poorly treated was soon sold South; it was in response to such threats that slaves "almost universally say that they are contented, and that their masters are kind" (19). When slaves from neighboring plantations visited the Lloyds, fights often erupted over the prowess of masters, "Colonel Lloyd's slaves contending that he was the richest, and Mr. Jepson's slaves that he was the smartest, and most of a man" (20). Douglass relates such confrontations with hardly a trace of irony; they represent the pained logic of the plantation, a logic of denial and shame. And yet

these memories are the more terrifying for the great psychological distance from which Douglass records them, for his experience was less
that of an oppressed child than of a beast:

> We were not regularly allowanced. Our...*mush*...was put into a large
> wooden tray or trough, and set down upon the ground. The children were
> then called, like so many pigs, and like so many pigs they would come
> and devour the mush; some with oyster-shells, others with pieces of shin-
> gle, some with naked hands, and none with spoons. He that ate fastest got
> most; he that was strongest secured the best place; and few left the trough
> satisfied. (27)

Even as Douglass relates the scene, he subtly removes himself, shifting
pronouns so as to deny his participation. He cannot fully acknowledge,
even now, his brutal chidhood. In a sense, by documenting these terrors, he was fulfilling the demands of the lecture platform, substituting
cruelty for interiority; but in a sense more terrifying still, this blankness was all he had: it served to fill up a childhood "dehumanized,"
without intrinsic meaning. It is almost as if the mature Douglass were
as eager to expunge his past as the slave boy called away to Hugh
Auld's in Baltimore, who washed himself so vigorously "not only to...
scrub off the *mange*, (as pig drovers would call it,) but the skin as well"
(*BF* 134).

Writing could not be used to make this experience intelligible to
slaves, but it could at least allow a freedman to portray his own struggle for meaning. Again, this was no simple task. It must constantly be
kept in mind that the *Narrative* was an apology to a white audience
that identified blacks by their capacity for punishment. Douglass was
not at liberty to produce an iconoclastic tract; his autobiography was
an extension of arguments he had been making for years among Garrisonians. But within these constraints he could at least seek control
over his own memories, by rendering the atrocities his audience demanded with an orator's skill. Here, for example, is the way he portrays
his second master, Thomas Auld:

> He was cruel, but cowardly. He commanded without firmness. In the en-
> forcement of his rules, he was at times rigid, and at times lax. At times he
> spoke to his slaves with the firmness of Napoleon and the fury of a demon;
> at other times, he might well be mistaken for an inquirer who had lost his
> way....His airs, words, and actions, were the airs, words, and actions of
> born slaveholders, and, being assumed, were awkward enough....He pos-
> sessed all the disposition to deceive, but wanted the power. Having no
> resources within himself, he was...forever the victim of inconsistency.
> ...He was a slaveholder without the ability to hold slaves. (53)

The entire passage turns on Douglass's use of antithesis and parallel-ism—the one device reflecting his distance from slavery, the other reflect-ing his ability to order its essential meaninglessness. As Douglass repeats his long phrases and turns them on his master, he himself ac-quires the firmness of Napoleon, rendering Auld's erratic temperament both meaningful and absurd. It is a technique that allows him to re-verse the most degrading aspects of slavery, in effect to render his mas-ter blank, to give balance to chaos.[18] Moreover, it allows him to reverse his scapegoat's marginality by "inhabiting" the figures he describes, as he evidences in more formidable subjects. Hence, Douglass describes the sadistic overseer Austin Gore, who once coolly killed a defiant slave, as "proud enough" to abuse blacks, but "quite servile enough" to fawn over the master, "ambitious enough" to crave power, yet "artful enough to descend to the lowest trickery, and obdurate enough to be in-sensible to the voice of a reproving conscience" (22). Like Thomas Auld's, Gore's temperament falls into patterns for which Douglass alone holds the key, patterns that turn on his skill at finding unity in contradiction. The darkness of the closet had produced balanced prose.

This, of course, is a direct effect of Douglass's platform manner, which shocked white audiences as much by his articulateness as by the horrors he portrayed. Occasionally in the *Narrative* he reproduces what amount to set speeches, purple passages designed to stir an audience in much the same way that his depiction of the beaten slave stirred those in Rochester in 1852. Once again, the sense of order and poise in his writing countermands the blank powerlessness he remembers. "She was nevertheless left a slave," he writes of his grandmother, "a slave for life—a slave in the hands of strangers; and in their hands she saw her children, her grandchildren, and her great-grandchildren divided, like so many sheep" (47–48). In this instance, Douglass masters dark-ness itself:

> She gropes her way, in the darkness of age, for a drink of water....And now, when weighed down by the pains and aches of old age, when the head inclines to the feet, when the beginning and ending of human exis-tence meet...at this time, this most needful time, the time for the exercise of that tenderness and affection which children only can exercise towards a declining parent—my poor old grandmother...is left all alone...before a few dim embers. (49)

And yet, the mastery is only temporary, for Douglass does much the same in his account of the "free" North. After his escape from Balti-more, the circumstances of which he conceals from the reader—an-other resonant lacuna—Douglass produces a stinging diatribe. Here was the first occasion in the text where the freedman could create scenes familiar to the white reader, make his plea on the basis of shared experience. Only let the reader imagine himself a fugitive, Douglass urges:

> let him place himself in my situation—without home or friends—without money or credit—wanting shelter, and no one to give it—wanting bread, and no money to buy it . . . in the midst of plenty, yet suffering the terrible gnawings of hunger,—in the midst of houses, yet having no home,—among fellow-men, yet feeling as if in the midst of wild beasts . . . then, and not till then, will he fully appreciate the hardships of . . . the . . . fugitive slave. (108–9)

But if this rhetoric were necessary in New York—if powerlessness still shadowed his prose—then what remained of his freedom? In effect, the same antithesis and parallelism that had subdued his masters now reenslaved him. Once again, he inhabited the borderline.

The genius of the *Narrative*, though, is that the borderline itself became the site of unity. If the Christian herd valued pity and suffering, Douglass found he could drive them like an overseer. Indeed, in forging such overtly sentimental appeals, of the kind favored by Garrison himself—it was Garrison who discerned "in him that union of head and heart, which is indispensable to an enlightenment of the heads and a winning of the hearts of others" (vi)—Douglass tapped a more basic, almost ritual impulse. Although Houston Baker is quite right to assert that the freedman could not often look to "philosophical and ideological justifications" and the "preexistent codes of his culture" in writing autobiography,[19] Douglass had the singular advantage of *The Columbian Orator* and its multiplied jeremiads. Hence, the play of antithesis and parallelism in the *Narrative*, the creation of unity through condemnation, and the suggestion that all experience with tyranny could be reduced to a single, sustained pattern—all this was dependent on Douglass's peculiar oratory—"that most sublime of all arts," declared one of Bingham's speakers, "that art, which could render one man more dreadful to a tyrant, than hostile fleets and armies . . . [t]hat refinement of taste, that laudable ambition to excel in every thing which does honor to humanity" (*CO* 33). The power of rhetoric to "make every spring in the human machine cooperate" with the speaker (31) was Douglass's most potent antislavery argument.

In fact, Douglass, like most contemporary slave narrators, relied on two cultural motifs to produce assent. A distinct, if subtle, theme in the *Narrative* is that of Christian conversion, the same theme found in countless spiritual autobiographies.[20] Although there are no explicit scenes of conviction of sin or repentance here, as there are, for example, in the slave narratives of Josiah Henson and John Thompson, there are pointed suggestions that Douglass's, too, was a spiritual journey. Of his sojourn in Baltimore he writes that "divine Providence" determined his fate: "This good spirit was from God, and to him I offer thanksgiving and praise" (31). At the climactic fight with Covey he declares, "It was a glorious resurrection, from the tomb of slavery, to the heaven of freedom" (73). And he refers to his early antislavery work as a "severe cross" (117), one he took up as a saint devotes his life to God. But despite the power of this appeal, Douglass does not allow it to dominate his text; indeed, he overturns it. He makes few direct references to Christ, and uses religion more as a wedge between himself and his audience than as a bond. Hence his savage diatribe in the appendix on "The Christianity of America," which will

> . . . loudly talk of Christ's reward,
> And bind his image with a cord,
> And scold, and swing the lash abhorred,
> And sell their brother in the Lord
>   To handcuffed heavenly union. (123)

A union of this kind, overborne by hypocrisy, rather prophesied destruction than grace. The soul of America had to be cleansed before it could be saved.

Much more potent is Douglass's appeal to the secular ideal of liberty. It was Garrison himself who proclaimed him an equal to "PATRICK HENRY" (v) in the cause of liberty, and Douglass never forgot the parallel. "The silver trump of freedom had roused my soul to eternal wakefulness," he writes of *The Columbian Orator*. "Freedom now appeared, to disappear no more forever" (41). In another set speech he retained through all his revisions, Douglass subsumes religious imagery within a more comprehensive, republican plea. "You are freedom's swift-winged angels," he addresses the ships on Chesapeake Bay,

> I am confined in bands of iron! O that I was free! O, that I were on one of your gallant decks, and under your protecting wing! . . . O, why was I born a man, of whom to make a brute! . . . I am left in the hottest hell of unending slavery. O God save me! God deliver me! Let me be free! (65–66)

His battle with Covey marks his ascent to a "heaven of freedom" (73), and his attempted escape from William Freeland is a "final struggle" (83). "We did more than Patrick Henry, when he resolved upon liberty or death," he writes of his escape plans. "With us it was a doubtful liberty at most, and almost certain death if we failed. For my part, I should prefer death to hopeless bondage" (85–86). On the eve of his successful escape he recalls the same theme: "The wretchedness of slavery, and the blessedness of freedom, were perpetually before me. It was life and death with me" (107). And, indeed, New Bedford, to the liberated slave, was the very heaven he had imagined, free from the "deep oaths or horrid curses" he had heard ever since childhood, and populated by republican saints—"sober, yet cheerful" men who had a proper sense of their own dignity (113)—this despite their overt racism. In his appeal to such republican virtues, Douglass was embracing truly national themes.

But once again, the appendix dismantles this theme. In his fury at religious bigots—an issue he pursues throughout the autobiography—Douglass produces a panorama of Southern hypocrisy, from Bible-quoting sadists to Christian fornicators, loading his prose with the barbed antithesis and parallelism that mark his sharpest passages:

> Revivals of religion and revivals in the slave-trade go hand in hand together. The slave prison and the church stand near each other. The clanking of fetters and the rattling of chains in the prison, and the pious psalm and solemn prayer in the church, may be heard at the same time. . . . Here we have religion and robbery the allies of each other—devils dressed in angels' robes, and hell presenting the semblance of paradise. (119–20)

American slaveholders had produced a corruption so monumental that only divine judgment could cleanse it—a judgment Douglass reproduces by quoting Christ's attack on the Pharisees in Matthew 23.4–28. But this fiercest of jeremiads points up the inherent weakness in the *Narrative*, for it effectively excludes almost all readers. If the "religion of this land" (118) were universally damned, then no freedman—not even Douglass—could hope to inhabit it. In effect, the entire nation became a borderline, a no-man's land awaiting vengeance. The rhetoric through which he asserted control leaves Douglass no choice. Antithesis and parallelism had allowed him to express his distance from the South; they could do no less for America.

Once again, then, Douglass had claimed the margin. In 1845 he was a devoted Garrisonian, with Garrison's scorn for compromise and union. The community he addressed was, in fact, a narrow one, an association of white ultraists, ardent yet faintly racist. It did not include slaves or many freedmen or most Christians, and it addressed Northern laborers, who refused Douglass dock work, with suspicion. Moreover, the *Narrative*, in its occasional attempts to portray Douglass as a providential agent or heroic autodidact, strives for an exemplariness almost entirely alien to white readers, who might have recognized the rhetoric but would have marvelled at the result. Only by insisting on the republican sentiments of *The Columbian Orator* could Douglass feel on somewhat firm ground, and yet here, too, the genre worked against him; for behind the taut prose and eloquent appeals, this remained a tale of whips and chains, a portrait of a vicious system that excluded him. The man had to fight for recognition not only in life, but in the text itself.

MY BONDAGE AND MY FREEDOM

"A man who can speak well to a public assembly, I must respect," wrote Ralph Waldo Emerson in 1846, "and he is *ipso facto* ennobled.... He has established his relation, representativeness, that he is a good apple of his kind, proved by the homage of apples, and not merely like your lonely man of genius, that he is an apple shaped like a cucumber."[21] In the decade between the publication of the *Narrative* and *My Bondage and My Freedom*, in England and America, Frederick Douglass strove to be "a good apple of his kind." His enthusiastic reception overseas showed him what it meant to be a man among men, and, returning with a writ of manumission from Thomas Auld, he soon established himself as an independent editor in Rochester. By 1853 he had embraced the Constitution, broken with Garrison, and proclaimed himself a representative American—"the test," as he would later put it, "of American civilization, American statesmanship, American refinement, and American Christianity."[22] With this wider culture he radically revised the *Narrative*, transforming a sectarian tract into what he hoped would be exemplary autobiography. His models now were literary—the novels, poetry, and popular fiction to which Sylvia Griffiths, English co-editor of the *North Star*, helped to introduce him. And yet these models, refracted by his extraordinary talent, paradoxically led him away from representativeness. Although he struggled to unite the elements of his contradictory status, his most powerful autobiography shows him less a good apple than a lonely genius.

Despite the troubling remoteness from slavery he acknowledged in the *Narrative*, Douglass continued to portray himself as a representative slave. "I have been one with them in their sorrow and... degradation," he wrote to a white friend in 1856, "one with them under a burning sun and the slavedriver's bloody lash" (*LW* 1:189). "Being ...so completely identified with the slaves" (1:189), he could give voice to their mute despair. "We are one with you under the ban of prejudice and proscription," he addressed them in the *North Star* a year later, using the editorial "we" to underscore the unity, "one with you in social and political disfranchisement. What you suffer, we suffer; what you endure, we endure. We are indissolubly united, and must fall or flourish together" (*LW* 1:283). At the same time, though, his own freedom allowed him to pursue wider issues. On the eve of the publication of *My Bondage and My Freedom*, Douglass enunciated an antislavery ideal that owes much to the Emerson of "Self-Reliance" and *Representative Men*. Whereas abolitionist speeches are ephemeral, he declares, the cause itself is immortal, a supreme inspiration to all: "Its incarnation in any one individual man, leaves the whole world a priesthood, occupying the highest moral eminence—even that of disinterested benevolence." Such a man "has the world at his feet, and is the world's teacher, as of divine right," a prophet who will "exemplify" wisdom by snatching "from the bosom of nature the latent facts of each individual man's experience," and display them "fresh and glowing" to humanity (*LW* 2:354). This is Emerson's Poet, "the complete man," who apprises all partial men "not of . . . wealth, but of the commonwealth."[23] It is also a fair statement of Douglass's larger intentions for *My Bondage*. No longer simply a slave narrator, he felt a wider responsibility, to address a literary culture in a language it would understand. Consequently, he would shape this autobiography to his readers' tastes; only thus could he compel America to acknowledge its moral duty to the slave.

My Bondage and My Freedom is less an antislavery tract than a success story portraying the rise of a shrewd, combative, often sardonic dissident, a social critic with a novelist's eye. Where the earlier version begins abruptly—"I was born in Tuckahoe, near Hillsborough, and about twelve miles from Easton, in Talbot county, Maryland" (1)—the revision sweeps the landscape and its history with an almost Dickensian eye:

> Decay and ruin are everywhere visible, and the thin population of the place would have quitted it long ago, but for the Choptank river, which runs through it, from which they take abundance of shad and herring, and plenty of ague and fever.
> It was in this dull, flat, and unthrifty district, or neighborhood, surrounded by a white population of the lowest order, indolent and drunken to a proverb, and among slaves, who seemed to ask, *"Oh! what's the use?"* every time they lifted a hoe, that I—without any fault of mine—was born and spent the first years of my childhood. (34)

Though a slave, he is no alien; the region interests and affects him as fully as it does white inhabitants, a point he subtly emphasizes in the slaves' eponymous hoe. Now the narrator is not a driven outcast but a wise observer, expressing general truths. "Children have their sorrows as well as men and women," he writes of his childhood, and adds: "SLAVE-children *are* children, and prove no exceptions to the general rule" (39). Often he affects such wisdom as to disappear in platitude:

> The germs of affection with which the Almighty, in his wisdom and mercy, arms the helpless infant against the ills and vicissitudes of his lot, had been directed in their growth toward that loving old grandmother, whose gentle hand and kind deportment it was the first effort of my infantile understanding to comprehend and appreciate. (53)

But he can also write memorably: "A man's troubles are always half disposed of, when he finds endurance his only remedy" (65). Such aphorisms assumed a wider audience, novel-readers as well as abolitionists.

Douglass had numerous models for this expanded version of his life. In his evocations of children, motherhood, and the human sufferings of slaves, he was reproducing major themes of the sentimental novel, chief popoular genre of its day.[24] Such works, as Philip Fisher notes, performed a radical social function by extending sympathy to the powerless, and allowing them to "ear[n] the right to human regard by means of the reality of their suffering." "Exotic" characters could be made intelligible "by means of...deep common feelings" readers shared, particularly those engendered by the helplessness Nietzsche assigned to the herd. It was the reader's generous compassion at the mere description of pain that occasioned what Rousseau called a "species-preserving" feeling,[25] an acknowledgment of community. Undoubtedly, Douglass was familiar with this literature. In England he read widely and began to salt his speeches with literary citations and effects—his description of the slave coffle in the Rochester address is only one prominent example of his facility. Indeed, it appears he often had specific writers in mind. The opening passage of *My Bondage*, describing the miasmatic conditions in Easton, echoes a similar description of Virginia in Charles Dickens's *American Notes*:

> In this district, as in all others where slavery sits brooding . . . there is an air of ruin and decay abroad, which is inseparable from the system. The barns and out-houses are mouldering away; the sheds are patched and half roofless; the log cabins . . . are squalid in the last degree. There is no look of decent comfort anywhere. . . . gloom and dejection are upon . . . all.[26]

His use of Harriet Beecher Stowe, whose *Uncle Tom's Cabin* he cites in the autobiography, is even more emphatic. Stowe described Kentucky's brand of slavery in this manner:

Perhaps the mildest form of the system of slavery is to be seen in the State of Kentucky. The general prevalence of agricultural pursuits of a quiet and gradual nature, not requiring those periodic seasons of hurry and pressure that are called for in the business of more southern districts, makes the Negro a more healthful and reasonable one.[27]

Here is how Douglass describes corresponding conditions in Maryland:

It is generally supposed that slavery, in the state of Maryland, exists in its mildest form, and that it is totally divested of those harsh and terrible peculiarities, which mark and characterize the slave system, in the southern and south-western states of the American union. The argument in favor of this opinion, is the contiguity of the free states, and the exposed condition of slavery in Maryland to the moral, religious and humane sentiment of the free states. (61)

To the sensitive reader, such echoes indicated that melodrama, piety, moral portrait were to be as important as whips and chains. Douglass, that is to say, had made a profound shift—from diatribe to feeling.

Other novelistic devices mark the text as well. Douglass frequently addresses his "dear reader" to summarize action or point a moral. "Think it not strange, dear reader, that so little sympathy of feeling existed between us," he writes of his siblings. "My poor mother, like many other slave-women, had *many children*, but NO FAMILY!" (48). At the end of a chapter on the Lloyd plantation, he attempts to render the exotic intelligible: "Such, kind reader, was the community, and such the place, in which my earliest and most lasting impressions of slavery, and of slave-life, were received" (78). This literary hand-holding creates a sympathy largely absent in the *Narrative*, a sympathy deepened by Douglass's constant appeal to the sentimental icons, hearth and death. New to this version is a long, loving description of his grandmother's cabin, "a noble structure" (37), surrounded by all the enchantments of childhood, including a "charm[ing]" ladder, on which he delighted to play (37). "The old cabin...was MY HOME," Douglass declares, "the only home I ever had; and I loved it, and all connected with it" (44). Then, too, he deplores slavery for its undignified treatment of death. "Scenes of sacred tenderness, around the deathbed, never forgotten, and which often arrest the vicious and confirm the virtuous during life, must be looked for among the free" (57). Even the death of his grandmother, imported from the *Narrative*, is given special status, set off in smaller type from the main text.

Douglass shows a novelist's care, too, in arranging several incidents of the revised text. The pathetic scene in which the young narrator, brutalized by Covey, appeals to a cold Thomas Auld is foreshadowed by an identical scene, in which a female cousin, beaten by her overseer, "traveled twelve miles, bare-footed, bare-necked, and bare-headed," suffering, as Douglass would, from "a blow on the head with a hickory club," only to hear from her master words similar to those uttered by Thomas Auld: "he 'believed she deserved every bit of it,' and if she did not go home instantly, he would himself take the remaining skin from her neck and back" (82, 83; cf. 229). More subtle is Douglass's foreshadowing of the first overseer he encountered at the Lloyd plantation, Mr. Sevier (denominated "Severe" in the *Narrative*). Trudging the twelve miles to the Great House with his grandmother, terrified by imaginary demons crouching in the woods, he confesses the walk "was quite a severe test of [his] . . . young legs," and would have been altogether too "severe" had not his grandmother carried him (46). The overseer, too, crouched in those woods, promising a terror not even a mother could evade. For white readers, such devices served to turn an alien life into a well-wrought tale.

Perhaps the most pervasive use of this appeal comes in Douglass's stress on his singular education. This appears far earlier here than in the *Narrative*, at a point soon after his arrival at the Lloyd plantation. "*Why am I a slave? Why are some people slaves and others masters?*" the boy begins to ask after emerging from the dark closet. The answer was soon in coming. "The appalling darkness faded away, and I was master of the subject." "*Even then*," he declares, he was "most strongly impressed with the idea of being a freeman some day" (89, 90, 91). As he traces the stages of his knowledge, he suggests his growing isolation. "I was more and more filled with a sense of my wretchedness," he writes as he leaves for Balitmore; his own severe deprivations, "and the terrible reports of wrong and outrage" made the child wish he had never been born (133). But this perception—another embroidery of the original text—stands in pointed contrast to a simultaneous sense of favor—the "first plain manifestation of that / 'Divinity that shapes our ends, / Rough hew them as we will'" (139). His sufferings, in other words, were seasoning him.

Douglass finds much the same message in Baltimore, where he now discloses that a figure named Uncle Lawson had foreseen great prospects. The " 'Lord had a great work for me to do,' " declared the old man, who "had been shown that I must preach the gospel" (168). By the time he is threatened with sale away from Baltimore, Douglass seems clearly conscious of his difference. "I probably suffered more than most of my fellow servants" in Captain Anthony's estate sale:

I had known what it was to experience, kind, and even tender treatment; they had known nothing of the sort. Life, to them, had been rough and thorny, as well as dark. They had—most of them—lived on my old master's farm in Tuckahoe, and had felt the reign of Mr. Plummer's rule....I had left a kind mistress at Baltimore, who was almost a mother to me. She was in tears when we parted. (177)

The slave valuation is all the more shocking because it threatened Douglass's evident promise, those gifts, as one biographer notes, that all his masters seemed to recognize.[28]

The revisions, then, emphasize Douglass's emergence from the blankness of slavery, his resolute acquisition of the means to succeed in spite of his origin. This is why he now subdues the language surrounding his climactic fight with Covey—a decision that has disturbed some critics.[29] The aphoristic "You have seen how a man was made a slave; you shall see how a slave was made a man" (*N* 65–66) now becomes: "You have, dear reader, seen me humbled, degraded, broken down, enslaved, and brutalized, and you understand how it was done; now let us see the converse of all this, and how it was brought about; and this will take us through the year 1834" (223). Similarly, his "resurrection" now was to "the heaven of *comparative* freedom" (247, emphasis added), as if he still had far to go. Douglass can be more modest about the event because it is merely another step in his education, a post on the road to prominence. In short, Douglass here traces his rise as a Romantic hero; he writes a kind of *Bildungsroman*.

This portrait of what Waldo Martin calls "self-conscious heroism"[30] has a long foreground in Romantic literature, from Wolfgang Goethe to Walter Scott. In America the Romantic hero acquired epic significance in Cooper's *Leatherstocking Tales*, and the young initiate, in Franklin's *Autobiography*. By invoking these models, Douglass was claiming a spiritual aristocracy, a status that placed him far above not only his brutalizing masters but also the brutalized slaves. None of the other plantation children could perceive their oppression; to them "*God, up in the sky*" simply "made *white* people to be masters and mistresses, and *black* people to be slaves" (89). When he returned to the region several years later, Douglass had already far outstripped such ignorance; he was the "pride" of the Eastern Shore, the only literate black (237). It was the same on William Freeland's farm, where he led others to revolt. "If any one is to blame for disturbing the quiet of the slaves and slavemasters of the neighborhood of St. Michaels," he proudly declares, "*I am the man*" (279). But as Frederick Garber notes, such heroic status could have unexpected consequences. In Romantic fiction, the political rebel who seeks to be a "redemptive figure" is forever battling contradiction. On the one hand he is aware of the richness of his talent; on the other, he recognizes the need to champion the oppressed. His very self-awareness "made clear to him how different he was from those with whom he had to deal."[31] As I have tried to show, Douglass was acutely aware of these contradictions separating his literate rendition of slavery from the mute sufferings of slaves, and depriving him of an audience for his passionate appeals. But in an autobiography that details his conversations with English lords and his hero's welcome overseas, the problems were even more severe. How could he hope to portray himself as Emersonian spirit and representative slave? How could he be a redemptive figure to white readers?

One solution was to use that very contradiction as an organizing theme. In a manner he had only suggested ten years before, the clash between aristocracy and community became the means toward an examination of Southern society itself, as if his personal struggle were social law. Douglass announces this theme in the *zeugma* informing the second paragraph of *My Bondage*: "Decay and ruin are everywhere visible, and the thin population of the place would have quitted it long ago, but for the Choptank river, which runs through it, from which they take abundance of shad and herring, and plenty of ague and fever" (34). The river is no less the resort of slaves than of their masters, and as all are nurtured by it, so they are equally infected. In the South, that ruinous region Dickens described, talent and aristocracy meant nothing, so great was the social decay. Nowhere is this more evident than at the Lloyd plantation, an extensive description of which Douglass added to *My Bondage*. In a pointed echo of the plantation novel, he describes this wealthiest of Maryland estates as a latter-day Eden, with its sweeping drives, its stately Great House and neatly painted outbuildings, "interspersed with grand old trees, ornamental and primitive, which afforded delightful shade in summer, and imparted to the scene a high degree of stately beauty" (67). There were parks, too, with all manner of wild game "playing about," and tall poplars "covered with...redwinged blackbirds, making all nature vocal with the joyous life and beauty of their wild, warbling notes" (68). But the Lloyd plantation was also the site of a chilling insularity, as heinous as that of any medieval fiefdom. All the produce, the trade, and the men were controlled by Lloyds, for the benefit of Lloyds alone, in the service of an all-consuming greed. "Lurking beneath all their dishes," Douglass warns after a list of their sumptuous meals, "are invisible spirits of evil, ready to feed the self-deluded gourmandizers with aches, pains, fierce temper, uncontrolled passions, dyspepsia, rheumatism, lumbago, and gout" (111). Ease ironically afflicts them, much as it afflicts Sophia Auld. That "most kind and tender-hearted woman" (152) who treated young Douglass with genuine warmth was soon corrupted by her unchecked power. She became a virago, enraged at the merest hint of her slave's independence and opposing his desire to read. "Slavery and social isolation" (183) had consumed her. "Does not wantonness enervate them?" demanded Galgachus in *The Columbian Orator*. "Do they not even go to excess in the most unmanly vices?" (187). Douglass could now reply with cool reserve:

> The slave is a subject, subjected by others; the slaveholder is a subject, but he is the author of his own subjection. There is more truth in the saying, that slavery is a greater evil to the master than to the slave, than many, who utter it, suppose. The self-executing laws of eternal justice follow close on the heels of the evil-doer here, as elsewhere; making escape from all its penalties impossible. (105–6)

The entire region was withering, as from a plague.

Douglass's interest in what Thomas de Pietro calls "slave institutions, class-analysis, or broad sociological generalizations"[32] gave rise to a pervasive literary device one might call "double irony." Just as the miasmatic Choptank infects master and slave, so slavery itself produced a peculiar discourse. Once again, the Lloyd plantation serves as a model:

> There are no conflicting rights of property, for all the people are owned by one man; and they can themselves own no property. Religion and politics are alike excluded. One class of the population is too high to be reached by the preacher; and the other class is too low to be cared for by the preacher. ...The politician keeps away, because the people have no votes, and the preacher keeps away, because the people have no money. The rich planter can afford to learn politics in the parlor, and to dispense with religion altogether. (64)

Here are the pointed antithesis and parallelism of the *Narrative*—but with a telling difference. Whereas the earlier style reflected Douglass's distant mastery of slavery, this written life suggests that no mastery is possible. Here master and slave are equally abject, and Douglass's prose does not restore order so much as depict utter depravity. He makes this disturbingly clear in a portrait of the slave Isaac Cooper, added to *My Bondage*. "Uncle" Cooper, one of the few slaves with a last name—even in the North, Douglass observes, blacks are likely to be addressed by their first names only—had charge of religious instruction among the Lloyd slaves. The old man was a tyrant and conducted recitals of the Lord's Prayer with the savagery of an overseer. "Our [t]hick tongues and unskilled ears, followed him to the best of our ability," Douglass recalled, but with as little success as tired field hands picked tobacco. "Everybody in the south, wants the privilege of whipping somebody else," and Cooper would use his hickory as freely as Mr. Plummer. His lessons mixed so much of "the tragic and comic" as to make the prayer a travesty (72). Once again, mastery turns on itself, corrupting blacks as fully as whites until no trace of dignity remains.

More disturbing still was the intolerance of the "free" North. Just as Captain Anthony might have been more "humane . . . and . . . respectable" (80) had he lived in a humane community, so Northern prejudice was merely a refinement of slavery. In an incident carefully suppressed from the *Narrative*, Douglass relates his outrage at a New Bedford minister who made sure all his white congregants had exited before offering Communion to blacks. "The colored members—poor, slavish souls—went forward, as invited. I went *out*"; and although Douglass sampled several churches, he found in all of them "the same spirit which held my brethren in chains" (353, 354). It was the same "stupid contentment" he discovered among slaves in Maryland, as he alone writhed with "the frightful dragon that was ready to pounce upon" him (160). His acute consciousness of wrong had robbed him of all peace, North or South. Once again, he was marginal.

Indeed, it is the supreme irony of *My Bondage*, that Douglass could find refuge from these republican cruelties only in aristocratic England. There, in a country that prized talent, he was treated civilly; he could go into any church or public hall without hearing America's motto, *"We don't allow niggers in here!"* (371). At home, even the abolitionists exuded a faint odor of racism: "In their eagerness, sometimes, to show their contempt for the feeling, they proved that they had not entirely recovered from it. . . . When it was said to me, 'Mr. Douglass, I will walk to meeting with you; I am not afraid of a black man,' I could not help thinking—'And why should you be?' " (398). And when Douglass finally asserted the same independence that once subdued Edward Covey, the Garrisonians excoriated him. In *My Bondage* he only hints at the acrimony surrounding his publication of the *North Star*:

> My American friends looked at me with astonishment! "A wood-sawyer" offering himself to the public as an editor! A slave, brought up in the very depths of ignorance, assuming to instruct the highly civilized people of the north in the principles of liberty, justice, and humanity! The thing looked absurd. (394)

In fact, the rift was far uglier. After a prolonged period of study, Douglass was forced to reject the Garrisonian contention that the Constitution was pro-slavery, a position that infuriated fellow abolitionists, who accused him of selling out to white patrons. Soon Garrison himself was remarking that "the Anti-Slavery cause . . . has transcended the ability of the sufferers from American Slavery and prejudice, *as a class*, to keep pace with it, or to perceive what are its demands, or to understand the philosophy of its operations." And what was worse, he accused Douglass of philandering with Julia Griffiths, who had "not only caused much unhappiness in his own household, but perniciously biased his own judgment."[33] Characteristically, Douglass sought comfort in print, defending himself in the *North Star*, and with greater tact in the autobiography. Yet the message remained clear: there was no heaven of freedom in the North, or anywhere in America, for a heroic black. No abolitionist would consent to be taught by a "nigger."

But if the miasma were pervasive, if no region were secure from racism, then Douglass's representativeness vanished. He had not, in *My Bondage and My Freedom*, succeeded in portraying the life of a common slave: he had been an uncommon slave, united with the rest only through the firmness of his rhetoric. And yet he must have known that his rhetorical appeals to white readers would equally fail. They were asked to see him as a representative American, one who overcame poverty to preach freedom; he remained a fluent propagandist, searching for a supportive audience. He had mastered the form but not the function of representativeness. Nowhere is this more clear than in his christening as a freedman. Like William Wells Brown, he had asked a patron for a surname, and accepted "Douglass," after Walter Scott's heroic highlander. Perhaps he reflected that the choice was faintly suspect, since Scott's work had been widely used by pro-slavery apologists; if so, the thought is nowhere recorded. It would have been too chilling an irony for even the most self-conscious hero.

THE RISE OF SOLITUDE

Ralph Ellison once remarked that "a writer did not so much create the novel as he was created *by* the novel."[34] In two autobiographies, Douglass had chosen to create himself through public discourse—in the *Narrative* through conventions of the lecture platform, in *My Bondage* through those of sentimental romance. His choice was not unique; it was shared by an obscure poet whose first volume appeared in the same year as *My Bondage*. Walt Whitman, too, had been stirred by the possibilities of oratory. As he wrote *Leaves of Grass*, he imagined a "wander-speaker," who "by powerful words, orations, uttered with copiousness and decision, with all the aid of art," would "rule over America"—opening sessions of Congress, inaugurating the president, calming in time of crisis—"and *always hold[ing] the ear of the people*."[35] This great American "champion," as Paul Zweig persuasively argues, became the speaker of "Song of Myself"—not only within the embossed green covers to which Whitman affixed Emerson's paean, but in the flesh. "The poems became Whitman's model," Zweig observes, "a template for a personality...longing to be whole" (116). The man he offered to readers was the democratic beast he sought to become—rustic, gregarious, "one in whom you will see the singularity which consists in no singularity," homely as "something you knew before, and was waiting for."[36] Fourteen years after the publication of "Self-Reliance," Whitman, too, was attempting to answer Emerson's call for a representative man, and like Douglass, he sought to do so by proclaiming a corporate self. It is one of literature's crueller ironies that both books appeared five years before the Civil War. But even if America at mid-century had retained the relative homogeneity it had possessed in Franklin's day, the experiment would still have been doubtful. The reason lay in a profound cultural shift that rendered the old corporate identity suspect—the triumph of individualism.

Although it is probable that what we now think of as American individualism—economic opportunism, political independence, psychological distinctiveness[37]—existed in various guises since the early colonial settlements, its real flowering did not occur until the nineteenth century. To be sure, it is possible to see pronounced individualistic tendencies a century earlier. As Richard Bushman, James Henretta, and others have argued,[38] the First Great Awakening helped to weaken corporate ties by stressing personal responsibility for salvation. What mattered was not the power of congregations to sanction grace, but the sinner's own ecstatic experience of salvation—a force ministers breathlessly pursued and tried to contain. Then, too, the sharp-dealing Yankee began to emerge during this period—the Quaker grandee who so disturbed Woolman, the wealthy planter, the Boston merchant. Certain trends in education, emphasizing the full development of the child's independent judgment, also encouraged the kind of self-regarding individual who would "*improve* his fortune by his honest industry, lest he should never be enabled to rise out of a state of dependence."[39] And the colonial towns, which had, for the first two generations at least, maintained themselves as "Christian Utopian Closed Corporate Communities," were, in many regions, yielding to the pressures of out-migration, legal bickering, and political conflict.[40] But although the Revolution is often cited as a watershed—the sanction of individual over corporate rights—the ethos of the new nation had not entirely changed. All revolutionary parties, Calvinists and rationalists alike, remained committed to corporate virtue, feared faction, and exhorted citizens to sacrifice for the common good. Even those who rose to wealth through rigorous self-interest often preached community, as Franklin's career demonstrates. One mark of this diffuse individualism emerged during the Revolution itself, when hungry sailors and militiamen took to the streets of Philadelphia, demanding that it was their "natural right" to have the city set a just price for grain—a practice characteristic of early Puritans rather than of nascent capitalists.[41] The new nation, in many ways, remained tied to the past.

It was the Second Great Awakening that substantially weakened this "old corporate theory of society,"[42] by extending pietism to large masses of Americans. From its inception in the early 1800s, to its crest in the 1820s and 1830s, the revival appealed, with an intensity unmatched in American experience, to the vagaries of the individual soul. "You will be called eccentric," proclaimed the great revivalist Charles Grandison Finney in 1835, "and probably you will deserve it. . . . I never knew a person who was filled with the Spirit, that was not called eccentric" (115). Salvation now depended on unique experience, an intimate relationship with God. The minister, Finney explained, could approach potential converts with only the most general expectations, and the greatest sensitivity: "The characters of individuals, affords [*sic*] an endless diversity. What is to be done with each one, and how he is to be converted, depends on his particular errors" (364). In one of his lectures on revivals, Finney offered a telling anecdote. Confronted with a score of unregenerate boarders, a pious woman resolved to save souls. Rather than engage them all in postprandial prayer, however, she decided on a different approach. Speaking earnestly to a single boarder, she soon found him "hopefully converted," and did the same with another, until, "one at a time," all were saved. "Now if she had brought the subject before the whole of them together," remarks Finney, "very likely they would have turned it all into ridicule. . . . But taking one alone, and treating him respectfully and kindly, he had no such motive for resistance as arises out of the presence of others" (159). Masses of Christians were now to be saved individually; the focus was on the solitary soul.

This "perfectionist" impulse, the notion that all progress hinged on the cleansing of individuals, came to dominate Jacksonian reform. As John L. Thomas argues in a classic essay, the liberated individual became the rationale for wide-ranging attacks on institutions—corporate bodies—whether the established church, the national bank, or the slave system. Northern intellectuals like Theodore Parker, William Ellery Channing, and Emerson urged the claims of the transcendent self, the "primitive atoms" upon whose individuality rested all true society.[43] "The country is full of rebellion," noted Emerson in "New England Reformers." "Hands off! let there be no control and no interference in the administration of this kingdom of me." The spirit of the age stressed "the private, self-supplied powers of the individual"; society was "perfect" only when all its members were "isolated."[44] To be sure, Emerson, along with other transcendentalists, viewed the individual less as an isolate than as a fragment of a cosmic community;[45] but the force of such perfectionism often fragmented the earthly community. Perhaps the best example of that is the abolitionist movement itself, which continually split over Garrison's come-outer philosophy. Even as Northern opposition to slavery became general in the decade before the war, the Garrisonians clung to their peculiar brand of "anarchism"[46] with a fervor not even Douglass could abide. Perfectionist individualism spurned all union.

But the liberated– perhaps "anomic"[47]—individual was only a symptom of much wider social change. The first third of the nineteenth century saw rapid modernization in almost all areas of American life. New roads, canals, and railroads spanned the Northeast and spread south and west. Factories sprang up and cities grew, disrupting old relations within families, guilds, and towns. Newly opened territories constantly lured the unsettled or ambitious, provoking what foreign observers saw as an inexplicable restlessness.[48] "In the United States," Tocqueville observed, "a man builds a house in which to spend his old age, and he sells it before the roof is on; he plants a garden and lets it just as the trees are coming into bearing; . . . he settles in a place, which he soon afterwards leaves to carry his changeable longings elsewhere."[49] Under these accumulated pressures Americans began to treat their expansiveness in a new way. The term "individualism" had originally been used by European conservatives to denounce the effects of market capitalism and the French Revolution; soon it was taken up by socialists who, like Honoré Balzac, thought unrestrained self-assertion "the most horrible of all evils."[50] Increasingly, however, American spokesmen transformed the term. "The course of civilization," wrote a contributor to *The United States Magazine and Democratic Review*, "is the progress of man from a state of savage individualism to that of an individualism more elevated, moral, and refined." American democracy

recognizes the distinct existence of individual man in himself as an independent end, and not barely as a means to be merged in a mass. . . . His in-

> stinctive conditions, his irrepressible desires, his boundless capacity for improvement, conspire . . . to make the doctrine of individual rights the greatest of political truths.[51]

Perfectionism, faith in progress, the cult of self-reliance, and the "boundlessness" of the period all combined to produce an ideology enshrined in the slogans "free society," "laissez faire," and "the common man"—an ethos given scientific status by the work of Herbert Spencer. The English syncretist, whose deductions from Darwin rapidly dominated American thought, saw civilization

> as a progress towards that constitution of man and society required for the complete manifestation of every one's individuality. . . . our advance must be towards a state in which this entire satisfaction of every desire, or perfect fulfillment of individual life, becomes possible. . . . And further progress must be towards increased sacredness of personal claims, and a subordination of whatever limits them.[52]

American optimism, competitiveness, and expansiveness converged in this apology for what Margaret Fuller once called the "mountainous me." The nation had found a cosmic ideology.

LIFE AND TIMES OF FREDERICK DOUGLASS

Although Douglass often appealed to the cult of the self-made man—indeed, became its spokesman late in life—he could not forego the social vision of *The Columbian Orator*. To do so would be to sacrifice that self he had so painfully created in two autobiographies, and was to extend in *Life and Times*.[53] But how could he resist so pervasive a trend and the increased marginality it promised? In large measure, Douglass was saved by an anachronism: his insistent identification with the jeremiad. As the crisis of civil war approached, Northern preachers once again discerned Apocalypse, that "first great conflict to precede the millennium" when, the Southern dragon subdued, there would dawn "such a day as Washington and Hancock and Adams pictured and dreamed about, and prayed for. It will come with blessings, and be greeted with Hallelujahs, it will be the Millennium of political glory, the Sabbath of Liberty, the Jubilee of Humanity."[54] Since the early days with Garrison, Douglass had been gazing on just these "contending armies" of the Union, awaiting only the "bolt of heaven" to engage; now, as the armies met, he, too, looked far into the future. "There is a general feeling amongst us," he declared to a Rochester audience in 1861, "that the control of events has been taken out of our hands, that we have fallen into the mighty current of eternal principles—invisible forces, which are shaping and fashioning events as they wish, using us only as instruments to work out their own results in our National destiny." In that first enthusiastic outburst, Douglass left no doubt about the "invisible" agent:

> In the apocalyptic vision, John describes a war in heaven. You have only to strip that vision of its gorgeous Oriental drapery ... clothe it in the simple and familiar language of common sense, and you will have before you the eternal conflict between right and wrong, good and evil, liberty and slavery ... Michael and his angels are still contending against the infernal host of bad passions ... and the fight will continue till one or the other is subdued. ... Such is the struggle now going on in the United States. The slaveholders had rather reign in hell than serve in heaven.

Here was the rhetoric of *The Columbian Orator* brought to life, the dawn of the great judgment that "would raise every slave in the world and prepare the earth for a millenium [*sic*] of righteousness and peace." Millennialism promised to save the isolated orator, attach him once again to a universal cause. Now, as at no time before, could Douglass declare: "In birth, in sentiment, in ideas, in hopes, in aspirations, and responsibilities, I am an American citizen."[55]

The conflict allowed Douglass to make crucial realignments. Sifting through the welter of antislavery movements, he endorsed ever larger political parties—performing an abrupt about-face in 1856 when he switched from Liberty men to Republicans. What he sought was a national party capable of opposing the growing slave power and advancing his world-historical cause. Events had left the ultraists far behind. No longer could the opponents of slavery afford moral purity; "the time had come for a new organization which should embrace all who were in any manner opposed to slavery and the slave power" (*LT* 344). Hence Douglass would compromise; he would support any party that "will forward what we conceive to be the highest interests of society," reserving his right, as Columbian orator, to reassert ideals:

> When this much is accomplished, invite the party to a higher ground; if they fail to come up, sound the alarm: "To your tents, O Israel"; and the Republican leaders will see, that while they were true to liberty, they could carry the masses with them, but when they undertake to impede the advancing hosts of freedom, the power will depart from them.[56]

Such pragmatism was to infuriate Douglass's critics, both before and after the war; yet so great was the man's sense of mission that he could support even the most suspect powers, if only their ends seemed just. And invariably, when challenged, he would advert to that republican rhetoric that made all local movements stages in millennial progress.

Hence, when war was declared, Douglass became a spokesman for the free North. Before the war, he had portrayed the North as aghast at "the kind of civilization to which *they* were linked" (*LT* 363, emphasis added). After Fort Sumter, his pronouns shift decisively. To a Rochester audience he declared:

> We (the people of the North) are a charitable people, and, in the excess of this feeling, we were disposed to put the very best construction upon the strange behavior of our southern brethren.... We could not but believe that there existed at the South a latent and powerful Union sentiment which would assert itself at last.... we could not be made to believe that the border States would plunge madly into the bloody vortex of rebellion. (408–9)

Perhaps among his listeners in Corinthian Hall were some who had heard his Independence Day address eight years before; if so, they would have detected the same links between personal and national concerns. "I confess to a feeling allied to satisfaction at the prospect of a conflict between the North and the South," he later wrote in *Life and Times*. "Standing outside the pale of American humanity, denied citizenship, unable to call the land of my birth my country . . . I was ready for any political upheaval which should bring about a change in the existing condition of things" (402). It was precisely the attitude he had earlier taken toward Edward Covey, with whom he attempted to provoke a second fight in order "to do him serious damage" (*BF* 249). The North had at last acted on his own maxim:

> Hereditary bondmen, know ye not
> Who would be free, themselves must strike the blow? (*BF* 249)

The Civil War was Douglass's first great proof that history could echo the inner life of an inspired orator. Under its influence he once again expanded his life. If his previous autobiography had been addressed to the sentimental reader, this one would be addressed to the culture at large. It would be less a romance than a chronicle, a vital voice in a cultural dialogue. Hence, as the war was a projection of his own fight for freedom, so later events recalled personal truths. After an interview with Andrew Johnson during which the president opposed enfranchising the freedmen, Douglass published an attack paraphrasing his comments on Covey. "Can it be that you recommend a policy which would arm the strong and cast down the defenceless?" he asks Johnson. "Experience proves that those are most abused who are whipped easiest" (468; cf. 59). More significant was his own dramatic rise. If the black were "the test of American civilization" (*LW* 2:448), then postbellum America had unmistakably advanced. In a remarkable conflation of personal and national affairs, Douglass records his reception as a delegate to the National Loyalist's Convention, in Philadelphia in 1866. His very selection by Rochester had been remarkable enough—a city with only two hundred black residents; and Douglass insisted on representing all despite the considerable opposition of wary Southern whites. When he arrived in the city and sought to take part in a parade to the convention hall, he found himself shunned by his own party—but not by the people of Philadelphia:

> I was myself utterly surprised by the heartiness and unanimity of the popular approval. We were marching through a city remarkable for the depth and bitterness of its hatred of the abolition movement; a city whose populace had mobbed anti-slavery meetings, burned temperance halls and churches owned by colored people, and burned down Pennsylvania Hall because it had opened its doors to people of different colors upon terms of equality. But now the children of those who had committed these outrages ...were applauding the very principles which their fathers had condemned. (476)

What was more, the children were applauding Douglass, who was reenacting that momentous change in Philadelphia's values. He had come to the city a shunned representative, and left a Representative Man.

But vindication did not stop there. Among the applauding crowd was Amanda Sears, the daughter of Thomas Auld. Her presence allows Douglass to make an apparent digression that is very much to the point. Seven years before, he recalls, on another visit to the city, he had received word that his "once mistress" had attended his lecture at National Hall. Skeptical yet stimulated, "eager to know if my kinsfolk still lived, and what was their condition" (478), Douglass agreed to visit her the next day. The affair had a theatrical quality. Douglass, desiring "to make the contrast between the slave and the free man as striking as possible" (479), put on his best suit and hired the finest carriage he could find. When he arrived, he was ushered into a large drawing room, where a curious *tableau vivant* greeted him. John Sears, "to test [his] memory," had arranged the large company so as to conceal his wife; on a chair before Douglass sat a slender impostor who bore a faint resemblance to the young Amanda. But the orator was not to be deceived. "Mr. Sears," he announced, "if you will allow me, I will select Miss Amanda from this company," and as he gestured toward her, his "once mistress" bounded into his arms (480). The parlor scene, like the street scene, is a dramatic reversal of a nation's values. Where formerly Douglass struggled with his own slave's blankness, now he confronted an audience of anonymous whites, with the power of conferring identity. And although he had come hoping to receive information of his own family, he was called upon to confirm Amanda's memories of Lucretia Auld. No longer an outcast, the slave's experience now provided a crucial link to a shared past:

> She also recollected that as I had had trials as a slave she had had her trials under the care of a stepmother, and that when she was harshly spoken to by her father's second wife she could always read in my dark face the sympathy of one who had often received kind words from the lips of her beloved mother. (480)

Indeed, Douglass repeats this scene at Amanda's deathbed, relating Lucretia's "personal appearance" and selecting, from among the Sears children, the one who most resembled her. His choice again confirms his sagacity: "Her name is Lucretia," Amanda told him, "after my mother" (481). This "digression," then, allows Douglass to confirm in life what he had formerly evoked in print. He had been embraced by a white audience, witnessed a deathbed scene, invoked motherhood. His writing had proved prophetic.

Much of the new material in *Life and Times* has this faintly celebratory air. In a chapter that has drawn the fire of many critics, Douglass relates two incidents underscoring his personal achievement. First, he revisits his erstwhile master, Thomas Auld. Like the Sears episode, this deathbed scene seems to have a "peculiar and poetic force" (533)—a representative status. The frail old man and the United States marshal establish an intimacy they never knew under slavery, and freely renounce their former antagonism. "Capt. Auld," Douglass declares in his most oratorical manner, " ...I did not run away from *you*, but from *slavery*; it was not that I loved Caesar less, but Rome more" (536–37). Repentant tyranny and republican virtue now join hands over old wrongs, in a scene that "might well enough be dramatized for the stage" (533): "Our courses had been determined for us, not by us. We had both been flung, by powers that did not ask our consent, upon a mighty current of life, which we could neither resist nor control.... but now our lives were verging towards a point where differences disappear" (535). It was the last act in a grand historical drama that Douglass had early identified as his own, one that epitomized that momentous century.

Even more momentous is his visit with the Lloyd clan. Forty years out of slavery, Douglass found himself on a federal ship off Easton, and sent for permission to visit the Great House. He was given a grand tour—the same Edenic grounds, with their "broad walks, hedged with box and adorned with fruit trees and flowers of almost every variety" (544), now wearing a distinctly different cast. He sat on the veranda overlooking the vacant slave quarters, sipping fine wine and dangling a bouquet of flowers presented him by the younger Lloyd, feeling in "every way gratif[ied]" (547). At last he had been conferred a position equal to his talent—had found in America what he once thought possible only in England. When he sat some days later conversing with a Lloyd daughter, he discovered "as little embarrassment as if I had been an old acquaintance and occupied an equal station with the most aristocratic of the Caucasian race" (547). It is perhaps easy to see such comments as fatuous egotism; but Douglass saw them as much more. They were America's imprimatur, its acknowledgment of a Representative Man.

It was James M'Cune Smith who had suggested, in the introduction to *My Bondage and My Freedom*, that Douglass was "a Representative American," having "passed through every gradation of rank comprised in our national make-up" (xxv, xxvi). Now in 1882, as at no other time in his career, Douglass was prepared to endorse that claim. He had lived, he concluded, "several lives in one"; as a slave, a fugitive, a freedman, a Union man, and a citizen, he had recapitulated the great historical movement of his time:

> To those who have suffered in slavery I can say, I, too, have suffered. To those who have taken some risks and encountered hardships in the flight from bondage I can say, I, too, have endured and risked. To those who have battled for liberty, brotherhood, and citizenship I can say, I, too, have battled. And to those who have lived to enjoy the fruits of victory I can say, I, too, live and rejoice. (582)

Here was the rhetoric of the *North Star* trained on the reunited republic—and yet the rhetoric now had currency. Douglass could now tour Easton or speak at Harper's Ferry and be applauded by white Southerners; he could revisit the very jail where William Freeland had imprisoned him, shake hands with his former jailer, and put up at a white hotel. He could serve as a bank president, a federal commissioner, a United States marshal. As he revised his autobiography from this eminence, he became convinced that his had been less a private life than a chronicle history, a record of the times. Like Shepard, Franklin, and Whitman, he had come to see his rise in ideological terms:

> I have aimed to assure . . . that knowledge can be obtained under difficulties; that poverty may give place to competency; that obscurity is not an absolute bar to distinction, and that a way is open to welfare and happiness

> to all who will resolutely and wisely pursue that way...that races, like individuals, must stand or fall by their own merits. (582)

Races and nations behaved like individuals, for, as Emerson declared, the individual confirmed national promise. The autobiographer was a *typos* for democracy.

Throughout the Reconstruction period Douglass had been plying this theme. His most popular lecture, "Self-Made Men,"[57] extolled those "who are what they are, without the aid of any of the favoring conditions by which other men usually rise in the world" (7). Theirs was not rare genius, but a capacity that would inaugurate the "millennium" (24). If so, the great age would be cast in Douglass's image. Successful Americans, he exhorted,

> are not brought up but...are obliged to come up, not only without the voluntary assistance or friendly co-operation of society, but often in open and derisive defiance of all the efforts of society and the tendency of circumstances to repress, retard and keep down. They are the men who, in a world of schools, academies, colleges and other institutions of learning, are often compelled by unfriendly circumstances to acquire their education elsewhere.... From the depths of poverty such as these have often come.... From hunger, rags and destitution, they have come; motherless and fatherless, they have come, and may come. (7)

All across the North, for six months in every year, Douglass preached this communal autobiography, and worked it into drafts of *Life and Times*. He muted, for example, the embarrassing ostracism in Philadelphia. The "committee of delegates" that counseled his withdrawal in an earlier version became "a committee of my *brother* delegates" in revision (473, emphasis added), and the admonition that his presence "would undoubtedly turn the scale against, and defeat the Republican candidates" became "a very slight circumstance...likely to turn the scale against *us*, and defeat *our* Congressional candidates" (473, emphasis added). Now it was his "brother" delegates who shunned him on the parade route—a parade in which "we" were nevertheless cheered (476). By 1882 Douglass saw his earlier impulse to stand apart from the American parade "strange"—such was "the progress which had been made" (472).

But there is a tension in *Life and Times*, an irony Douglass did not fully grasp, undercutting his buoyant prose as surely as individualism had undercut his vision. All too often, as he recounts his prophetic achievements, he is forced to explain away failure. The pattern begins fairly early, when, after a meeting with Lincoln, he is promised a commission as a Union officer, only to find it obstructed by Secretary

Stanton; he was prized for his influence with black recruits, he concluded, not for his military service. After the Civil War he was induced to move to Washington, D.C., on the promise of a prestigious editorial post. *The National Era* was to be a liberal journal with a national voice, yet Douglass soon discovered it a phantom corporation. "I found myself alone," he confesses; the journal's affairs "had been so managed by the agent appointed by this invisible company, or corporate body, as to compel me to bear the burden alone, and to become the sole owner" (486). The wording is significant: Douglass expects unity and finds isolation; he expects to be "incorporated," and finds himself alone. The paper's failure two years later cost him ten thousand dollars.

More devastating still was the Freedman's Bank debacle. This institution, founded by Northern liberals in 1865, had grown unwieldy by the early 1870s, with far-flung branches making questionable loans, yet promising great wealth to black depositors. Its Washington headquarters, with its "towering height, and ... perfect appointments," its elegant young clerks flipping through stacks of crisp bills, was the very symbol of black progress; and when Douglass was elected the bank's president in 1874, he savored the symbolism:

> I could not help reflecting on the contrast between Frederick the slave boy, running about at Col. Lloyd's with only a tow linen shirt to cover him, and Frederick—President of a bank counting its assets by millions. I had heard of golden dreams, but such dreams had no comparison with this reality. (489)

But the bank, too, was a phantom. Years of mismanagement and the panic of 1873 had gutted it before Douglass arrived; in fact, he had been elected in a desperate attempt to save it by the sheer force of his prestige. Instead, he presided over failure, reporting its difficulties to a congressional committee that soon compelled the bank to close. In the process, Douglass was villified, with "an amount of abuse and detraction greater than any encountered in any other part of my life" (492). Since this statement includes his life as a slave, his bitterness must have been considerable: his representativeness itself had been betrayed.

Less tangible but equally troubling was Douglass's involvement in a number of policy questions. A staunch supporter of President Grant, he received, in 1871, an appointment as commissioner to Santo Domingo. For over a year, under the prodding of his business cronies, Grant had been pressing for annexation; now he found himself blocked by a skeptical Charles Sumner, chairman of the Senate Committee on

Foreign Relations, who had defeated a proposed treaty. The Douglass appointment was a manipulation: if the distinguished commission—there were three white members, including the reformer Samuel Gridley Howe—were to return a favorable report, the Senate might be persuaded to annex. The effort failed; and although Douglass cannot be blamed for the machinations of Grant, he can be censured on other grounds. Once again, he prizes status. Grant had given strict instructions to treat the black commissioner with every mark of respect, and Douglass duly notes "the spectacle presented by a colored man seated at the captain's table" during the passage as unprecedented in "the history of the United States navy" (501). It was "another point indicating the differences between the OLD TIME and the NEW," a black man "in the society of gentlemen, scientists, and statesmen" (500). Indeed, the only troubling aspect of the trip was the demeanor of the black waiters, who failed to perceive the difference, and would rather have seen him in steerage. As for the Dominicans, Douglass once again invoked republican rhetoric:

> When the slave power bore rule, and a spirit of injustice and oppression animated and controlled every part of our government, I was for limiting our domain to the smallest possible margin; but since liberty and equality have become the law of our land, I am for extending our dominion whenever and wherever such extension can . . . be accomplished. (496)

Why should not blacks of Santo Domingo share in the NEW TIME? Annexation would give "to a part the strength of the whole, and lif[t] what must be despised for its isolation into an organization and relationship which would compel consideration and respect" (499). As Douglass rose, so rose the people. And yet, as events proved, this was another phantom corporation, one that exploited Douglass as surely as it would Dominicans. The NEW TIME was not the Millennium he had foreseen.

More telling still is a sectarian issue on which Douglass took a surprising stand. In the mid-1870s, in response to severe repression, black leaders began calling for mass black migration from the South; by 1878 a Louisiana entrepreneur had recruited almost 100,000 people for resettlement in the Midwest.[58] Called on to support the movement, Douglass lashed out at it instead. Not only was it a betrayal of the Constitution, which promised equal protection for all, it was also a denial of the black man's own instincts. In a speech before a "Social Congress" at Saratoga, Douglass drew a vivid picture of the impoverished freedman, his tatters whipped by the fierce winds of a Kansas winter as the land speculators made off with his last dollar. "The Negro . . . is preeminently a Southern man," Douglass declared. "He will not only take with him to the North southern modes of labor, but southern modes of life." He was adapted to the hot sun, the hard work, and the grim waste of the Deep South, and had adopted "careless and improvident habits" that could not "be set aside in a generation" (531). But this is a curious argument from a native Southerner, one whose own "improvidence" vanished as soon as he reached New Bedford. Indeed, as Philip Foner argues, his very success may well have put Douglass out of touch with a region he had not toured in forty years. As the sharecroppers were "fluttering in rags and wretchedness" (527), Douglass was commanding as much as two hundred dollars a lecture, and occupying a mansion in Washington (455). Although he should not be condemned for success, he seems, nevertheless, a victim of his own rhetoric. A stump speech he made during the period captures his entrapment. "It is the same old conflict," he declared of his Democratic opponents. "Liberty, union and civilization on the one hand and Slavery, disunion and barbarism on the other."[59] As political conditions changed, Douglass remained the Columbian orator.

By the 1870s Doulgass may indeed have been overtaken by his own success. Having left Rochester, which had installed his bust in its university and hailed him as "the greatest of our citizens" (565), he entered the avaricious world of Washington, a city as terrifying, in its manner, as New York had been to the fugitive. It was a venal world, where any distinction brought with it "disparagement and abuse of the successful man" (512)—Nietzsche's *rancune* for what is great; and one has the feeling that Douglass was ever wary of those "ferocious beasts" he once sensed on Broadway (*N* 111). When he discusses his activities as a government functionary, he is quick to defend himself against charges of impropriety, on the one hand, and timidity on the other. It was not true, for example, that as United States marshal he despised the capital, nor was it true that he had allowed all blacks to be snubbed by President Hayes's refusal to invite him to the White House on state occasions. That was the president's prerogative, Douglass contended, and he was civilly treated at other times. There is even a pathetic quality in his strict adherence to form. After delivering a bold jeremiad in Maryland, in which he criticized the racist attributes of Washington, Douglass was so inundated with abuse that he was forced to reiterate the Promise in the local press. "Elsewhere we may belong to a section," he wrote, "but here we belong to a whole country, and the whole country belongs to us." One can only imagine his outrage as he repeated to political enemies the conclusion of his speech. Washington was indeed

a redeemed city, beautiful to the eye and attractive to the heart, a bond of perpetual union, an angel of peace on earth and good will to men, a common ground upon which Americans of all races . . . , North and South, may meet and shake hands, not over a chasm of blood, but over a free, united, and progressive republic. (516)

It was a city that honored his oration at the unveiling of a Lincoln Monument erected by blacks, but said nothing when, in the same year, he was barred from speaking at the Centennial Exhibition in Philadelphia. It was a city where white party hacks praised him and blacks accused him of "desert[ing] to the old master class" (523). As he faced such cruel ironies, it is not surprising that even the representative Douglass occasionally glimpsed a tragic isolation. Twice in *Life and Times* he pictures himself an American Othello, declaring his "occupation . . . gone" (453) at the end of the Civil War, and imagining himself an embattled general after the Freedman's Bank fiasco. He had been summoned to resuscitate the bank, by "some drugs, some charms, some conjuration, or some mighty magic," and had found instead "the malicious and envious assaults of unscrupulous aspirants who vainly fancy that they lift themselves into consideration by wanton attacks upon the characters of men who receive a larger share of respect and esteem than themselves" (493). The black orator had discovered the tragic limits of heroism.

"While sociologists gleefully count his bastards and prostitutes," W. E. B. Du Bois would write of this period, "the very soul of the toiling, sweating black man is darkened by the shadow of a vast despair. . . . The bright ideals of the past,—physical freedom, political power, the training of brains and the training of hands,—all these in turn have waxed and waned, until even the last grows dim and overcast."[60] Nothing so fully measures the distance Douglass had traveled than this subdued, elegiac prose. The representative writer of *Life and Times* had remained faithful to his past, and to the shrill republican rhetoric that had marked his rise. Now approaching seventy, he looked back over a remarkable life and felt justified in discerning the signs of the times. A self-made man, he had been enshrined in the nation's capital as a symbol of cultural progress: he embodied the best of the era. Like the Whitman of *Specimen Days*, he struggled, through severe trials, to preserve that identity—did preserve it, despite the ironies surrounding him. Yet those very ironies suggest that, toward the end of the century, the myth of republican unity, too, had aged. Perhaps the problems of world power, class antagonism, and race hatred could no longer support the boundless vision of a Representative Man.

THE REVISED *LIFE AND TIMES*

The revised, 1892 edition of *Life and Times*[61] provides a curious coda. Here again, Douglass is quick to note the epiphanies of the intervening decade. As marshal at President Garfield's inauguration, he once again remarks the contrast between slave boy and dignitary—between an abused pariah and the official "having under [his] care and guidance the sacred persons of an ex-President and of the President-elect of a nation of sixty millions" (627). "The precedent was valuable," he declares; and yet, there is a note of tentativeness, almost world-weariness in the appraisal. It was a mere moment in the history of an abused race, a single pinnacle from which the "tide" would recede, perhaps to the desperate ebb noted by Du Bois. Indeed, Douglass here considerably masked his feelings. One of the earliest drafts of the passage almost scorns the ceremony:

> I did not fail to see that I was still a member of a proscribed ~~people~~ class. and that the high place I had was . . . accidental, not regular. ~~I know~~ that my presence ~~on that occasion~~ was tolerated ~~rather than sought~~ not invited, endured not sought or desired by the majority of the American people. Yet I was not sorry that for once at least that the face of a colored man ~~was~~ should be seen by this nation and by the civilized world on an occasion so august and commanding.[62]

The event merely underscores a darker truth, "that the American people are much . . . mystified about the mere matter of color as connected with manhood," that they equate blackness with immorality, and "do not feel quite reconciled to the idea that a man of different color from themselves should have all the human rights claimed by themselves" (621). It is hard to imagine a statement of such profound bitterness in the earlier edition; harder to imagine his acerbic comments on "the Afro-American press" (643), whose malicious rumors of the marshal's great wealth excited "numerous and persistent beggars" (643). The dry remark that he "could not exactly see how or why I should be called upon to pay the debt for the whole four millions of liberated people" (643) is a sign, perhaps, that the Representative American had once more shifted ground. Although he preserves the earlier text with few revisions, he grafts a final warning, the fire of a last jeremiad.

Once again, it is Europe that provides the damning contrast—aristocratic Europe that confers equality. At the age of seventy, with his second wife, Douglass undertook a grand tour. As with all events of his life, this, too, had symbolic resonance: it was the ex-slave's claiming world culture on equal terms with whites. As he visited Paris, Athens, and Rome, gazed at the dome of St. Peter's and at Paganini's violin, he found a temporary freedom from caste. He noted with interest the darkening complexions of Europeans as he traveled south, and even found precedents for the Civil War in the dim battlegrounds of the Continent, where civilization and barbarism, "the old and the new ... fought out the irrepressible conflict" (682). Like Whitman's late tour of the Rockies, Douglass's experience gives him a new universality. He saw not only contemporary Europe but also the ruins of Memphis and Crete, the Temple of Dionysus, and the Parthenon. The ex-slave reclaims that culture denied him "on the banks of the Chesapeake" (713)—projects what all might become in some more liberal future, instructed by his experience.

But the trip also serves as a warning, a summons to racist America; for now, from this last summit, Douglass unleashes a jeremiad. Only Europe is color-blind: in America

> a white scoundrel, because he is white, is preferred to an honest and educated black man.... Nowhere in the world are the worth and dignity of manhood more exalted in speech and press than they are here, and nowhere is manhood pure and simple more despised than here. We affect contempt for the castes and aristocracies of the old world and laugh at their assumptions, but at home foster pretensions far less rational and much more ridiculous. (648)

It is a final oratorical turn, the menace concealed in millennial promise—underscored by Douglass's principled resistance to governmental corruption. In 1889 Douglass received the patronage appointment he had always desired, a consulship to Haiti. As with his earlier commission to Santo Domingo, the post had a Machiavellian dimension; the Harrison administration hoped to convince the Haitians to cede a valuable port to the United States Navy. Douglass, who was hailed by Haitian President Hyppolite as "the illustrious champion of all men sprung from the African race, ... one of the most remarkable products ... on the American continent,"[63] was expected to provide leverage. But as if to atone for Santo Domingo, he refused: when naval gunboats appeared off the island to support the "negotiations," he resigned his post and wrote a stinging exposé for the *North American Review*:

> Is the weakness of a nation a reason for our robbing it? Are we to take advantage, not only of its weakness, but of its fears? Are we to wring from it by dread of our power what we cannot obtain by appeals to its justice and reason? If this is the policy of this great nation, I own that my assailants were right when they said that I was not the man to represent the United States in Haiti. (731)

No longer would his representativeness mask racism.

The revised *Life and Times* is a kind of prose archeology. One uncovers the layers of a remarkable rhetoric, now caustic, now self-gratulatory, as Douglass works through his public stance. Preserved there are the bombast and the anger of a complex man who could never quite come to terms with his culture. Yet though his prose varies, as he attempts to meet near maddening demands, he preserves a certain configuration, an American essence. There is an anecdote in his last autobiography that captures that essence. During the Egyptian tour, Douglass was "tempted ... to ascend to the top of the highest Pyramid." The feat was by no means a simple one: the thick, irregular blocks offered few sure footholds; the desert heat soon wearied the young tourist, and Douglass was seventy years old. "Neither in ascending nor descending [was] it safe to look down" (711). Yet the old man—two Arabs tugging above and two pushing below—reached the summit. "The main work I had to do myself," he remarks, and he "paid dearly for the venture." But the view from that desert pinnacle, overlooking the monuments of a civilization, justified the pain:

> the great unexplained and inexplicable Sphinx, the Pyramids and other wonders of Sakkara, the winding river valley of the Nile, the silent, solemn and measureless desert, the seats of ancient Memphis and Heliopolis, the distant mosques, minarets, and stately palaces, the ages and events that have swept over the scene and the millions on millions that lived, wrought and died there—

the old orator viewed them all (711). Throughout his career Douglass struggled to ascend that pinnacle. His labored, often inspired autobiographies mark the majesty of his passage.

6 | *Reluctant Modern:*
Gertrude Stein

In the summer of 1904, a reserved and rather wealthy American confronted modernity in a room off the Avenue du Bois de Boulogne. Henry Adams, brooding on the multiplied failures that had shattered his "medieval" world, drew a wry sketch for his autobiography—of a "howling, steaming, exploding, Marconiing, radiumating, automobiling maniac" longing for the "primitive" 1830s. "A world so different from that of my childhood or middle-life can't belong to the same scheme," he wrote to a friend. There had been a "rupture of continuity," destroying old unities;[1] and as he wrote "A Grammar of Science," Adams foresaw "a new world": "a land where no one had ever penetrated before; where order was an accidental relation obnoxious to nature ... against which every free energy of the universe revolted; and which, being merely occasional, resolved itself back into anarchy at last."[2] Adams, nearing death, observed the new order with clear-eyed, atavistic horror. "It is time to quit," he confessed, "and I shall be glad to take leave."[3] Not far away in the rue de Fleurus, a younger American began to formulate a grammar of her own. While Adams wrote his *Education*, Gertrude Stein assembled the complicated sentences of *Three Lives*. She was striving for an art to express the new century, one rendering consciousness in a "prolonged present"[4] sealed off from the past. The nineteenth century had preached grand unities—science and progress, evolution and Esperanto; the twentieth century, she was convinced, demanded private, even gnomic reflection, instantaneous impressions captured in fugitive prose. And yet as the mature Stein pursued these ideals, with a rigor that often defied comprehension, she, too, seemed to shudder at modernity.[5] The woman who championed one of the most radical revolts in the history of art could write wanly of a "splendid...time when everything cracks, where everything is destroyed, everything isolates itself...,"[6] and of a literature whose most interesting characters were "dead."[7] Isolated from American readers, she struggled increasingly to accommodate her genius to her audience, her conservative temper to cataclysmic change. Stein's four autobiographies—*The Autobiography of Alice B. Toklas* (1933), *Everybody's Autobiography* (1937), *Paris France* (1940), and *Wars I Have Seen* (1945)—record her halting recovery of those forgotten unities.

DIS/UNITY IN A NEW AGE

"Naturally if you were born in the nineteenth century," Stein remarks in *Wars I Have Seen*, "when evolution first began to be known, and everything was being understood...then there would be progress and everything could be and would be understood."[8] Stein was born in 1874, a decade after Herbert Spencer's *First Principles* had appeared, and the very year in which John Fiske, Spencer's most prominent American disciple, published his multi-volume *Outlines of Cosmic Philosophy*. The years following Darwin's great work had seen a swarm of unnatural progeny, eclectic thinkers and strident popularizers who used evolutionary theory to their own ends. Spencer, whom Nietzsche would call the philosopher of "Anglo-angelic shopkeeperdom" (*WP* §944, 489), sought to gather all knowledge under a single evolutionary law. The parallels he traced through astronomy, geology, biology, sociology, psychology, and other disciplines were no mere coincidence:

> when we recognize these divisions as mere conventional groupings, made to facilitate the arrangement and acquisition of knowledge—when we remember that the different existences with which they severally deal are component parts of one Cosmos; we see at once that there are not several kinds of Evolution having certain traits in common, but one Evolution going on everywhere after the same manner.[9]

Spencer demonstrated that unity in a monumental "synthetic philosophy," a summation of all knowledge. John Fiske more modestly traced evolution through astronomy and physics, geology and religion before arriving at his "theory of the universe," that "sublime synthesis" that made "all previous philosophic speculation...fragmentary, crude, and unsatisfying."[10] To anxious Americans, this news was particularly welcome, and the popularizers made sure to speak in familiar terms. "All imperfection must disappear," declared Spencer, invoking the millennial dream. "Thus the ultimate development of the ideal man is logically certain—as certain as any conclusion in which we place the most explicit faith."[11] Fiske was even more emphatic. History would inevitably yield global harmony, "When the kindly earth shall slumber, lapt in a universal law ... [exhibiting] the highest possible ... integration among the units of the community."[12] Then would humanity as a single soul greet the new age: "Peace and love shall reign supreme ... and ... we may look forward to the time when in the truest sense the kingdoms of this world shall become the kingdom of Christ, and he shall reign for ever and ever, king of kings and lord of lords."[13] At last, the Millennium had been scientifically sanctioned.

Doubtless, Fiske's promise had little appeal to a bookish young Jew from Oakland, California; but when Stein arrived at Radcliffe, she became caught up in the issue in another way. In the year of Nietzsche's mental collapse, William James, who would remain one of her strongest "influences" (*WIHS* 63), had published *Principles of Psychology*,[14] his first of many attacks on that monolithic unity Christian evolutionists preached. What consciousness reveals, James asserted, is not a cluster of timeless truths, invariable responses to an inflexible world, but an exquisitely subtle organ in constant change. Although "each present brain-state" (1:234) potentially contains the whole history of its owner, successive moments of consciousness are discrete, discontinuous. The mind was less an immutable entity than "a kaleidoscope [in which] ... the figures are always rearranging themselves" (1:246). The self, then, was a receptacle, and consciousness a Heracleitean stream:

> For ... it is obvious and palpable that our state of mind is never precisely the same. Every thought we have of a given fact is, strictly speaking, unique, and only bears a resemblance of kind with our other thoughts of the same fact. When the identical fact recurs, we *must* think of it in a fresh manner, see it under a somewhat different angle, apprehend it in different relations from those in which it last appeared. (1:233)

States of consciousness could not be predicted by any simple law; like Nietzsche, James found "a certain amount of loose play" in our responses to the world.[15] And since the "prevision" of psychology would "never foretell ... the actual way in which each individual emergency is resolved," Spencerians must acknowledge "that the order of uniform causation ... may be enveloped in a wider order, on which [science] has no claims at all" (2:576). Free play, James concluded, may well reflect cosmic law.

But James did not opt for randomness. In a curious formulation that would affect Stein's writing, he threaded a sinuous argument between the obvious fact of sustained thought, and the mental discontinuity his theory seemed to imply. If the stream of consciousness were ever-changing, then the psychologist could observe only the present moment. How, then, could one be assured that thought bore any necessary relationship to the past—that the self perdured? James answered the question in two ways, neither of them entirely satisfactory. He likened thought to a series of hooks "from which the chain of past selves dangles"; as each present moment subsides, its thought is "treated as an object and appropriated by a new Thought in the new present which will serve as living hook in turn" (1:340, 341). James supplemented his conveyor belt metaphor with a more vital one, in which the present self continuously recognized the "living" thought as its own. There was thus a synecdochic relationship between the present and the historical self, akin to Nietzsche's revisionary *typos*, with each "section" of consciousness knowing its products, "and knowing, hug[ging] to itself and adopt[ing], all those that went before,— thus standing as the *representative* of the entire past stream" (1:340). All this was occasioned by James's rigorous phenomenalism, his refusal to assume "any transcendent . . . sort of an Arch-Ego" in consciousness (1:340), any absolute self. The psychology Stein learned at Cambridge, then—and carried with her to France—was self-consciously ambiguous: asserting free play, it sought the laws of thought; asserting the radical discontinuity of thought, it clung to a sustained self. One need not be a determinist to see here a source of Stein's own literary subtleties.

Across the ocean Stein found similar discontinuities. Henri Bergson, who himself had mastered James's work, was rapidly becoming the most influential thinker in France, and although Stein rarely mentioned him, their affinities are manifest. Like James, Bergson insists on the constancy of change, the mental fact "that every sensation is altered by repetition."[16] "This is not a mere illusion; for if today's impression were absolutely identical with that of yesterday, what difference would there be between perceiving and recognizing, between learning and remembering?" (130). Like James, too, Bergson opposed determinist psychology, which, he felt, sought to reduce complex mental states to the absurd simplicity of "letters of the alphabet" (237). So great was his distaste for that alphabet that he posited a profound, "durative" consciousness beneath normal thought—well beyond the reach of associationists. As early as 1903, the year Stein reached Paris, Bergson was distinguishing between two modes of perception, the "relative," in which "I place myself outside the object itself," and the "absolute," in which "I insert myself into [the object] through an effort of imagination."[17] By 1910, when Stein was working on *Tender Buttons*, the relative and the absolute—the outside and the inside—had become the fixed poles of Bergson's thought. Mental life consisted of the understanding, open to the manipulation of determinists, and "the depths of the organized and living intelligence, [where] we ... witness the joining together or rather the blending of many ideas which, when once dissociated, seem to exclude one another as logically as contradictory terms" (*T* 136). But if logic did not aply to these depths, how, then could one know the inner life? In *Time and Free Will* Bergson answered that question with studied ambiguity. Since language itself was part of the determinist alphabet, no direct description of deep thought could be given at all:

> the word with well-defined outlines, the rough and ready word, which stores up the stable, common, and consequently impersonal element in the impressions of mankind, overwhelms or at least covers over the delicate and fugitive impressions of our individual consciousness. To maintain the struggle on equal terms, the latter ought to express themselves in precise words; but these words, as soon as they were formed, would turn against the sensation which gave birth to them, and, invented to show that the sensation is unstable, they would impose on it their own stability. (132)

To express a fugitive consciousness one needed a fugitive language, as distinct from normal speech as intuition was from thought. Only thus could thought be truly free.

Common to both psychologists was an emphasis on process, a view of self in the Nietzschean sense, as an interplay of forces. That view, like so many others in the late nineteenth century, harks back to Darwin, for whom nature was a product of imperceptible laws. "It has been said that I speak of natural selection as an active power or Deity," Darwin wrote in 1876; but nature was no more intelligent than gravity, an "aggregate action" of innumerable unconscious events.[18] For rationalists, "nothing ... [was] more difficult to believe" (404) than that orderly life evolved through chance; but even human reason, Darwin insisted, was "gradually perfected through natural selection."[19] There need be no central intelligence in nature. For Darwin's disciple, Herbert Spencer, "Force" was "the ultimate of ultimates" (*FP* 132), driving the universe as it drove consciousness. "Grant but sensibility with no established power of thought," and Force could still be detected in the mind. For since thought was constant change, "the ultimate datum of consciousness" must be the Persistence of Force (132). All human activities, Spencer maintained, were aspects of "a single metamorphosis universally progressing" (439)—the cosmic Law of Evolution.

But such grand forces, as the maneuverings of James and Bergson suggest, could also threaten; for if natural selection invaded even human reason, then the self promised to dissolve into blind law. No nineteenth-century American sensed this more keenly than Henry Adams, who capped his education with a "dynamic theory of history." Adams took for granted that "the forces of nature capture man":

> The sum of force attracts; the feeble atom or molecule called man is attracted; he suffers education or growth; he is the sum of forces that attract him; his body and his thought are alike their product; the movement of the forces controls the progress of his mind, since he can know nothing but the motions which impinge on his senses, whose sum makes education. (*EHA* 474)

The corollary was that mind could well vanish, so "violent" were the forces it confronted (496). Indeed, the narrator of *The Education* was himself a "manikin, ... the only measure of motion, of proportion, of human condition"—a bundle of crotchets with only a faint "air of reality" (xvi). Darwin had seen "gradual perfect[ion]" in the anonymous play of forces;[20] Nietzsche had seen a joyful wisdom. For Adams, the result was chaos.

How, then, to write an autobiography? If the central self was dissolving into a mist of molecules, what attitude could capture consciousness? Paul L. Jay suggests that Adams found the task forbidding; hence his constant professions of failure, his reference to himself as "a bundle of disconnected memories" (*EHA* 20), and his fragmenting into such "manikins" as Odysseus, Gibbon, and Teufelsdröckh.[21] But if *The Education* is a precursor to modernism, as Jay claims, it is also a study in resistance to change. For behind the playful, painful testament to failure lies a stubborn intelligence observing and recording all. Adams may have been dead, as he often joked, a wraith reporting on life from beyond the grave, but life produced an education that was his alone. Hence the frequent references to his uniqueness, as if in defiance of multiplicity. The boy who learned fairly late in life that all children did not have presidents for grandfathers became the man who alone among men could triangulate the forces of history. He had sensed his singularity among the dynamos in Chicago, where for "the first time" a historian "sat down helpless before a mechanical sequence" (342). Later, the forces pursued him to the Arctic Circle, where hourly telegraphs of McKinley's death convinced him that "no such strange chance had ever happened to a historian before" (413)—as he was convinced in 1893, when economic forces nearly ruined him. Most men "died like flies under the strain"; he "alone waxed fat and happy, for at last he had got hold of his world" (338). This was no mere contrarian impulse, the asperity of old money. Rather, by the subtlety and grace of his insight, Adams defied multiplicity and change.

The broad cycles of his education assert as much. Although he felt himself on the verge of an uncharted world, his autobiography maps his constant returns to Paris, to Washington, to the steps of Ara Coeli. His was "the Pursuit of Ignorance in Silence," a pilgrimage that always "began anew" (359). Hence, when he returns to Harvard College, symbol of his failed education, it is to lodge in the same room he had visited as a boy (299); and when he finds himself bankrupt in Boston, the shock is "a starting-point" for a new education (337). Even his attempt to map the forces of history—one that placed him alone at the focal point of civilization—was a kind of renewal, as if he had defied historians and "started afresh" (376) with only the laws of change. In a curious way, then, Adams's goal was not merely to name the dissolution he foresaw, but to insist on his origins in spite of it. If Americans were "drifting" into the new century "as their solar system was said to be drifting toward some point in space," Adams would provide the sextant—the "fixed" point from which all relations could be observed (343). And if the new world was nothing but "chance collisions" of imperceptible particles, then a dynamic theory of history would provide that "known ray at the end of the scale" by which all could be measured (381–82). Adams insisted on his isolation, his consciousness, his reserve—and thereby sheltered himself from chaos. As for many moderns after him, mind became his refuge from change.

Yet the distance between Adams and another "posthumous" autobiographer points up the limitations of this stance. For Nietzsche, too, lived as his father's corpse, felt cut off from his homeland, considered himself unique. He, too, Adams noted, was preoccupied with the problem of force (485), and he, too, feared the dissolution of self, as his attacks on rancorous readers make clear. But there remain substantial differences between the two—and for that matter, between Nietzsche and James or Bergson—that will have important consequences for a reading of Stein. Despite his "dynamic theory," for example, Adams's thought tends to confine change to two grand abstractions, Unity and Multiplicity, like the two wheels of a historical cart joined by the axle "Force." Change thus becomes unpredictably lawful, lawfully unpredictable, as Adams's numerous attempts to triangulate it suggest; even the "vertiginous violence" (495) of a scarred future could be softened by the curve of the past. Conversely, the individual in this scheme becomes little more than transported stuff—or, as Adams has it, the fleeting ion of a Dynamo—driven irresistibly by time. And since the most a historian could manage was comprehension, his sole strength lay in re-treat: like the scholar who found unity in twelfth-century France, one sought shelter in the ruins of self. The latter impulse was also largely true of Bergson and the early James: both responded to the play of anonymous forces by burrowing deep down, to some substratum they could claim, however precariously, as genuine. Not so for Nietzsche. Although he discerned historical periods of his own, culminating in the European nihilism he strove to overcome, Nietzsche saw all force, his-torical or psychic, as deeply personal:

> This world; a monster [*Ungeheuer*] of energy, without beginning, without end; a firm, iron magnitude of force that does not grow bigger or smaller, that does not expend itself but only transforms itself; . . . a household with-out expenses or losses, but likewise without increase or income; . . . a play of forces and waves of forces . . . eternally changing, eternally flooding back, with tremendous [*ungeheuren*] years of recurrence, . . . out of the sim-plest forms striving toward the most complex . . . and then again returning home to the simple . . . still affirming itself . . . blessing itself as that which must return eternally, as a becoming that knows no satiety, no dis-gust, no weariness: this, my *Dionysian* world. . . . (*WP* §1067, 550; *KG* 7, 3: 38 [12], 338)

These are the same terms Nietzsche uses to describe himself in *Ecce Homo*—the man of monstrous, Dionysian contradictions, a *"force ma-jeure*, a destiny" (*EH* 333). For such a man, historical action is a joyous affirmation captured in the Eternal Return, a tremendous re-vision in which all knowledge is self-knowledge, and from which nothing is ex-cluded. Nietzsche's self is that eternal Yes-sayer, bringing "incompa-rable things" from his depths to the dawn's light (*EH* 290) or proclaiming a *"great noon"* for humanity (291). It is in this clear light that one may best read Stein, a writer with the prowess of Friedrich Nietzsche and the instincts of Henry Adams.

FIRST DRAFTS: *THE MAKING OF AMERICANS* AND *A LONG GAY BOOK*

James's notions of consciousness first fully enter Stein's writing in her *magnum opus, The Making of Americans*[22]—the book she claimed inaugurated modern literature. As was often the case with Stein's proj-ects, the work is experimental in the strictest sense: it represents her la-bored search for a form equal to her theoretical assumptions. Hence the tortuously varied sentences—"He was being living every day. He was knowing every day that he was being living on that day. He was know-ing every day that he was being living. He would know that he was meaning being one being living every day" (864)—reflecting the variable

repetitions of Jamesian thought. Hence the search for "bottom natures," those deep patterns underlying habits as intuition underlay reflection. But *The Making of Americans* cannot be so easily reduced; it is
an eclectic work into which Stein poured many preoccupations, and
numerous contradictions. Although the repetitive prose approximates
the "continuous present" James and Bergson ascribe to consciousness,
her dogged catalogs of bottom natures rather reflect a rage for order, the
universal laws of a Henry Adams. Spurred by the taxonomies of Otto
Weininger, whose *Sex and Character* had appeared in 1908, Stein pursued an almost Spencerian vision. "Sometime then there will be a history of all women and all men," she promised, "of every one of them, of
the mixtures in them of the bottom nature and other natures in them
...of all their being and how it comes out from them from their beginning to their ending" (176–77).[23] Then, too, when she did define the
bottom nature in one of her characters, Stein betrayed a very Jamesian
ambiguity. One can trace her progress from an inchoate sense of normal behavior in the opening pages to the mature formula, appearing
two hundred pages later: "there are then always to my thinking in all
of them the two kinds of them the dependent independent, the independent dependent; the first have resisting as the fighting power in
them, the second have attacking as their natural way of fighting" (192).
This was the "complete description of something" she claimed, thirty
years later, to have learned from James; but the terms of the matrix
are so close as to be indistinguishable, even to the careful observer.[24]
This fusion of opposites, recalling James's wedding of unity and multiplicity in thought, would become one of Stein's most characteristic
gestures, the sign of her struggle with modernity.

But the novel's greatest contradiction has less to do with James
than with Whitman. Stein's intention, after all, is to portray an epically
representative family, one that would describe "how every one who
ever lived eats and drinks and loves and sleeps and talks and walks
and wakes and forgets and quarrels and likes and dislikes and works
and sits" (*EA* 138). The sentence itself reads like one of Whitman's
panoramas, and one hears echoes of "Song of Myself" in many of
Stein's catalogs:

> always as one looks more and more at each one, as one sees them walking,
> eating, sitting, sewing, working, sleeping, being babies, children, young
> grown men and women, grown up men and women, growing old men and
> women, old men and old women, as one sees them every moment in their
> being there must be sometime a history of them. (177)

Stein also seems to share Whitman's penchant for self-projection; a third of *The Making of Americans* is concealed autobiography, examining her childhood in Oakland, and much of the remainder stems from her observations of Baltimore cousins. Nevertheless, this is not another exercise in synecdoche, for Stein is more interested in the motions of her own thought than in the natures of Americans. The book is punctuated with asides depicting the artist at work—"Always then I am thinking and feeling the repeating in each one as I know them. Always then slowly each one comes to be a whole one to me" (301)—and, at last, Stein fairly abandons description in favor of her own ruminations:

> Everywhere something is done. Everywhere where that thing is done it is done by some one. Everywhere where the thing that is done by some one comes to be done it is done and done by some one. Certainly every where where something is done it is done and done by some one. Certainly some are doing something and it is done and done by each one of them. (920)

This is James's stream of consciousness apprehending its subject, not the subject itself; it is Bergson's "inside" view. As Richard Bridgman observes, Stein's grand plan to sum up all human existence ended in the reflections of "a single mind"[25]—the modern's ephemeral self.

In this respect, *The Making of Americans* is typical of the later autobiographies. After trying to reduce the world to pattern and feeling overwhelmed in the attempt, Stein turned inward, where she found a similar but more manageable multiplicity. And although she would not often admit it, her retreat was as much motivated by fear as by theory. "Confusion always was strong in her," she wrote of Martha Hersland, her autobiographical character. "All of her when it was in motion just was sort of knocking together" (*MOA* 411). From the inside, at least, she might record that chaotic motion.

Stein's encyclopedic passion, however, did not exhaust itself in *The Making of Americans*. Her next work, *A Long Gay Book*,[26] was to be the promised "history of every man and woman"—and her failure to complete it marks a decisive shift in her attitude toward science and determinism, those hallmarks of the nineteenth century. The book begins more abstractly than its predecessor, with an examination of "kinds" rather than of family members. There are long ruminations on the life cycle, on how it feels to be a baby or an "old one," and there are acute passages that may well be confessional: "When they are a little older they know they are beginning to be afraid of changing thinking about ageing, they are beginning then to know something of being uncertain about what is being young and what is being old, they are beginning then to be afraid of everything" (25). In due course, Stein decides to examine pairs of acquaintances, running through a list of characteristics and illustrating them in gnomic fashion; but when she reaches H. P. Roché, whom she calls "Vrais," she makes an important discovery. Roché would make a brief appearance in *The Autobiography of Alice B. Toklas*; his salient feature was his habit of repeating "Good good, excellent" at any piece of news. What Stein realized through his behavior was that any repetition—including that of her own prose—could be constricting: "In continuing he was being one being the one who was saying good good, excellent but in continuing he was needing that he was believing that he was aspiring to be one continuing to be able to be saying good good, excellent" (53). Bergson had suggested that intuition was indeterminate, wholly free; here was evidence that Stein's attempt to render the free play of consciousness was itself constrained. The very intent to capture thought in writing had distorted, just as Bergson claimed. Her scrupulousness betrayed her.

Gradually, then, Stein's writing began to shade into the associations of *Tender Buttons*,[27] as a means to greater freedom. Random words now enter her prose: "if the color is dark and the passing away of walking is not too quick then all that was expected from asking was that what had been done had not had any way of laughing" (84). Fractured syllogisms appear: "If stumbling is continuing then a side-walk is restoring. If a side-walk is restoring then eating is satisfying. If eating is satisfying then undertaking is beguiling" (85). Tautologies stress the identity of all thought, no matter how obscure: "In the time there is that time which is all of the whole of it where there is not anything that is not where there is one and one that is one and one" (90). As Jayne Walker notes, Stein had recognized that "the inherent order of language is...alien...to the chaotic richness of immediate perceptual experience."[28] By so wrecking her plan for the book, she was pursuing a more important aim—the inner freedom James and Bergson had defined. Her plan was simple: "Largely additional and then completely exploding is one way to deny authorisation" (98)—by shattering her continuous prose she could resist determinism. "Something has changed," she declared; "alarming looking at each one had begun" (95, 90).

This obscure style was to characterize Stein's writing for the next twenty years; she abandoned it for her first autobiography, and then only reluctantly. Nevertheless, obscurity would not wholly solve the problem of freedom, or, indeed, that of her own unity; for the most radical of her experiments communicated little at all. "A type oh oh new new not no not knealer knealer of old show beef-steak, neither

neither," reads her description of an orange in *Tender Buttons* (495). Many critics have attempted to decode these *aperçus*, relying on associations, onomatopoeia, and the like to reproduce Stein's thought. But no reading of *Tender Buttons* can hope to exhaust the text's essential elusiveness, its free play. The *aperçus*, as Stein intended, lost their meaning as soon as they left her pen; they were instantaneous impressions, unique impulses. As Neil Schmitz notes, her object was to decenter discourse, to present "everything [as] contingent, changing as it moves and the mind moves."[29] To the puzzled reader, her prose is "all inside." Stein was thus forced into a paradoxical position: she wrote for an audience that her artistic premises excluded, about a self she could never recover. And by the same terms, when she imposed continuity on her thought, she violated her will to freedom. "Breakfast," in *Tender Buttons*, evokes the following reflections: "A white cup means a wedding. A wet cup means a vacation. A strong cup means an especial regulation. A single cup means a capital arrangement between the drawer and the place that is open" (484). The formula permits the reader to glimpse her meaning, but only by constraining Stein's thought; it imposes continuity on a radically discontinuous process, a false permanence on the self. The dilemma was one Bergson himself had scouted: thought was discontinuous and free; language was continuous and lawful. The two could not be joined. And beneath this contradiction lay one even more intractable: how could a perduring "self" be fashioned from a bundle of discontinuities? Stein had just begun to grasp the problems of subjectivity Nietzsche had confronted in *Ecce Homo*, but found no rigorous solution. Logically, then, she was left to defend a middle ground, asserting the identity of opposed principles. Hers had become an art of ambivalence.

AMBIVALENT MODERNS

" 'Science gets on only by adopting different theories, sometimes contradictory,' " noted Henry Adams, much to his distaste (*EHA* 497). The remark might serve as a motto for the "age of acceleration" he described. For Adams's sense of ambiguity and contradiction suffused prewar Paris, that "broken world" (*LGB* 15) so different from the nineteenth century. Thomas Kuhn has described such momentous changes in scientific thought as shifts in "paradigms," those periodic upheavals when old theories are "blurr[ed]" as new ones incorporate "old terms, concepts, and experiments ... into new relationships."[30] But Kuhn's model has far wider application. Betty Craige, for example, suggests a "modern," relativist paradigm, one based on "multiple points of reference," multiple meanings "for individuals, things, and events that take the place of the single meaning . . . adopted in a world of absolute truth."[31] And Nietzsche himself, whose work had begun to disseminate throughout Europe as Stein wrote *Tender Buttons*, characterized modernity by the "Overabundant development of intermediary forms" in which "traditions" and "schools" break off (*WP* §74, 48). When, as Adams tells us, chaos became "the law of nature" (*EHA* 451), when Einstein shattered the fixity of Newton's universe, all else was cast in doubt. To the "generation of 1914," the world was changing at a dizzying pace, as the links between subject and object, time and sequence, truth and utility were shattered.[32] Indeed, the old notions of fixed forms and absolute relations were yielding to a new, "ambivalen[t]" mode.[33] One sees this in Freud's association of love and hate; in Jung's notion of "enantiodromia"—the turning of each thing into its opposite; in the quantum physicist, for whom light was both wave and particle, "yet in a strict sense neither" (*M* 84–85). One sees it in the increasingly ambivalent responses to the fragmenting self—in Paul Valéry's "moi," "composed of bits and pieces that never coexisted"[34]; in Nietzsche's *Ecce Homo*. And everywhere, one sees this shift in the arts—in Hermann Hesse's *Demian*, whose hermaphroditic deity, Abraxas, "is both . . . god and devil"; in James Joyce's Bella Cohen, the mannish woman, magically transformed into Bello Cohen, the womanish man; in Rilke's desire to express "the identity of terror and bliss" and "oneness of life and death" (*M* 86–87). "For me," wrote Hesse, "the highest words of humankind are those few mysterious phrases and images in which the great opposites of the world are seen to be both necessary and illusory at one and the same time" (*M* 87). In the most literal sense, then, the twentieth century was attended by radical contradiction, a clash of worldviews.

During her early years in Paris, Stein was preoccupied with the modern view. Although her cubist friends little understood the theorists of the "new reality," they never tired of citing them in their manifestos. André Salmon, who had acted so scandalously at Picasso's banquet for Rousseau, declared in 1912 that the scientists had provided an "only guide for seekers" who wanted to experience "all angles" of an object.[35] Guillaume Apollinaire invoked the "fourth dimension" in his defense of the new perspective, and Jean Metzinger looked, as Adams had, to the work of the French mathematician Henri Poincaré (*I* 30, 36). Also circulating was the concept of simultaneity, derived from Bergson's "duration." Leon Metzinger urged painters to "seize" the object "from . . . several successive aspects," and halt time by "fus[ing] them together" (*I* 31). Others likened their excursions into "non-Euclidean geometry" to the actions of a kaleidoscope or other mechanical *trompes l'oeil* (36), in order to achieve what a recent commentator calls "fluctuant representation." According to Winthrop Judkins, cubist painting sought a comprehensive ambiguity. Among the characteristics he lists are these:

> parts of an object displaced from the whole so that its recognition is made elusive, fugitive, intermittent;
> objects seen from two (or more) directions at once;
> sections of objects shifted and adjusted so that they become either involved in other continuities or new forms.[36]

Most important, claims Judkins, is the quality of "diametric opposition or ambivalence," the representation of an image along with its "polar opposite" (36). Planes at once transparent and opaque; objects that form their own backgrounds; surfaces that simultaneously obscure and project other surfaces; shadows that become substance; interlocking forms that seem simultaneously to advance and recede—all these were the apparatus of Picasso, Braque, and their followers (21–22), including Stein. "I was alone at this time in understanding" Picasso, she would later write, "perhaps because I was expressing the same thing in literature"—a claim supported by several recent studies.[37] And though one might not want to argue that all this was a conscious response to a paradigm shift, there seems little question that in art, as in literature, the modern courted ambiguity, committing himself, as McFarlane puts it, "neither wholly to the notion of 'both/and,' nor wholly to the notion of 'either/or,' but (as it were) to both—and to neither. Dauntingly, then, the Modernist formula becomes 'both/and and and/or or either/or' " (88). Stein herself could not have put the matter better.

There were, however, particular reasons for Stein's attraction to this formula—reasons that mark her as less a charter member of the avant-garde than a somewhat timid figure, like Adams, reluctantly backing into modernity. One must tread carefully here: despite her four autobiographies, Gertrude Stein's was an extraordinarily concealed life. She comes down to us almost solely as a function of her craft, and after two weighty biographies, there is still much we do not know—about her fears, her relationship with Alice Toklas, her childhood. It is the mark of her shrewdness in all matters of publicity that what we now possess is the official Stein: confident, ebullient, witty. Nevertheless, she has left numerous hints of a much more complex life. If one is to believe her descriptions in *The Making of Americans*, Stein's world was, from birth, marked continuously by radical, often inexplicable change. She was born in Allegheny, Pennsylvania, as she was fond of repeating, but when she was eight months old her father broke up the house and shipped the family to Vienna, where Amelia Stein was soon forced to care for them alone while Daniel pursued business elsewhere. When Gertrude was four her father summoned the family again—this time to Oakland, where he established them in a removed, rather poor neighborhood. Here they lived a divided life, with a "half and half feeling" of the well-off among the poor, and the city-bred among the rural (92). And always there was Daniel Stein, with his impulses and his passion for experiment:

> Now he wanted the children not to have their english spoiled by french and german. Now he was certain that music was a thing no one could learn when they were children . . . children should have freedom, should have an out of doors gymnasium, should have swimming and public school living, should have a governess. (241)

Stein captured the man's feverish unpredictability in a telling anecdote. Often he would demand that the children sit down with him to a game of cards; but after a few minutes he would bolt from the table muttering, "here you just finish up I haven't time to go on playing" (129). The children, who had joined only to oblige him, "felt it . . . hard on them," particularly when he stalked in to check on their progress. It is no wonder that the Stein children found Daniel's regime "a great trouble to them . . . when they first began to be young grown men and women" (52), and that Gertrude remained troubled "whenever anything unexpected happens."[38] Like Martha Hersland, she may well have been resisting the shocks of a strenuous childhood.

Chief among those shocks was death. In *Wars I Have Seen* Stein confesses to a "posthumous fear" when she discovers that the Gestapo had broken into her Paris apartment while she was hiding in Culoz (255). But she had known that fear much longer, for childhood had yielded a similar discovery. Her parents had wanted five children; Leo and Gertrude replaced two who had died. This belatedness seems to have engendered a precocious sense of mortality. At the age of eight Gertrude anxiously scanned the Old Testament, but found no assurance "about a future life or eternity" (*EA* 114). The Book of Revelation gave no more comfort, nor did the realization that civilizations died, or that space was a vast, lifeless void. The knowledge touched off what she later called "the dark and dreadful days of adolescence, in which predominated the fear of death, not so much of death as of dissolution" (*WIHS* 14), and from which the only refuge was a mythical infancy when, "knowing nothing," she had enjoyed an "everlasting feeling" (*LGB* 15). The rest, to Stein, was a "broken world" (*LGB* 15).

To regain that remote beatitude from the shattered present became her lifelong preoccupation.[39] One sees it in her refusal to acknowledge historical change, even as she entertains the avant-garde; in her notion of genius, which exists "without any internal recognition of time" (*EA* 243); in her curious assessment of France, a nation so rooted in "reality" that it saw history as mere "fashion."[40] And one sees it in her stylistic peculiarities, that "continuous present" in which she discarded the past tense for the present participle. In short, Stein inhabited a divided world. She was the bourgeois patron of the avant-garde, the "half and half" American who lived in France for forty years, the artist who wrote obsessively about time in order to deny its importance. She rejected the nineteenth century's psychology, yet clung to an almost Emersonian notion of genius; professed a multiplicity of impulses, yet sought a continuous self. She was a reluctant modern. Ironically, this believer in "monotonous tradition" (*MOA* 34) became the chronicler of modern art, in an autobiography as elusive as its narrator.

THE AUTOBIOGRAPHY OF ALICE B. TOKLAS

In a sense, Gertrude Stein had been practicing self-portraiture for two decades preceding *The Autobiography of Alice B. Toklas*. Yet the *Autobiography* is no simple adaptation of earlier techniques; it is a distinct departure, in which Stein inverted many of her artistic practices. If before she had rendered people from within consciousness, now she would see them through another's eyes. If before she had striven for a timeless present, now she would describe development and change. And if she had once written in an allusive, private language, now she had to write for an audience that, friends assured her, would make the book a best-seller. In short, she decided to turn herself inside out (cf. *ABT* 192). As Richard Bridgman demonstrates, the change did not come easily. In "Stanzas in Meditation," a companion to the *Autobiography*, Stein confessed her anxiety: "Can they like me oh can they like me"; and then with the old insouciance: "Let me listen to me and not to them."[41] But with Alice Toklas pouncing on any sign of obscurity, Stein was forced to listen in a different way: she would write an autobiography that performed two tasks at once. For "them" she would narrate the making of modern art—the "endless" succession of geniuses and near-geniuses who paraded past her throne in the rue de Fleurus. In effect, this was the multiple, impulsive self of *Tender Buttons*: the purveyor of disconnected gossip, witty remarks, casual portraits, unpredictable acts. The life she told to herself, however, resisted audience and change: it presented a revolving structure of repetitions, *aperçus*, and characterizations that continued her private obsessions. The Gertrude Stein of the *Autobiography* is a divided figure—both buoyant artist and pioneer, caught up in bohemia, and remote genius, insulated from the world she describes, an autobiographer as Other. And yet there is no grappling here, as in Nietzsche, with the presence and priority of this textual Other. Rather, like *The Education of Henry Adams*, Stein's first self-portrait is an artful denial, a work of dazzling concealment.[42]

The chief way Stein hid from her audience lay in her decision to have Toklas narrate. This was by no means a serene achievement. In a first draft of chapter 1, preserved at Yale University, she interrupts the narrative line to indulge the continuous present. "I myself have had no liking for violence,"[43] reads Toklas's crisp voice, to which Stein's arises, as if in protest:

> but in spite of that which is what I wish to say I have had more reason [?] to feel what violence is.... In this way there can be no doubt, no doubt, that in no way there is any doubt that having to have that which I have had and have that which I have. As I say I have had reason to have anything which I do not have to have but I have and I have had to have ... and I will have it. (cf. *ABT* 3)

Clearly, Stein had not yet mastered this historical voice; she plays with tenses, deliberately confusing them in order to negate any time but the moment of writing. After several such passages—"How does one begin," she asks—Stein broke off. When she resumed, she had apparently solved the problem: the *Autobiography* unfolds much as it would appear in published form. But she had to steel herself to the task, eliminating any traces of the old manner. Repetitions disappeared: "I was seriously interested in music, ~~very seriously interested in music~~" (cf. *ABT* 4); "But to return to the pictures. ~~There were at this time pictures on the white washed walls right up to the ceiling.~~ As I say they completely covered the white washed walls right up to the very high ceiling" (cf. *ABT* 11); "Madame Matisse was an admirable house keeper. Her place was small but immaculate. ~~She was one of those admirable house keepers~~" (cf. *ABT* 43). Where Stein was lax, Toklas herself enforced the principle. Once she put her red pencil through the phrase "I cannot help repeating," and often reminded Stein, with pointed redundancy, "have already typed this earlier." Also eliminated were several suggestions of the writer's present. The first draft of chapter 4 ended not with Bromfield's approval of *Q.E.D.*, but with an intention: "When we ~~get home~~ return to Paris this autumn ~~we~~ I will read it" (cf. 104). Toklas excised the comment. She also crossed off a reference to "this year" in a discussion of Mildred Aldrich; and both women collaborated on this excision:

> We found that Belley was the birth place of Brillat Savarin, we now in ~~the~~ Bilignin are in the enjoyment of [illeg.] the house of Brillat Savarin which house belongs to the ~~young landlady~~ owner of this house ~~and Francis Rose just the other day acquired wall paper off the wall of Brillat Savarin's house because it having been rented they have just been tearing off the old wall paper~~. (cf. 274)

It was in this sense, as Bridgman suggests, that the work was a "collabora[tion]" (216); Alice Toklas forced Stein to preserve the past.

This is not to say that Stein treated the past conventionally. As any reader of the *Autobiography* knows, the first third of the text is broken up, much like a cubist painting. After a brief introduction, in which Stein establishes her narrator, time slows, as Alice Toklas describes her first visits to the atelier and to the Independent Salon. Thereafter, personalities drive the narrative—Picasso and Fernande, the spinach-eating Van Dongen, the adulterous Alice Princet—until the march is halted and Stein retreats to her first years "in the heart of an art movement of which the outside world . . . knew nothing" (34). After recounting the publication of *Three Lives* in 1909, she halts once more, for a brief account of her childhood and youth, whence the narrative proceeds, with frequent digressions, through the war years and beyond. Yet the reader never loses sight of chronology. Before the war, the artists hold sway: Picasso progresses by way of his portrait of Stein, from the harlequin period to the *Demoiselles d'Avignon*; Matisse regresses from the clarity of *Bonheur de Vivre* to the indifferent productions of his school; Braque and Juan Gris and Picabia struggle to express, or refine, or reject. After the war the writers take over, the American crowd led by Hemingway and Sherwood Anderson, whose careers seem to grace Stein's. And straddling the two is the spectacle of Stein and Toklas confronting the war from the cab of an ambulance named "Auntie." Throughout runs the tale of Stein's own artistic progress, from the anonymous manuscript given to Bromfield, through *The Making of Americans* and the portraits, ending with Toklas's methodical publication of the Plain Edition. But it is a progress obliquely rendered, as if Stein could still not bear sustained narrative.

In fact, the text is held together by a number of devices Stein might have once rejected. She seems to have an arbitrary fondness for threes—the three geniuses Toklas names, the three dancers she favors (167). Fernande had "three subjects" (31), Miss Mars described "three types" of make-up (16), and Stein herself had three favorite saints

(107). A triumvirate of works—Stein's *Three Lives*, Matisse's *Bonheur de Vivre*, and Picasso's "strange complicated picture of three women" (7)—marks the heroic year 1907, as Picasso's three landscapes of Spain inaugurate cubism (109). The faithful Alfy Maurer "followed, followed, followed" (13). The device even allows for some Steinian repetition: "Sentences not only words but sentences and always sentences have been Gertrude Stein's life long passion" (50). Many of her digressions fulfill a similar function. It was the San Francisco earthquake that first brought the Stein family to the attention of Alice Toklas, who was later struck by Gertrude Stein's French notebooks "with pictures of earthquakes and explorations" (10) when Toklas herself began to explore Paris. To his Oxford admirers, Picasso seemed to have a halo— the same one Stein imagined when she "first knew him" (150, 271). Stein's wonder at how much young artists could achieve in a year introduces chapters 2 and 7 (7, 237), and references to drab Japanese prints (56, 246), Stein's haircut (70, 304), and copying or reading proof (64, 138, 264, 266, 275) abound. Remarks also pass, like literary motifs, from figure to figure:

> Gertrude Stein always says the chicagoans spend so much energy losing Chicago that often it is difficult to know what they are. They have to lose the Chicago voice and to do so they do many things. Some lower their voices, some raise them, some get an english accent, some drawl, some speak in a very high tense voice, and some go chinese or spanish and do not move the lips. (210)

> [Hemingway] said, when you matriculate at the University of Chicago you write down just what accent you will have and they give it to you when you graduate. You can have a sixteenth century or modern, whatever you like. (245–46)

In 1910, Stein would have viewed such recurrences as limiting imagination; in 1933 they became structural principles, Jamesian "hooks" for the multiple self.

Repetition allowed Stein to convey the almost maddening diversity of her public life economically. Yet despite the preoccupation with others, it seems appropriate to think of these motifs scattered throughout the text—the verbal equivalents of cubist portraiture—as serving more private ends. Stein's 1923 portrait of Picasso had used the cubist approach in a more radical way—"If Napoleon if I told him if I told him if Napoleon. Would he like it if I told him if I told him if Napoleon. Would he like it if Napoleon if Napoleon if I told him. . . . If I told him would he like it would he like it if I told him"[44]—evoking her association of painter and general in a rhythmic structure imitating the facets of, for example, Picasso's *Portrait of Daniel-Henry Kahnweiler*. By extending the analogy, one might account for other features of the *Autobiography* as well—notably Stein's penchant for ambiguity. Presiding as she did over a weekly menage of egotists, Stein was privy to endless gossip, and she delighted in twice-told tales. Her first dinner with Carl Van Vechten, for example, was preceded by a lugubrious session with his ex-wife, during which the man who would prove her most useful friend was portrayed as a "hero or villain" (168). She was amused by a quarrel between Wyndham Lewis and Roger Fry, both of whom "told exactly the same story only it was different, very different" (150), and she noted wryly the artistic consciences of two friends—Matisse, who bought the pictures of others as the best legacy for his children, and Picasso, who bought his own for the same purpose (45). She details her purchase of Matisse's *La Femme au Chapeau* from opposite perspectives, those of buyer and seller, overlaying her own pleasure with Matisse's anxiety (41–49). Paradoxes serve the same purpose. The winter of 1914 was a "strange" one in which "nothing and everything happened" (195); the Paris atelier became so popular that "anybody came and no one made any difference" (151). And above all, the fictional narrator renders the entire text ambiguous, blurring the distinction between memory and artifice in precisely the way "fluctuant" cubist images meld and emerge. All the work is Stein's; none of the work is Stein's, mimicking Picasso's remark on her portrait: "everybody says that she does not look like it but that does not make any difference, she will" (14). The text is and is not autobiography.

Perhaps the central metaphor for this complex arrangement is one the cubists shared with William James, that of the kaleidoscope. Saturday evenings in the rue de Fleurus were "like a kaleidoscope slowly turning" (109)—filled with the remarks, the stories, the fragments of gossip and shop talk that swell the *Autobiography*. In Stein's kaleidoscope, however, there is no symmetry, only an amorphous set of loosely recurring scenarios punctuated by the words "endless" and "always"—patterns that allow for unity in dispersion. Scarcely a page passes in which Stein does not evoke a habitual remark, a recurrent incident, a witty truism—all revolving in thought like the atelier visitors who thronged about her high-backed Renaissance chair. Two passages might illustrate Stein's intent. The temporary building in which the Independent Salon was housed suggested the permanence of change:

> In France they always put things up just for the day or for a few days and then take them down again. Gertrude Stein's elder brother always says

that the secret of the chronic employment or lack of unemployment in France is due to the number of men actively engaged in putting up and taking down temporary buildings. Human nature is so permanent in France that they can afford to be as temporary as they like with their buildings. (19–20)

Here Stein has taken three elements—Toklas's first visit to the Salon, the distinctive building, and her brother's remark—to fashion a repetitive, "timeless" structure much like deep consciousness itself. Montmartre provides the same opportunity: "We go there every now and then. It is a place where you were always standing and sometimes waiting, not for anything to happen, but just standing" (25). The poverty of bohemians, who could afford few chairs, becomes an emblem for the continuous present—a refuge from change.

The aphorisms of friends, which Stein parades in "endless variety" (151), also have this timeless quality. A reference to her bric-a-brac, for example, allows her to draw in all young painters and an older, more rueful, Picasso. The pleasure of collecting, Stein insists, is the recurrent adventure of finding new objects: "That is what she always says about young painters, about anything, once everybody knows they are good the adventure is over. And adds Picasso with a sigh, even after everybody knows they are good not any more people really like them than they did when only the few knew they were good" (107). The remark, reflecting Stein's career, seems to apply to all artists everywhere. Then too, much of the fascinating gossip reveals Stein's passion for endless variety. For weeks the talk of Montmartre had been Apollinaire's duel; when the principals settled, there were still bills to pay:

In these was itemised each time they had a cup of coffee and of course they had to have a cup of coffee every time they sat down at one or other café with one or other principal, and again when the two seconds sat with each other. There was also the question under what circumstances were they under the absolute necessity of having a glass of brandy with the cup of coffee. And how often would they have had coffee if they had not been seconds. All this led to endless meetings and endless discussion and endless additional items. (72)

And yet beneath this multiplicity lies an abiding self whose continuity is revealed in the patterns it discerns. It is all rather like a transatlantic *Making of Americans*: Stein continues to study the endless repetitions of her friends, to observe, record, and catalog as if she were seeking bottom natures. In this regard, she is no longer writing historically: she is abstracting timeless essences.

The most obvious signs of this impulse are the sixteen illustrations scattered through the text.[45] Man Ray's photographs literally freeze time, many in ways suggestive of the text itself. The photographs of the atelier, for example, show a dominant object in a cluster of paintings: "Room with Oil Lamp" (40) has a central lamp above a Renaissance chair, surrounded by ten framed paintings and numerous curios; "Room with Bonheur de Vivre and Cézanne" (50) is dominated by the two paintings, flanked by four smaller ones and parts of five more; "Room with Gas (Femme au chapeau and Picasso Portrait)" (56) places Stein's somewhat obscured portrait on the same plane as the lamp in the foreground, beneath which hang eight paintings. Such compositions reflect the atelier's visitors, the talented and the anonymous, illuminated by Stein. Two other photographs show Stein amid a crowd. "Gertrude Stein at Johns Hopkins Medical School" (104) has her squinting through a microscope flanked by a crammed bookcase, a stack of papers, and a *memento mori*, a skull almost level with her head. In "Gertrude Stein and Alice B. Toklas in front of Saint Mark's, Venice" (108), the two women sit in the foreground, surrounded by milling pigeons. Directly above them are the multiple columns of Saint Mark's, below which stand a score of other visitors. Stein is the still center of this turning world, the massive constant around which all others congregate—the central self.[46] And with her sure sense of recurrence, she ends the text with a photograph of the first manuscript page, suggesting an eternal repetition of the same. The effect, from this point of view, is to make the *Autobiography* a succession of timeless moments, arrested by Stein's "exac[t]" prose (259).

But the multitude surrounding Stein is not always a stable one. Alice Toklas attests to the "confus[ion]" (120) this torrent of art could cause, and Stein herself makes a discrete association between that feverish world and her own writing. When she discovered Cézanne in Vollard's gallery, she must have sensed another metaphor for the creative intelligence:

> It was an incredible place. It did not look like a picture gallery. Inside there were a couple of canvases turned to the wall, in one corner was a small pile of big and little canvases thrown pell mell on top of one another, in the centre of the room stood a huge dark man glooming. This was Vollard cheerful. When he was really cheerless he put his huge frame against the glass door that led to the street, his arms above his head, his hands on each upper corner of the portal and gloomed darkly into the street. Nobody thought then of trying to come in. (36)

Here once again is the central, presiding spirit, but his environment has none of the regularity of an atelier wall. It is an "incredible," chaotic place, this storehouse of modern art, and a menacing one. Perhaps for this very reason Stein's initial photograph seeks to reverse these impressions. In the frontispiece, "Alice B. Toklas at the door, photograph by Man Ray," the fictional autobiographer stands, framed by a doorway in the background, not cheerless, like Vollard, but expectant. In the foreground and partially in shadow, sits Gertrude Stein, absorbed in her writing. The room is filled with precise planes—the strong verticals of the transom, the foreshortened table and illuminated arms of Stein's chair, the partially obscured curios precisely lining a shelf. This is a retreat literally ordered by Stein's writing, the only retreat she had from that creative unrest swirling about her atelier. As an emblem of the peculiar authorship of this text, the frontispiece suggests Stein's "inner" intent: her autobiography would evoke timeless repose.

Indeed, the largest source of chaos in the years Stein details is almost entirely expunged. The war, when Stein chooses to enter it, becomes an extension of the atelier, a source of anecdotes and *aperçus*. There are the "endless stories of french village life" their maid told in Mallorca (204); the endless doughboys for whom they "always stopped" (214) their ambulance; the conquered Alsatian villages in which they "talked to everybody and everybody talked" to them (233). Bristling generals, drunken soldiers, witty peasants march across Stein's canvas disclosing French or American charm—yet the war itself is obscured: no talk of casualties, no devastation, no suffering. Even the scarred battlefields, which evoked such haunting descriptions from others, become ghostly suggestions—"un paysage passionant" (230), as a French nurse calls them. Rather than confront these scenes, Stein attempts to subsume them within an omniscient art. When she and Picasso first see a camouflaged cannon on a Paris street, the painter is thunderstruck: "C'est nous qui avons fait ça" (110); "the whole theory of art and its inevitability" (231) was evident there. And since cubist experiments with color had anticipated the war by a decade, the war could be ignored. Apollinaire, indeed, was a casualty; Kahnweiler and Marie Laurencin were forced to flee, even the cubist movement succumbed—but none of this seemed to affect Stein, who drove forthrightly forward in "Auntie," rarely in reverse. Expunged, too, was her considerable fear. Although she is fretful in Mallorca and weeps over the saving of Paris, she is never directly touched by the destruction, nor could she be. "Anything can scare her but anything," reads an excised passage from the manuscript; but for Stein the war remains a remote, absorbing theater. "All the nations marched differently," she wrote of the victory parade beneath Jessie Whitehead's hotel window, "some slowly, some quickly, the french carry their flags the best of all, Pershing and his officer carrying the flag behind him were perhaps the most perfectly spaced" (236). For the concealed autobiographer, the war ends as it began, with a multitude to be martialled in repose.

This oblique manner was both Stein's liability and her charm. By giving the *Autobiography* the fragmentary permanence of cubist portraiture, she was able to suggest the depths of her own art. But this "outer" portrait of the artist was also a protest, a *tour de force* in which the writer wrapped herself in her corduroy mantle and disappeared behind her prose. The Gertrude Stein she gives us is a mythical modern who thrives on cataclysmic change; the woman Alice Toklas knew was a "dependent independent" who could not bear contradiction or disorder. There is a moment during her first visit to the atelier that captures Stein's temperament. In a corner of the room Toklas observed a large table on which were displayed "horseshoe nails and pebbles and little pipe cigarette holders which one looked at curiously but did not touch," as if they were in a museum cabinet (11). These were the random "accumulations from the pockets of Picasso and Gertrude Stein"—preserved, ordered, untouchable. In that secure corner Stein arranged the materials of genius, and allowed the world to stare in silent wonder.

EVERYBODY'S AUTOBIOGRAPHY

In the largest sense, *The Autobiography of Alice B. Toklas* raised the problem of alienation only to ignore it. Like Nietzsche's "uncanny" writing, Toklas was the Other inhabiting Stein, allowing the writer to reflect on her activities from a point at once external to and deep within the self. Nietzsche treated this multiplicity through the dyad isolation/union, representing not only his split consciousness but his desire for intimacy with "monstrous" readers. Stein entertained multiplicity in her atelier, with a graciousness that belied her aversion. Yet these superficial similarities mask the degree to which she simply evaded problems that Nietzsche had worked through in *Ecce Homo*. Having Toklas narrate was a witty device, but little more, since the text never stages a confrontation between self and Other akin to that between the dead and living selves of Nietzsche's corpus.[47] Moreover, although Stein reviews her writings, she makes no attempt to "read" them in Nietzsche's manner—to make the repetition of textuality a structural principle of the self. Repetition in the *Autobiography* is rather a means toward stasis: it permits a retreat from, rather than an engagement with, the play of forces surrounding the atelier. The *Autobiography* opts, in short, for a naive, deep self, a vitalist reserve of consciousness.

Within that reserve lay the dilemma Stein had learned from James. To write accessibly was to submit to grammar and structure, principles she had long since dismissed. Readers represented necessity, and the age demanded freedom. Yet readers also bestowed recognition—the ground tone of the *Autobiography*. For what other purpose did she present her life as a cynosure? She had never denied her desire for "la gloire," and now that the *Autobiography* was a success, and publishers were clamoring for more, she found herself the most famous unknown writer in France. Requests soon came for interviews and an American lecture tour, but her "serious" manuscripts remained untouched, and even Alfred Harcourt was daunted by *The Making of Americans*. Her art remained free but unread; a readership threatened to distort those "exact" sentences—and yet, had not Picasso become a wealthy man? Once again, it seemed, Stein was confronting the crisis of modern art, and she set about methodically, and at length, to answer it. Her solution was two-fold and characteristically ambivalent: by splitting off creativity, as Bergson had intuition, she attempted to preserve the artist's freedom, while she indulged the lower functions of mundane life, the world of newspapers and common sense. Even a genius, after all, could go on tour. The artist, like Adams's historian, "had nothing to do" with mass life, yet she was entitled to transform it through patient thought. The world of her American readers Stein would call "human nature"; only a genius could occupy the "human mind."

An incident Stein related to her American audiences illustrates the strategy. When she was eight she had her first epiphany before a work of art, a panorama of the battle of Waterloo. The viewer mounted a platform, and was encircled by the spectacle:

> It was an oil painting a continuous oil painting, one was surrounded by an oil painting and I who lived continuously out of doors ... felt that this was all different and very exciting.... I remember standing on the little platform in the center and almost consciously knowing there was no air.... it just was an oil painting and it had a life of its own ... and it was a real thing which looked like something that I knew because the feeling was not at all ... the feeling which I had when I saw anything that was really what the oil painting showed.[48]

Art represented, but had no connection with nature and history, just as Stein's later visit to the site of the battle of Metz ceased to "look like an oil painting" (*LIA* 64) when two old mourners entered the scene. Conversely, the audience for a great work of art lost its historical perspective and was swept up in the continuous present of the artifact. This is what Stein meant by "recognition," that the audience "must be at one with the writing, must be at one with the recognition must have nothing of knowing anything before or after the recognition."[49] On such terms there would be no difference between reader and writer; Nietzsche's "monster of...curiosity" would be subdued; and Stein could indulge her consciousness, her sense of unity.

That was the ideal; in practice, perhaps, only a fellow artist could achieve the timelessness a work of art required. The reason derived from James: "If you exist any day you are not the same as any other day no nor any minute of the day because you have inside you being existing" (*N* 38). Time meant multiplicity, destroying recognition for all but the most disciplined observers, those who were always attending "anything that is happening everything that is happening." Discipline, then, constituted genius—"to be always going on doing this thing at one and the same time listening and telling really listening and telling" (*N* 34)—that monumental pigeon-holing that produced *The Making of Americans*. But it was not just superior acuity that characterized genius; more important was the mantra-like resolve to defeat time, to deny the "sense of anything being successively happening, moving is in every direction beginning and ending is not really exciting, anything is anything, anything is happening and anybody can know anything at any time and anything is happening" (*N* 19). Genius, then, was timeless and exclusive, monumental and indifferent, less a Nietzschean *typos* than a fortress self. Before her mystified but enthusiastic audiences, the artist reasserted her freedom.

Stein distilled these notions in a long, playful meditation published after the tour. *The Geographical History of America* attempts to give what Thornton Wilder called a "metaphysic[al]" sanction to her reticence.[50] The "human mind," she now claimed, had nothing to do with memory, fighting, money, speech—even autobiography; the mind was the realm of pure art, of timeless motives recognized after "thousands of years or no years it makes no difference" (80). And since it had no identity, the mind had no audience to link it to history and change. In a sense, this was a retreat to the pristine days of anonymity, when Stein wrote a thousand pages while all Paris slept; but the problem of her popularity remained. "As long as nothing or very little that you write is published it is all sacred," she remarks, "but after it is a great deal of it published is it everything that you write is it as sacred" (25). The answer, once again, was yes and no:

> Well yes it can it cannot sound like writing because if it sounds like writing then anybody can see it being written, and the human mind nobody sees the human mind while it is being existing, and master-pieces well master-

pieces may not be other than that that they do not exist as anybody seeing them and yet there they are. (146)

Stein never solved this problem, either here or in any of the works stemming from the tour. Her best response was to invoke James Boswell, who "conceived himself as an audience an audience achieving recognition at one and the same time that Johnson achieved recognition of the thing he Johnson was saying . . . by the intensity of his merging himself in the immediacy of Johnson" (*N* 60). The model was the one she had used in *The Autobiography of Alice B. Toklas*, and yet it was not entirely satisfying: the oracular artist was still forced to merge. Unlike Nietzsche, whose suspicion that he did not live betrayed a deep need for disciples, Stein still shrank from audience. What she desired was insularity; what she accepted, in her next autobiography, was an articulate ambivalence.

Everybody's Autobiography is Stein's richest. It possesses the complexity of a meditation and the closure of a novel, even as it examines its own artistic premises.[51] Like its predecessor, it presents a central disruption—tour rather than war—but it does not seek to evade; rather, it uses the tour as an epitome for the problems of autobiography. In Depression America, Stein's stature approached that she had once wryly assigned to Joyce—she was the "incomprehensibl[e] que tout le mond peut comprendre" (*ABT* 260), the darling of the uninspired. That knowledge gives the autobiography a peculiar urgency, for if Stein's was an authentic genius, she would have to absorb even these faceless multitudes within her art. It was the crux she had abandoned with *The Making of Americans*, returned with a vengeance. In America she had received the longed-for "shock of recognition" (175); how then could she acknowledge "everybody" while remaining free? The answer, partially glimpsed in the last pages of the work, was to become an audience herself.

The germ of the text lies in Stein's artistic crisis following *The Autobiography of Alice B. Toklas*. For six months, she and Toklas celebrated their success with receptions and tailored dresses, a new Ford, even a coat for their poodle, Basket. Stein, now near sixty, was no longer equal to the prodigious writing of her youth, and as the publicity continued, her output faltered. With that came a blow to identity itself: "I had always been I because I had words that had to be written inside me and now any word I had inside me could be spoken it did not need to be written. . . . was I I when I had no written word inside me. It was very bothersome" (64). Textuality and selfhood merge; and yet the effect is agonizing. In the impasse, her faith in autobiography is shaken. The need to recollect, revise, and submit her life to others seemed almost a physical violation, and Stein was critical of every step of the process. Recollection was a contradiction in terms, because "you are never yourself to yourself except as you remember yourself and then of course you do not believe yourself." The "trouble" with autobiography was that life constantly changed, "and if you do remember right it does not sound right and of course it does not sound right because it is not right. You are of course never yourself" (68). Then, too, her recollections were not universally applauded. In 1935, Eugene and Maria Jolas published a sharply critical issue of *transition* in which several principals of the Rousseau banquet accused Stein not only of error but of ignorance. "It is evident," wrote André Salmon, "that Miss Stein understood little of the tendency we all had.... what confusion. What incomprehension of an epoch!"[52] Even Francis Picabia, one of the near-geniuses Stein praised, pointed out an omission. There were not two Spaniards at the show where Leo Stein first saw Picassos, but three, "and... he was the third one." "In those days," Stein writes apologetically, "I never heard anything about a third one" (*EA* 43). Multiplicity shattered public and private selves alike. Indeed, such criticisms struck at the heart of her aesthetic—her putative refusal to revise. "After all," she remarked to Harlan Miller, "what is in your head comes down into your hand and if it has come down it can never come again no not again" (311). And yet she would return now to many of the same memories, even the same scenes she had described in other texts, as if sudden success had forced her back upon her origins. It was not writing alone, but autobiography that troubled Stein.

Everybody's Autobiography is the expression of that ambivalence. What happened to identity, she began to ask, as an autobiography passed from reader to reader—or for that matter, from culture to culture? Alice Toklas had already protested: "If it has to be at all it should be Alice Toklas and in the French translation it was ... but in America and England too Alice B. Toklas was more than Alice Toklas" (3). The letter was less important than the "be-ing"—and yet one's identity seemed almost an accident of language. The *Autobiography* had the same relation to its subjects as the wooden umbrella of a Paris acquaintance, which looked "exactly like a real one even to the little button and the rubber string that holds it together" (3). Both were artifacts, counterfeits, yet they identified their possessors; which was real? And if, as Toklas feared, the *Autobiography* would spur imitators, how could the original be told from the counterfeits? "Even if there were lots of others it would not make any difference," rejoins Stein, as if recognition from Toklas were all she desired (3). But the pressure of "everybody" now haunted her prose. Like Miss Hennessy in the rain, she, too, might "loo[k] a little foolish" (3) to an anonymous audience for whom all identity was counterfeit. Nobody was anybody.

But the problem was not confined to autobiographers. In an anecdote about Dashiell Hammett, whom Stein met at a Beverly Hills dinner party, she portrays the successful writer as elusive, neurotic, almost invisible. Touted in California as she had been throughout the country, Stein was allowed to choose the guest list for the affair, but the novelist proved as mysterious as his work. He was neither in San Francisco nor in New York, as her hostess had been told; finally located in Los Angeles, he did not at first believe the message. At dinner the two discussed the tentativeness of modern men who, unlike their nineteenth-century counterparts, could write about no one but themselves. Hammett readily admits the charge: men "have no confidence and so...they have to hold on to themselves not having any confidence" (5). He was himself considering a novel about a father and son to see if he could not somehow "make another one." Stein, as ever, is "interest[ed]," but the talk of "others" raises more disturbing questions. Both self-involved writers had looked to the same strategy— Hammett expressing himself through a double, Stein using Toklas for that purpose. Yet Hammett's works were mysteries in which the principal character was "dead," and though, as an artist, he could have bestowed recognition, Hammett was more a "puzzle" himself. What, then, was Stein, who also could not "make another one"—was she, too, inhabited by a corpse? And if not, how was she to address herself to an audience?

In answer, she provides two quick vignettes. At an earlier New York party, Mary Pickford had accosted her, and proposed that they be photographed together. So delighted was Stein at the prospect, that the actress paled and slipped away, sensing that "it would not be good for her audience" (8). Like Hammett, the successful Pickford fairly "melted" before Stein's eyes, as if the awful public had made her a nonentity. In contrast was the recognition of a black woman on Fifth Avenue, who pointed wordlessly to Stein's photograph on the cover of *Portraits and Prayers*, displayed in a nearby window. The woman acknowledged an image, an artifact, just as Toklas, in the *Autobiography*, had acknowledged Stein. There was no mystery, no diffidence— and no language. If Stein were to retain her identity, she would, it seemed, have to do so in some realm beyond words.

That recognition ending the preface supports Stein's contention to Alfred Harcourt that her "extraordinary welcome" did not come "from the books of mine that they do understand like the Autobiography but the books of mine they did not understand" (8). The troubling audience was a function of her obscurity, a comforting thought to one whose very being was caught up with language. But the converse of that was equally true: Stein's relative clarity in the best-seller had confirmed that she was less than ever a public figure. She feared the life of a Mary Pickford, who, like Fernande's idol, Eveline Thaw, was "so blonde, so pale, so nothing" (*ABT* 33). It was all very much like her maid, Hélène's remark: "there is too much of nothing or there is never enough of anything" (6)—a sturdy French translation of her own ambivalence. Decoded, the clauses are either contradictory or complementary. If "nothing" has substance, then there is too much of that substance, contradicting the second assertion. But if one considers the entire sentence, then "there is too much of nothing" means that there is no product in abundance—that is, there is not enough of anything. This formula, which might be expressed as "A $\gneqq$ B"—McFarlane's "both/and and either/or"—captures Stein's creative dilemma. It may be seen in her attitude toward her public and writing, in the difficulties of other artists—Hammett, Sarbates, Dali, Picasso; in the rise of fascism in Europe, about which Stein is troubled and indifferent; in the contradictions of speech and writing, poverty and money; in the memories of her childhood, aroused by the West Coast trip. "One thing is certain," she wrote of that experience, "nothing can happen that is different from what you expected and when that happens and it mostly does happen everything is different from what you expected" (39). Once again she had confirmed the modernist paradox.

Stein, who could always recognize her own ambivalence more easily in others, examines the problem in a sly portrait of Picasso. In 1936 the painter had renounced his art forever, preferring the poet's idling in cafés. In Stein's judgment he was an eminently bad poet—a poet who was not a poet—and she makes the most of her annoyance. At a party where both he and Francis Picabia were present, she teases the little Spaniard for his resemblance to his rival. Picasso had branded the Frenchman a false painter, and yet people persisted in confusing the two: "I made them get up and stand together and they were the same height and they had the same shoes on" (20). Indeed, if the two did not resemble one another, the fault was Picasso's. When the Spaniard confessed to being "terrified" of the American custom of hitchhiking, it was Picabia who drew Stein's approval: "Picabia had soon stopped listening, nothing is real to him that is not painting and so knowing anything can not frighten him" (21). The indifference of genius eluded Picasso. Had he not succumbed to a Russian wife who understood him as little as he understood himself? "Superficially" the two were alike, "and gradually then they come to the part where they are not alike and then it is hopeless because all that is alike is in the covering" (21). And had he not surrounded himself with equally false friends? Sabartes had led "a long life of permanently installing himself somewhere," only to prove the maxim that "nothing is so impermanent as a permanent residence" (19). His rooming with Picasso, who "was living all alone," only intensified the painter's contradictions. But many other painters seemed to share his ambivalence. Dali, too, had married a Russian; had recently painted a picture on which he scrawled the legend, "I spit upon the face of my mother," whom he adored (28); had demonstrated "a violence in freedom but [was] never free" (26)—a remark that could equally apply to Jean Cocteau and Marcel Duchamp. Perhaps, Stein reflected, the problem lay in painting itself, for art was constant evasion. "Having done anything you naturally want to do it again and if you do it again then you know you are doing it again and it is not interesting" (28). Roché's paradox persisted. But though she claimed that writers, who worked from memory, were less bothered by repetition, the remark was clearly confessional. Like her painter friends, Stein, too, was paralyzed.

So great were the contradictions, that thought itself seemed subversive. In a conversation with an Egyptian acquaintance, Stein tried to draw a favorite distinction between writing and speech, functions of the human mind as against human nature. In Egypt, she discovered, lovers and heroes once spoke in "an exalted and fanciful language that has now become a written language," a decayed form of the Saussurean original. Stein's response is revealing:

> That is very interesting *I said*, now the English language *I said* has gone just the other way, they always tried to write like anybody talked and it is only comparatively lately that, it is true that the written language knows that that is of no interest . . . because everybody talks as the newspapers and movies and radios tell them . . . and so gradually the written language says something and says it differently than the spoken language. (13, emphasis added)

The distinction, rendered in suspect speech, collapses even as she makes it, just as the writer herself feared infection by movie-minded readers. A piece Stein wrote for the *Saturday Evening Post* during this period betrays the same confusion. Success, she told her readers, brought crisis, since "when your public knows you and does not want to pay for you and when your public knows you and does want to pay for you, you are not the same you" (44–45). Her habit of projection made this a universal law; all had to decide whether "money is money or ... money isn't money," and although most accepted wealth, the belief was unstable. How else could one explain the coexistence of communism and the Depression? "That is the way it is if you believe in anything deeply enough it turns into something else and so money turns into not money" (41). There was her banker cousin who said "he could not believe really believe that the depression was a depression although he did believe it and that worried him" (105), and the father of a Paris friend who saw his income rise from $2,000 to $25,000 after the war, only to lose it all in the crash (94). All the world seemed to share her pain. Perhaps even Stein's tools—words themselves—were suspect. A rose was a rose, according to the famous maxim, but naming, too, imposed false permanence, a Nietszchean posthumous identity. Hadn't she herself been named after a dead grandmother (115)? Indeed, her autobiography was a kind of death sentence. "That is very funny if you write all about any one they do not exist any more ..." (119), she observed, confirming Nietzsche's insight in *Ecce Homo*. Language, wealth, history conspired against her, upending her ordered world.

In part her anxiety reflected the times. No longer could Stein, worried about her own death, ignore unrest in France. In Paris, fascists, communists, republicans agitated on street corners. A royalist crank had even urged a Merovingian restoration, and a stranger passing her and her poodle, Basket, had chanted in the tones of class-warfare: "Piss you dog piss against the side of a house in passing, if it was my house I would take a gun and shoot you" (97). That winter they would watch the revolution, she grimly assured Bennett Cerf. All this was the era's accelerated grimace, turning children of the armistice into adults in a mere two years (94), and threatening to destroy Stein's settled life. As always, she resisted by martialling anecdotes of French permanence. A noted provincial hotel had managed to stay in business, despite family tragedy; her lovely country house attracted numerous visitors because "nothing has ever been changed ... nothing has ever been done" (128). "After all," she asserts, "revolutions are a matter of habit" (52). But the denial did not fully satisfy. When William Seabrook came to Bilignin, his questions stirred up a long reflection on her childhood, distorted now in light of social change. "There is too much fathering going on just now," she writes, as if Daniel Stein had returned to haunt Europe. "There is father Mussolini and father Hitler and father Roosevelt and father Stalin and father Lewis and father Blum and father Franco ... and there are ever so many more ready to be one" (133). It was the same for her as it was for the Jews, who were very much attached to and "very much given not to want a father and not to have one" (142); hence the score of pages devoted to life without father—to her siblings, her eldest brother, her Baltimore cousins. The deeply skewed recollections, interspersed with remarks on money, street railroads, feudalism, Spaniards, are as evasive as any Stein recorded, yet they are not free. Through them runs the theme of death and depression and the limitations of one's era. "After all it is very simple," she concluded, "we are on the earth and we have to live on it and there is...no extending it" (154). When the world seemed to share Stein's anxieties, evasion was as useless as repose.

This is why the American tour was such a liberation. The expatriate could declare her country unchanged, even after a war, a crash, and a depression. She visited Bryn Mawr College and slept in a room identical to those she knew in Radcliffe, complete with the same photographs (184); she found the students at her lectures identical to those of her own generation; she was introduced to people whom she might have known for years. America became an enormous platform from which Stein asserted, as she always had, that grammar did not make any difference, that pictures could evade their frames, that "the American way has been not to need that generations are existing" (*LIA* 166). There is a naive charm in her account of her lion's life, her delight in being pampered and having her whims satisfied. And yet she is too honest to ignore her ambivalence, even here. True, she had decided not to read American newspapers, since in Paris "nothing did happen that made any difference whether we knew it or not" (185), but she saw enough to excite doubt. Even as she asserted her cosmopolitan indifference, she was struck by New York, which seemed "as if we had come often but really it was not just the same" (169). She was troubled by the news of her arrival displayed in Times Square, a "shock of recognition and non-recognition" (175)—and by the streets that "did not look real" (171). In Chicago, the two impulses jarred rudely. At a dinner with Mortimer Adler she defended the timeless significance of writers, for whom ideas did not derive from "groups," but from the "human being to himself inside him" (206). That night she is taken on a tour of low haunts by the Chicago police and confronts the opposite extreme, an anonymous homicide victim. "He was of no importance," she was told, "he had nobody nobody knew him...nobody had any kind of feeling about him and one night...he was shot down dead" (209). The account must have stirred her anxieties, for she follows it with another parody of her lectures. In "Portraits and Repetition" she asserted that Americans had achieved her own stasis: "In short this generation has conceived an intensity of movement so great that it has not to be seen against something else to be known, and therefore, this generation does not connect itself with anything..." (*LIA* 166). The young confirmed her desire for unity in disorder. But if constant movement meant freedom, it also implied futility, as she discovered that night at a walking marathon. "Here there was nothing," she related, "neither waking nor sleeping, they were all young ones and they were moving as their bodies were drooping" (209). These were the desperate counterparts of her college audience, reduced to death-like trance after six weeks of constant motion. Although Stein does not address the irony, she was clearly disturbed, declining an opportunity "to be photographed with them." Such "timeless" images mocked genius.

Most disturbing of all was her visit to Oakland, for which her recollections with Seabrook had ostensibly prepared her. Here was no question of pleasing variety or exalted notions of permanence; she was thrown back upon the painful scenes of her childhood, without even the luxury of digression. All the pleasant fixtures of the Oakland estate, the big garden, the eucalyptus and the roses, were gone now, and Stein, who had canonized the scene in *The Making of Americans*, found herself before an illusion: "I did not like the feeling, who has to be themselves inside them, not any one and what is the use of having been if you are to be going on being and if not why is it different and if it is different why not. I did not like anything that was happening" (291). The identity she had fixed in writing had disappeared—what, then, was she? It was the question she had discussed with Hammett, yet after a seven-months' proclamation of her genius, she was no closer to an answer. She was an absence to herself; despite all the talk of timeless constancy, the trip had resolved nothing. True, she returned to France with Cerf's promise to publish anything she liked, but the trip had left her with a more compelling need. Once again, she had to free herself from herself.

In many ways, Stein's return to Oakland, a simulacrum of the larger textual crisis, recalls Nietzsche's visit to Bayreuth. There, too, a return to the past unsettled old verities, divorcing Nietzsche from "selflessness," from philology—from Germany—and allowing the corpse of his father to emerge, that parasite of writing that exposed his "nethermost self" (*EH* 287). So, too, Stein's tour of America exposed her to the Other she had evaded in France, the interminable multiplicity constituting the self. In Paris, her desire for unity had led her out of time; but the tour threw her face to face with a dispersion she could not deny. Nietzsche had confronted such demons by writing *Human, All-Too-Human*, in which he "put a sudden end to all [his] infections with

'higher swindle,' 'idealism,' 'beautiful feelings,' and other effemina-
cies" (*EH* 288)—disposing of the *pharmakos* he called "Wagner." For
Stein, too, recovery would come through writing in which she staged
the recognition she desired.

The return to France produced her "meditations"—*Four in America*, *The Geographical History of America*—texts in which she hugged
her genius somewhat more fiercely, addressed the world more forcefully. Part of her difficulty in Oakland, she realized, had been the very
absence of audience. When Seabrook, Chester Arthur, or the Abdys visited her at Bilignin, she had no trouble recollecting her past. Such sympathetic listeners "make you feel full inside you of why you are what
you are and so you tell them all there is to tell" (298). She had also
failed to narrate her life as simply as it was happening, a point she discussed during long strolls with Thornton Wilder. What she sought was
a new immediacy linking autobiographer and reader, as if both were
living the present moment. "The first autobiography was not that," she
realized, "it was a description and a creation of something that having
happened was in a way happening not again but as it had been which
is history which is newspaper . . . but is not a simple narrative of what
is happening" (302–3). Recognition demanded the vividness of shared
perception—like her best American lectures—and the intensity of a
continuous present; she had to find a way to make her audience share
her consciousness. Although she continued to insist on the rarity of
genius, she now implied that genius was a shared attribute, that to
succeed, her prose had to be typical. She had chronicled French artists
and lectured to Americans; now, in a final scene, she would teach them
how to read.

The occasion was a performance of "A Wedding Bouquet," a ballet
adapted from her play, *They Must. Be Wedded. to their Wife*. Stein was
invited to the final week of rehearsals and to opening night; as such,
she was a spectator to a work that was no longer hers, just as in
Oakland she had viewed scenes she could no longer identify. The crucial difference was art: "I liked hearing my words and I like it being
a play and I liked it being something to look at and I liked their doing
it again and I like the music going on" (316). Her response is a deliberate merging of past associations and present performance—a continuous present in which she discovers herself through movement and
language. Hence, as Stein describes the scene, she verges toward that
immediate description she had promised Wilder: "Tomorrow . . . we
will go to the theatre again and see how it is done when there is an
audience there. Tomorrow then" (317). And as she witnesses the performance—reported, significantly, in a shifting tense—her experience

approximates James's description of consciousness: "each time a musician does something with the words it makes it do what they [words]
never did do, this time it made them do as if the last word had heard
the next word and the next word had heard not the last word but the
next word" (317). The present performance had no history, and yet it
embraced the past as Jamesian thought embraced the self. Moreover,
the experience captured precisely what Nietzsche meant by revision:
the subject's desire to be "reborn in the guise of an interpreter," to
overcome dispersion by re-viewing her texts. So, too, an audience,
reading Stein, would recognize in her memories the materials of their
own lives—not particular histories but the common sense of moving
in time. For Stein, that sense was now vital. "Perhaps I am not I even
if my little dog knows me," she concludes, acknowledging the possibility of change, "but anyway I like what I have and now it is today"
(318). Her autobiography, all lives, confirmed the present moment.

Everybody's Autobiography was not the work Stein had discussed
with Wilder—it was not an evocation of life "as if it is existing simply"
(303). She was too preoccupied with identity and doubt for that. But
the work was a serious attempt to adapt her dense meditations to a
wider audience. Stein was still struggling with her genius. She could
not yet acknowledge herself as typical, nor could she admit all readers
into the sanctum of art; so she adopted a middle ground. The obli-
quities in the text—the odd associations, the repetitions defying logic,
the sudden shifts in emphasis—competed with the linear description
of the tour, much in the manner of her first autobiography. Americans
would respond to her warm account, rendered somewhat strange by
the odd sweep of this foreign observer; and if they demanded clarity,
Stein was ready with a response. "Explanations are clear," she had
told Joseph Alsop in New York, "but since no one to whom a thing is
explained can connect the explanations with what is really clear, therefore explanations are not clear" (171). Her audience had yet to achieve
that obscure clarity Stein so rigorously defended, as she had yet to
write a truly popular work. It would take another cataclysm to bring
about the recognition she desired.

PARIS FRANCE

When the French declared war in 1939, Stein was in the department of
Ain, where she was to remain until the Liberation. She had always
looked to the French to confirm her traditionalism, and as the Germans
advanced, she took comfort in peasant wisdom, recorded in a slight but
significant autobiography, *Paris France*. The book has none of the tech-
nical brilliance of *Alice B. Toklas*, or the intellectual depth of *Every-*

body's Autobiography; it is a flat denial of change, congratulating French reserve. But in Stein's struggle with audience it is a distinct advance, for it tries to close the gap between writer and culture. The truisms Stein puts into the mouths of her neighbors are reflections of her own thought, and as she gathers charming anecdotes, she approaches that recognition she so prized. The war was a common trial; Stein recorded common claims.

The text announces its conservative intent by using the same anecdotes, even the same language, Stein had used in the past. Here again is the meditation on the *Panorama of the Battle of Waterloo*, in which the painting's flat surface mimics timeless prose. Here, too, is Baronne Pierlot's remark that "nature . . . is not natural," a paradox first appearing in *Everybody's Autobiography*. When Mrs. Lindbergh came to Paris, the two women discussed the perils of publicity, much as Stein had done in America, and there is the familiar claim for artists, first made thirteen years before in "Composition as Explanation": "after all the way everything is remembered is by writers and painters of the period, nobody really lives who had not been well written about . . ." (21)—another testament to the "posthumous" nature of writing. Stein also records her confusion before drastic change. When Basket dies she is given sharply contradictory advice. One friend said to get another dog "as like Basket as possible call him by the same name and gradually there will be confusion and you will not know which Basket it is" (69–70). Picasso disagreed, since a replica would only "remind" her of the old one, and make her grieve the more. Stein opts for both measures: "we tried to have the same and not to have the same . . . I cannot say that the confusion between the old and the new had not taken place but certainly le roi est mort vive le roi, is a normal attitude of mind" (70). And, as ever, Stein displays paradox. War, she notes, increases isolation because "there are so many more people, animals and fowls and children" (95); the uniforms she sees her neighbors wear "make every one younger," only to make them "that much older" when they remove them (66). Most important, her neighbors confirmed her contradictory sense of permanence: "all French men had to be revolutionary . . . not for publicity but for civilization. How could you be civilised if you had not passed through a period of revolt, and then you had to return to your pre-revolt stage and there you were you were civilised" (58). They were merely proving Stein's assertion that even the radical could become classic.[53] The war would vindicate her art.

But this war does not share the invisibility of World War I; it is a haunting, disorienting experience, captured in the interpolated story of Helen Button. The girl's gnomic observations, so much like Stein's, depict life in uncanny terms, at once intimate and alien. In war, animals and children were naughtier or more frightened; dogs were more likely to kill chickens; nuns in cities wore gas masks in place of coiffes. Even the distinction between night and day had disappeared: "The nights were black and the days were dark and there was no morning. Not in war-time" (84). Once when Helen went out at night she was nearly run down by a car; another time she saw the carcass of an enormous animal without tail or ears. Over all was a strange and sinister wonder. People and animals appeared and disappeared, never to be seen again, and an aunt displayed an odd foresight: "She knew when any enemy was going to be dead, she knew how often a clock would strike, she knew who was not going to eat eggs, she knew who was going to buy a hat, she knew everything" (88). In *Wars I Have Seen* Stein would herself become this child; here she used the figure to convey her mute fear of a world once again riddled with mystery. A neighbor's horse, too old for military service, was mistaken for a younger one and requisitioned, but never found again, and the whole region worried how German bombers could find them in the mountains (78). It was Trotsky who had defined twentieth-century warfare as "neither war nor peace" (73); now, as that uneasy status settled on Bilignin, Stein struggled to maintain her balance.

One refuge was memory. As she sought out recurrences she returned to prewar France, to prove the world stable. Thirty years before they had kept their houses warm with pressed coal, "and now . . . everybody wants their boulets fire back again." Even the old hearth grates, long abandoned, were in demand, and Stein was lucky to find one in her own attic, "which dates from we do not know when" (116). Young men now seemed to be more "athletic and clean," but as they aged they more resembled their own contemporaries (113). The fashions of France, too, had a certain permanence. "When we came to Paris," she recalls, "the men wearing their silk hats on the side of their head and leaning heavily on their cane toward the other side ma[de] a balance" (111), the same balance she detected in French temperament. The image is a metaphor for all she finds comforting. When an octogenarian friend could not recall her father's occupation, the answer was found, like the fire grate, in the attic: a piece of old ermine identified him as a judge. "There are fashions that change and fashions that do not change or fashions that change slowly but there are always fashions," concludes Stein (29). This was French wisdom. When, a century before, the English panted after progress, the French recognized progress as mere fashion, and returned to their own rich culture (39). When the

French talked politics, they insisted that all change was temporary, mere fashion. "They talk about cutting off the heads of the grosses têtes but now we know that there will be other grosses têtes and they will be all the same" (28); what, then, was the use of revolution? A worker once called it "atavism" (32), this sense that "France cannot change it can always have its fashions but it cannot change" (33). Stein had always called it freedom.

To remain "completely conservative...particularly traditional" (38) had long been Stein's response to change; in her sixty-fifth year she discovered that response throughout a culture. The paean to France was little more than projection, as she saw the continuous present wherever she looked:

> I once wrote and said what is the use of being a boy if you are to grow up to be a man what is the use....But in France a boy is a man of his age the age he is and so there is no question of a boy growing up to be a man and what is the use, because at every stage of being alive he is completely a man alive at that time. (27–28)

All that mattered to her compatriots was the "daily life" (22) she had explored for years, the timeless present that, in the twentieth century, "was so completely dominating" (40). Soon Stein concluded that the century itself shared her attributes. Like her childhood, it had begun "in uncertainty" (117), and had endured a dismal adolescence marked by war, "a period of fashion without style, of systems without disorder, of reforming everybody which is persecution, and of violence without hope" (119). Only now was the century coming into its own, amid a crisis Stein vainly hoped would confirm her "enjoyment of ordinary living" (119). Perhaps no phrase in all her writing more accurately reflects Stein's true ignorance of the present. She was wrong about the serenity of France, and almost dead wrong about her own safety; only the machinations of Bernard Fäy, who was later jailed as a collaborator, would preserve her from the gas chamber. But as she shrank from history, her art expanded. No longer was she the isolated genius, fearful of mass life; she had begun to embrace mass life—the whole century—whose development now mirrored her own. The times demanded that "anybody can be free, free to be civilised and to be" (120). It was a claim she would renew in her final autobiography, *Wars I Have Seen*.

WARS I HAVE SEEN

In its simplicity, its clarity, and its preoccupation with the present, *Wars I Have Seen* resembles another American war diary, Whitman's *Specimen Days*. Like Whitman among the wounded or hobbling around

Stafford farm, Stein concerns herself with the immediate—the mundane affairs of Culoz, where she spent most of the Occupation. No longer can she evade war; it engulfs her now with a dread fully equal to that of Whitman's most vivid battle scenes, forcing her to observe. But beneath the village life, Stein is absorbed in a larger question. Like the aging Whitman struggling to glimpse national glory, Stein returns to the problem of modernity, to the role of art and self in a chaotic world. Her solution is characteristically Nietzschean: in her last work, Stein transforms her life into universal history.

An Emotional Autobiography and *Wars I Remember* were two of the rejected titles for this work. Both express Stein's radical departure. As if history were forcing her to confront her own death, she turned decisively to the past, and discussed it as she never had before. Now the uncertainties, the sense of absence that had so disturbed her in Oakland, suffused the text in a rhetoric of constraint:

> I do not know whether to put in the things I do not remember as well as the things I do remember. . . . I was not born during the night but about eight o'clock in the morning . . . I do not know whether the four living and the two dead older children had not been born equally perfect babies. (3)

Her mother's family was "not rich"; as tanners they did not like business, "but tanning is not really a business at least it was not in those days" (4). When she was eight months old she was left with an uncle, "why was never explained" (4); at four she visited Paris, but "I do not know whether I really remembered much" (51). What was the use of being a boy if one grew up to be a man, she had asked—how could identity survive the fragments of memory? Her answer now was to link these fragments to the eternal recurrence of death itself, death in the guise of war. In her mother's Baltimore—she did "not quite know how"—a "mysterious uncle . . . went all through the war and came out with or without or only with or only without a pair of shoes" (6). With uncanny irony, Stein turned the Civil War, her "favorite," into an emblem for uncertainty and loss, and traced her growth by a succession of other wars—the Boer War, the Russo-Japanese War, and Balkan War. Just as her youth was marked by constant change, so "modern wars all wars are like that, they go places, where they never heard of in many cases, and between babyhood and fourteen there had been so many changes of scene" (15). The pain of rejection, of sensing enemies, returned to her in reports of the Spanish-American War; and now that she was surrounded by death, the world itself seemed to be replicating her childhood. When she was young, she confesses, it was "a struggle not to die . . . not not to actually die . . . but . . . not to know that death is there" (21). Now, as the Germans requisitioned food, and some timid neighbors starved, Stein felt the same withering anxiety:

> War is like that, it goes on like that it keeps going on like that and soon nobody has anything to eat . . . and so I was then so am I now. . . . A fish bone can even be a worry anything that can happen or has happened or has not happened can be a worry and that is what war is, and so what is the difference between life and war. There is none. (15)

Self and Other, unity and dispersion had merged in the same vast negative, as the Germans aroused Stein's deepest fears.

The region around Bilignin was not officially occupied by German forces, although there was a large garrison in nearby Belley, and a detachment at Culoz, where Stein and Toklas soon moved. Indeed, as the war progressed, the Germans became more of a nuisance than a menace. They controlled the towns, and periodically threatened the mayors, but they simply had too few men to impose their will, and the village life wore warily on. Nevertheless, there were unsettling disruptions. Village boys were shipped off to German factories, troops often billeted in the farmhouses, and curfews were constantly imposed and amended. Toward the end of the war, bands of partisans tormented villagers they deemed collaborators, and the Germans were always on the watch for *maquis*. What Stein quickly sensed was a confusion as threatening as that of Vollard's gallery—or of her childhood. The young men were sent away without notice; "some of them run away and when they run away they do not know where and a great many of them are taken away they do not know where and this is all as it was between babyhood and fourteen" (15). The times seemed almost "mediaeval" in their instability: "you take a train, you disappear, you move away your house is gone, your children too, your crops are taken away" (26). Everyone was unsettled, confused. "Nobody seems to really know what they do want" (162), she observed:

> Everybody is so uncertain as to what they hope for and what they despair of, so confused that it is not necessary to know what they think, they think so many things, so very many things and all of them at once. . . . How they can have such a variety of emotions and convictions at the same time and so many of them completely opposed is perfectly wonderful. (171)

The French welcomed the Germans after the armistice, yet they despised the Occupation; they longed for the American invasion, but feared American influence; they cheered the Allied war effort, but disliked the bombing of German factories, where many of their own sons worked. And every night, Stein would listen to the propaganda of both sides—the Germans claiming that Americans would oppress France, the Americans claiming that they fought to make each person's home secure. For Stein, "the general confusion, the general fear, the general helplessness, the general nervousness" (13) must have seemed familiar indeed, for it recalled, in sharper terms, conditions in prewar Paris. The ferment that had surrounded the modernist movement, she now realized, had become synonymous with her life.

With the imaginative freedom that had always characterized her art, Stein began to embroider this theme. She divided her early life into two broad periods, centered on adolescence, and, like Nietzsche reading himself into history, gradually drew in all the phenomena she was observing. Her early life, "between babyhood and fourteen," was "legendary," a period when she naively accepted the world and its laws. That status precluded "remembering": "I was a legend then, of course I was, to myself and . . . I was struggling not to be dying that is not to know that dying was dying and frightening was not only frightening but connected with any thing" (21). From fifteen to twenty-four—about the time she lost interest in medical school—she began to wrestle with the world, a condition she variously describes as "pioneer" or "mediaeval." This was the period of "Money, possessions, eternity, enemies, the fear of death . . . and sorrow," the time when "you can begin to write . . . which makes the depth and consolation of disappointment and sorrow" (36). That is, along with knowledge of death, adolescence brought the self-consciousness of art. The distinction was crucial: even as Stein reassembled her past, she rejected that attitude she had always associated with genius—the denial of memory and death. Writing, she now realized, was bound up with the two principles dominating her world.

That truth, in turn, allowed her to project her own experience. Stein had reached maturity at the turn of the century, joining the modern movement with the publication of *Three Lives* in 1909. Was not her youth, then, a preparation for modernity itself, a "killing off" of the nineteenth century? The last century had been an age of naive beliefs—in progress and evolution, Esperanto and the white man's burden—false universals, as "legendary" as a child's naive sense of her own limbs. Only in the twentieth century had mankind achieved maturity. As adolescence brought literacy, so the modern world had learned to "read and write," and to dispel its illusions:

> now in the twentieth century anybody can listen to the radio, in any language and everybody is civilised enough to do that, but wars are more than ever and now everybody knows that although everybody is civilised there is no progress and everybody knows even though anybody flies higher and

> higher they cannot explain eternity any more than before, and everybody
> can persecute anybody just as much if not more than ever, it is rather
> ridiculous so much science, so much civilisation...and they persecute
> anybody, and put books on the index, that and ban them publicly just
> like that. (62–63)

This was the goal of the twentieth century, of her own maturity: to kill
the latter century "dead, quite dead" (105) by means of writing. It was
a movement that had begun with the First World War, as she noted in
Paris France; now the French, the Allies, Hitler himself were all con-
spiring to extinguish the "romantic" (15) notions of the past. The nineteenth century had been "very resistant strong obstinate and
convinced of its service to humanity," but at last it was dead: "Hitler
killed it, and like a very Samson he fell down with it and was killed in
its ruins" (73). History had at last overtaken Gertrude Stein.

For Stein, this ritual sacrifice was an ingenious compromise: she
could satisfy her loathing for the past, and still write with peculiar conviction. Part of the past—the part that had so troubled her in Oakland—was as dead as the century; what remained was the imaginative
kernel, the continuities she had always sought through her writing.
Hence, in a move identical to Nietzsche's Eternal Return, she now insists on the utter contemporaneity of literature. In the long days under
curfew, she had returned to Shakespeare, and was astonished at the
similarities with France. At times she was moved by the tragedies,
which "said that nothing was anything that human beings had no
meaning, that not anything had meaning" (13); again, she found parallels between troop movements in *Henry V* and talk of the Allied invasion (39). And with a peasant love of superstition, she searched for signs
of the times:

> what is so terrifying is that it is all just like what is happening now, Mac-
> beth seeing ghosts well...is not Mussolini seeing the ghost of his son-in-
> law...take the kings in Shakespeare there is no reason why they all kill
> each other all the time, it is not like orderly wars when you meet and
> fight, but it is all just violence and there is no object to be attained, no
> glory to be won, just like Henry the Sixth and Richard the Third and
> Macbeth. (161)

The sense of being surrounded by enemies, including the French, who
might "denounce you," recalled Cooper's *Wyandotte* and *The Spy*; and
even the radio announcements seemed strangely literary. On the eve of
the invasion, the Americans advised them to study the local terrain for
potential landing sites, "and it was just like being in a theatre with a romantic drama, the things we heard when we were young, Secret Ser-

vice and Alabama and The Girl I Left Behind Me and Curfew Shall Not Ring To-night and Shenandoah" (187). Her provincial life had become a theater of war.

Those literary parallels affected her prose. Throughout her career, Stein had eschewed stories with "a beginning and a middle and an ending" (*GHA* 84), but the stories of her neighbors so moved her, that she began to salt the autobiography with interpolated tales. Two young villagers make a daring escape from Germany, outwitting border guards and disguising themselves as Italian troops; Stein provides the details. Another youth visits his brother in a German prison, in a vignette that could have come from Hemingway:

> He came in with two soldiers with guns and fixed bayonets at his back and it upset me so I began to cry but he said to me sternly control yourself do not show emotion, and we sat down at a table together and we talked and we compared photographs . . . and the adjutant who was there to listen to us said suddenly he is giving you photographs, how dare you said my brother accuse me of such a thing, apologise I insist that you apologise, first examine these photographs and then apologise, and the man said but it is all right, no said my brother look, look at them count them and examine them and then apologise, which the adjutant had to do. (136–37)

It was "like a piece out of Dumas," Stein comments, "and yet happening" (137). Literature had always been Stein's elite preserve, the refuge of genius; now, as life and history converged, her own writing could become historical. Perhaps for the first time in her career, she had fully embraced the past.

The confusion in Culoz, the sense of *déjà vu* in life and literature, all this gave new meaning to another one of Stein's obsessions. Cut off from the rest of the world, walking as much as sixteen kilometers a day for a few eggs or a loaf of bread, sitting in a neighbor's kitchen and worrying about the Germans, Stein was absorbed in unadorned daily life.[54] She had always been a sharp observer of character and habit, but at a safe remove; now her very insecurity freed her. If the times recapitulated her childhood, the reason was that there were no longer young lives and old lives, but simply lives (7). The young never talked about the future, there being "no futures for this generation" (190), and children were so open that they "mingl[ed]" (7) with their elders. "And so it being now war and I seeing . . . and knowing of the feeling of children of any age I do not now have to remember about my feeling" (7). No longer were there gaps in her inner life; she knew "what it is to be any age now that there is a war and so remembering back is not only remembering but might be being" (11). As she had once defined contemporaneity as constant motion, so now "everybody" was "on the roads" and "moving around" (167), as all Europe seemed to meld into a continuous present:

> It is the soothing thing about history that it does repeat itself, sometimes it has worse attacks of it than at other times, sometimes it is that history has a perfect outbreak of repetitions...just now that is November 1943 it is full of them full of repetitions nothing but repetitions. It repeats all the Balkan wars all the difficulties between France and England all the German defeats, and it repeats all Italian history. (96)

But she was witnessing more than recurrence. The war, she announced, was millennial.

Stein wrote with peculiar conviction. Circulating throughout the region were the prophecies of Saint Odile, whose oracles described the war much as Stein's pronouncements described modernity. Daily she sought assurance in the saint's apocalyptic scenario:

> the world would go on and there would come the worst war of all and the fire would be thrown down from the heavens and there would be freezing and heating and rivers running and at last there would be winning by the enemy and everybody would say and how can they be so strong, and everybody would say and give us peace. (59)

Satan would be unchained for Armageddon, which would end in the fall of Moscow and Rome—the very course of the war. It was the timeless history Stein had always sought, now unfolding with absolute millennial clarity before her eyes. Under its pressure, Stein's prose at last assumed the present tense she had promised at the end of *Everybody's Autobiography*. "Alice Toklas has just commenced typewriting this book," she confides, as the Germans begin to leave, "and then we can be peaceful...until the Americans come, then that will finish the book" (229, 233). Writing, text, self, and history had at last merged in a continuous present.

Audience, in Stein's American tour, had been a metaphysical challenge; now, as the Americans approached, it was a passionate desire. Cut off from her country for over four years, Stein sought out reporters as eagerly as she did generals, and only days after Culoz was liberated, she was broadcasting to America. What she told them was that they had finally come to resemble her. The American soldiers she met— and she met them all—had none of the reserve of doughboys, none of the hesitancy; "they talked and they listened and they had a sureness, they were quite certain of themselves, they had no doubts or uncertainties and they had not to make any explanations" (251). The sureness, the poise bordering on arrogance—this was the face Stein herself presented to the world, and as she continued to "meditat[e]," she discovered new similarities: "That is the great change in the Americans, they are interested, they are observant, they are accustomed to various types of people and ways of being, they have plenty of curiosity, but not any criticism" (252). All the G.I.s were aware of it; they told her it had to do with the Depression, which destroyed old illusions. But Stein had another explanation, one that made American maturity a mirror image of her own. Unlike other countries, which had developed distinctive languages, America had to use a borrowed one, even after it had its own "habits [and] feelings" (259). The long American search for identity was thus bound up with language; Americans asserted their freedom "by choosing words which they liked better than other words, by putting words next to each other in a different way than the English way, by shoving the language around" (259). The process had accelerated during the First World War and the Depression, and now it was done: "the G.I. Joes have this language that is theirs, they do not have to worry about it, they dominate their language and in dominating their language which is now all theirs they have ceased to be adolescents and have become men" (259). Americans gained maturity, that is, by emulating Stein's career—by rejecting, distorting, and finally dominating traditional language in a form that was distinctly theirs. In listening to them talk, watching them at the train depot, swapping stories and cheap novels, Stein was seeing herself. Twenty years before, she had asserted that war "advanced... recognition" (*C* 521); now, as her last war ended, Stein had recognized herself. She had become a *typos*, an exemplary American.

With that apprehension, Stein completed the course of self-overcoming mapped out by Nietzsche in *Ecce Homo*. She, too, had confronted the monstrous Other in the guise of the Germans, who had violated not only her houses in Culoz and Paris, but her very art. Possessed by a posthumous fear, she was soon forced to acknowledge the presence of death in herself—the corpse of the father within the living female. And just as writing, for Nietzsche, became the uncanny embodiment of this Other, so for Stein, writing and war coincided in tableaux as frightening as they were commonplace. Faced with this obliteration of self, Nietzsche embraced a more comprehensive identity that saw all his labors as Dionysian; so Stein read her life into time, recovering herself in the eternal recurrence of war. But just as Nietzsche's achievement was incomplete—his spirit distorted by the occupiers of France—so was Stein's epiphany a partial one. There is a photograph of her, in James R. Mellow's superb biography, taken a few months before her death. She sits rather woodenly in a lounge chair, facing a wooden Alice Toklas several yards away, and between them a row of G.I.s casually draped across a stone wall overlooking hills. The two women seem almost ill at ease, as if conscious of their belatedness, afraid to claim what the soldiers had taken by force; for they were sitting in Hitler's furniture. The American army had taken them on a Liberation tour, and stopped to visit the Berghof, Hitler's mountain retreat. There is an eerie serenity to the image: the easy mastery of the soldiers, almost unaware of the camera, balanced by Stein's formal pose, as if the mind of the artist had arranged the scene. Her sense of form brought them to life, these massed Americans, and they, in turn, sustained her in this savage refuge where only months before she would have been murdered. The balance, the calm, the anonymous audience, and the hidden terror—all were part of this late portrait, a coda to a career. And yet there is no closure, no sense of security here; for Stein is not situated in the photograph. She neither belongs with the liberators, nor can she be dissociated from them. They are gregarious and easy, largely in shadow; she remains formal and isolated, bathed in light; and it is they, not she, who have faced down death. Indeed, the image suggests that their places ought to be reversed. Wedged in her easy chair, she, not the soldiers, continues to straddle a boundary, the margin between freedom and fear.

"Writing," observes Roland Barthes, "is [a] compromise between freedom and remembrance."[55] The physical distance Gertrude Stein put between herself and her country signifies her fierce struggle for freedom—for a language divorced from tense and a literature divorced from history. In part, she wrote with the urgency of denial, sweeping aside all evidence of loss, of memory, and change; in part she wrote with that superior acuity that sensed the drift of her age. Above all, Stein wrote to bridge those discontinuities she saw throughout the modern world. She had begun her career by exploding all the old unities, even that of intelligibility, and ended by asserting, as she had in her lectures, that her work had become "classic." Only thus could this stubborn isolate acknowledge what another "Conservative Anarchist" had once taken for his code. "We are all . . . shifting symbols of the same unity," wrote Henry Adams, the "varying forms" of a single soul.[56]

Conclusion

Gertrude Stein's discovery that autobiography confers glory was not her only lesson to successors, many of whom have written multiple versions of their lives. Like Stein, Lillian Hellman became a best-selling author in three late autobiographies. Maya Angelou has written five; W. E. B. Du Bois published four autobiographical works at twenty-year intervals; and Mary McCarthy, in *How I Grew*, recently returned to a Catholic girlhood first examined more than three decades ago. Then, too, these writers share Stein's suspicion—at times scorn—of audience, as they attempt to define themselves against hostile Others. Hellman's texts, for example, chart a course of increasing rebellion, culminating in Stalinism and the cool defiance of *Scoundrel Time*. Angelou repeatedly proves the hostility of whites in her long journey from Arkansas to Ghana, where Du Bois, too, had taken refuge from American "lying, stealing, and killing."[1] Indeed, even Stein's uneasiness with the past now seems prescient. McCarthy's *Memories of a Catholic Girlhood* is a study in the treacheries of recollection; Hellman's autobiographical portraits in *Pentimento* often adopt a plotted, quasi-fictional stance, and her last published work, *Maybe*, abandons autobiography for the kind of loosely associative structure Stein used in *Ida*. What, then, has become of the millennial strain in American autobiography? Has a cultural center survived somehow, to be incorporated, however obliquely, in these attenuated lives, or is the notion of an American *typos* another of those twentieth-century casualties, like evolution and Esperanto, killed quite dead by empire and world war?

One's initial response is that the very notion of an integral self has succumbed to the forces Nietzsche foresaw more than a century ago. McCarthy's almost ritual uncertainty in *Memories of a Catholic Girlhood*,[2] for example, suggests the alienating power of a textual corpus, sharpened by the sense that all writing is a kind of lie. Hence the fragmentary nature of the narrative—brief, evocative vignettes in which the writer tries to recall her youth in a series of barren settings: the ominously palatial home of the McCarthy grandparents and the prison-like orphanage of Uncle Myers; the repressive convent and seminary; the Prestons' Seattle house, which "you would have thought . . . empty when everyone was home" (229), and the Bents' house in Montana, "the middle of nowhere" (176). Amid such aridity language itself ceases to signify, and McCarthy details her repeated perplexity as texts turn against her. Uncle Myers punishes her for a prize essay, "lest I become stuck-up" (63), and pockets the prize money. In Forest Ridge Convent her desire for attention mushrooms into theological debates over faith, in which the priests inexplicably accuse her of reading atheistic literature (122); her classmates assign her an inscrutable nickname, which turns her "into an outsider" (135). A later identification with the Diviciacus of Caesar's *Commentaries* revealed the treachery of "the archetypal quisling" (159)—a treachery McCarthy increasingly assigns to her own self-justifying texts. Returning from Montana, she puzzles over the lies she must tell her grandfather: "Were there mountains [in Yellowstone] . . . ? What tribes of Indians? What kind of rock? Did we stay in a hotel or camp out and if so, where? . . . The paucity of my information made me conscious of the enormity of the deception I was going to have to put over" (187). That Preston, sensing the deception, asked few questions only sharpened McCarthy's uncertainty, as all authority returned to that impenetrable vacancy later claimed by his wife. "She recognized the faces," the autobiographer wrote of her senile grandmother perusing photographs, "but she was vague about the names. 'My father,' she decided after studying an obituary photograph of Grandpa, clipped out of a newspaper. 'Son,' 'husband,' and 'father' were all one to her" (195–96). The old woman's failing memory is symbolic of McCarthy's struggle with the fragments of her own irrecoverable past.[3]

In Nietzsche's heroic revision the autobiographer masters severe doubt by reading himself into history; his texts all denote the effloration of a sustaining self. McCarthy undertakes the reading, but doubts the result. Repeatedly, in the editorial afterthoughts, she is forced back on the word "lie." "There are several dubious points in this memoir," she writes of "Yonder Peasant, Who is He?" (47). "The Blackguard" is "highly fictionalized"; "true in substance, but the details have been invented or guessed at" (97). Even so authentic a story as "C'est le Premier Pas Qui Coûte" bristles with inaccuracies, so much so "that I find it almost impossible to sort out the guessed-at and the half-remembered from the undeniably real" (124). These doubts, McCarthy recognizes, are in part the result of her orphanhood and the train of contradictory authorities who took her parents' place. But this, too, is a partial truth, for one sees the same disclaimers in the work of a more privileged rebel whose best fiction explored the continuity of generations—Lillian Hellman.

In the introduction to her collected autobiographies, published in 1979, Hellman, too, wrestles with truth, claiming that some of the texts "seem to have been written by a woman I don't know very well," and that she had often "kept much" from herself and might never know the truth.[4] Although Hellman's interchapters are more combative and self-justificatory than McCarthy's, one cannot escape the impression that her lapses are not merely the arrogant lies for which McCarthy chastised her. Just as McCarthy's conference with Madame MacIllvra (in which the woman inexplicably interprets a bleeding cut as a sign of menstruation) becomes an emblem for the maternal warmth the girl both needed and feared,[5] so the young Hellman's running away becomes a descent into the terrors of sexuality. When the lock of a boy's hair broke the wristwatch she stuffed it into, Hellman left home rather than face her father's anger, passing through foul bathrooms and brothels, fouling herself with urine, vomit, and finally menstrual blood as she comes of age. The first night she hid in an oversized doll house; her father found her in a flophouse (*UW* 30–39). That this account is no less—or more—shaped than McCarthy's points to an ineluctable fact of autobiography Hellman affirmed shortly before her death: "*What I have written is the truth as I saw it, but the truth as I saw it, of course, doesn't have much to do with the truth. It's as if I have fitted parts of a picture puzzle and then a child overturned it and threw out some pieces.*"[6] The impossibility of recovering all the pieces suggests the limits of autobiographical revision.

But there may be other reasons, more powerful than contemporary *Angst*, to explain the lacunae in these autobiographies: the absence of sustained narrative may indicate social oppression. As Estelle Jelinek and others have argued, the review of *public* works—career, publications, conquests—is a function of autobiographies written by men permitted to engage in such activities; the more oblique structures of many women's autobiographies reflect what Patricia Spacks calls "selves in hiding."[7] Indeed, one of the sustained tensions in the autobiographies of McCarthy, Hellman, Angelou, and Du Bois involves images of constraint and release, echoing the writers' struggle to control their bodies in a hostile world. Hellman's escape into New Orleans, announced by her huddling in a "ridiculous small" doll house and ending with her passing blood, "dizzy and nauseated" in a strange room (*UW* 31, 37), suggests her futile desire to purge herself of oppressive influences. Similarly, in *Pentimento*, the young Hellman, attacked by a cousin on a staircase, is overcome by a sneezing fit, the "violent" force of which drove the boy away (364). In like manner, McCarthy reopened a cut in order to quiet the absurd Madame MacIllvra, and during her Montana trip vomited repeatedly as she found herself prodded in automobiles or pinned beneath strange arms in a strange bed (182). For these women, power is but another kind of lie.

Most emphatic in this regard is Maya Angelou, whose childhood struggles with the rigid South are manifest in her inability to control bodily functions. As *I Know Why the Caged Bird Sings* opens, she is running from church, embarrassed by her gangly black features exaggerated by a hand-sewn dress, unsuccessfully attempting to hold her urine. "I knew I'd have to let it go," she recalls, "or it would probably run right back up to my head and my poor head would burst like a dropped watermelon, and all the brains and spit and tongue and eyes would roll all over the place."[8] Yet the punishment that would certainly follow release was no less terrifying. A similar fantasy emerges at her high school graduation, when the appalling prospect of racism triggers visions of holocaust, "a pyramid of flesh with the whitefolks on the bottom, as the broad base, then the Indians with their silly tomahawks, ... the Negroes with their mops and recipes and cotton sacks and spirituals sticking out of their mouths" (153). Such visions of release, however, proved just as impotent as capitulation. With her brother Bailey, who once explained that when frightened "his soul just crawled behind his heart and curled up and went to sleep" (166), she flees to California; yet, after wider wandering at sea and on the Southern Pacific Railroad, Bailey ends in the prison he could never elude. The Veil, as Du Bois called it, shadowed his every move.

But Angelou's was not a case, as it was so often for Douglass, of an impotent petitioning of white codes. Rather, each of these writers takes radical action—McCarthy and Hellman through leftist causes, Angelou through Nkrumah and Malcolm X, and Du Bois, as an old man, through communism. "Democratic government in the United States has almost ceased to function," he wrote shortly before renouncing his American citizenship. "We are ruled by those who control wealth and who by that power buy or coerce public opinion" (*A* 57). Under such conditions it may well be impossible to speak of a revisionary *typos* or national soul. Du Bois himself would seem to be proof of the collapse of millennial identity. Born in Massachusetts, educated at Fisk, Harvard, and Berlin, enjoying a life that spanned Reconstruction and the civil rights movement, he could well have portrayed himself, like Douglass, as an exemplar of national progress. Instead he projects a stubborn independence, divorcing himself from almost every American institution he joined—Wilberforce College, the University of Pennsylvania, Atlanta University (twice), the NAACP (twice)—and ending an embittered expatriate:

> There was a day when the world rightly called Americans honest even if crude; earning their living by hard work; telling the truth no matter whom it hurt; and going to war only in what they believed a just cause after nothing else seemed possible.... today we use science to help us deceive our fellows; we take wealth that we never earned and we are devoting all our energies to kill, maim and drive insane, men, women, and children who dare refuse to do what we want done. No nation threatens us. We threaten the world. (*A* 415)

This bald diatribe, coming at the end of his last autobiography, seems finally to qualify Nietzschean revision as the property of a white Western European male, comfortable with his culture if not with his country. Nietzsche's remedy may have nothing to do with that culture's victims.

And yet there are unmistakable signs, in these autobiographies, that the millennial *typos* survives, albeit in radically altered form. Unchanged, apparently, is the very need to return to autobiography, to make the repeated text the site of self-authentication. Hence McCarthy, the most obsessive doubter among these writers, is also the most obsessive reviser, having culled the chapters of *Catholic Girlhood* from previously published work, revised them, and commented on the revisions. Hellman, too, whose autobiographical project seems to decay from chronological overview, to diary fragments, to thematic vignettes, publishes reflections on her initial reflections, relentlessly pursuing themes of rebellion, betrayal, and trust. Angelou turns her life into an autobiographical project, prompting one to ask, in the manner of Paul de Man, whether the self is the ground or the consequence of the project. But the lie—the possibility that the textual self may fragment into a heap of broken images—is no necessary compromise of revisionary self-fashioning; for it allows, as I suspect Hellman discovered, an expansion of one's narrow significance toward larger themes. The range of Hellman's portraits in the three autobiographies in effect gives a harried era an image of its evasions. Ever moving between extremes—New York and New Orleans, Hollywood and Moscow, Cambridge and Berlin—she surveys all the centers of radical activity and finds them wanting. Even in Madrid, which she later calls the last line of resistance to Hitler, and with Russian troops in Poland, she manages to be obtuse about history—the big moments Hemingway craved—while capturing those silent alternatives the combatants missed. In Madrid she recovers China bottles and a photograph from a bombed apartment; "I have carried them with me to many houses for many years" (*UW* 116). She would rather remain in a quiet forest than push with the Russians toward Warsaw. She retains the image of a woman in nanny's uniform with a fur-coated child moving slowly past a bombed Lublin building (*UW* 167). The images coincide with what she most approves in her ruinous and eccentric friends: the ability to remain compassionate amid chaos. As such, Hellman, manages to combine her sharp anger, in the manner of a Douglass or Woolman, with a saving alternative.

That alternative is equally crucial to the work of Maya Angelou, whose recorded life provides a panorama of black American selves. Much like Douglass, she embraces all facets of black life, from the segregated South to the postwar industrial North and West; from cook, waitress, and prostitute to poet, dancer, and journalist. She is with Martin Luther King in New York and with Malcolm X in Ghana; is courted by a Greek sailor and a New York bail bondsman, by a Malian millionaire and a South African revolutionary. She performs in Paris and Cairo, in San Francisco, and on Broadway. In effect, her journey is one long flight from Stamps, that racist enclave where her most basic needs were stifled, including the need for language. It was in Stamps that she could not openly acknowledge Shakespeare, her "first white love" (*CB* 11), for fear of offending her rigid grandmother, and in Stamps that she expressed her shock at the world's betrayal by remaining silent for months after an incestuous rape; Stamps where, some years later, she was nearly lynched for berating a white sales clerk. That defiance continues to goad her whenever she faces arbitrary restraint. In Yugoslavia, for example, courted by a quaint admirer, she challenges travel restrictions by recalling her background: "I was myself. That is, I was Marguerite Johnson, from Stamps, Arkansas, from the General Merchandise Store and the C. M. E. Church. I was the too tall, unpretty colored girl who had been born to unhappy parents and raised in the dirt roads of Arkansas."[9] In a Cairo news bureau, confronted by the hostility of African men, she consoles herself with a childhood tale of Brer Rabbit's wit.[10] And, in pointed contrast to the impoverished hospitality of Stamps blacks pinched by racism, she describes the generosity of Ghanian villagers in calm control of their destiny.[11] Her past is both a burden and a bond.

These contradictory needs for escape and return collide during a protest in Ghana after the death of Du Bois. Although black Americans could live out their lives in "mother Africa," Angelou realized, they must remain expatriates. In America

> we had learned to live on the head of burnt matches, and sleep in holes in the ground. In Arkansas and Chattanooga, Tennessee, we had decided to be no man's creature. . . . We had learned the power of power in Chicago, and met in Detroit insatiable greed. We had our first loves in the corn brakes of Mississippi, in the cotton fields of Georgia we experienced the thundering pleasure of sex, and on 125th Street and 7th Avenue in Harlem the Holy Spirit called us to be His own. (*AGC* 127)

Angelou experiences the same difficulties with community that Douglass felt in America. But whereas Douglass struggled to unite the contradictory elements of a divided society, Angelou seeks unity in an encompassing black world—and finds it. At a village in Ghana she has an uncanny sense of return. Everything disturbs her: Keta's bridge seems inexplicably terrifying, a report of the coastline's erosion makes her stifle tears, and she is frightened in the village market. Wherever she turns, she encounters African women unnerved at the very sight of her, demanding to see her passport and wailing in sudden grief. The explanation that she is "someone else" (*AGC* 204)—no kin—does not satisfy, and at length she understands: the villagers had recognized a fellowship that stretched back three hundred years, when Angelou's ancestors had been sold into slavery. "And here in my last days in Africa," she concludes, "descendants of a pillaged past saw their history in my face and heard their ancestors speak through my voice" (207). The wandering expatriate becomes a sign of community.

Angelou, that is to say—at the current stage of her unfolding narrative—has reenacted the millennial role in a new key. Sensing otherness as a condition of her American experience, she embraces ever wider black communities until she discovers her true origin, a village compassionate and dignified in a manner Stamps could never achieve. That the recognition should come in Ghana following Du Bois's death is another of those elements that bring autobiography so close to fiction, for it was Du Bois, preeminently, who defined Angelou's role. Explicity identifying himself with black American history, Du Bois seems almost reluctant to stand forth from the Veil. His reminiscences in *The Souls of Black Folk* are concealed in sociological treatments of rural education, the black church, or the black university. *Darkwater* interleaves occasional self-revelations and an extended discussion of his ancestors with fiction and poetry, blurring autobiography, and *Dusk of Dawn*, in which the revelations are more extensive, remains "the autobiography of a concept of race."[12] In part this is necessary modesty, for Du Bois was acutely conscious of another veil, that separating the highly trained intellectual from common folk. "I sit with Shakespeare and he winces not," he writes in heightened, almost precious prose. "Across the color line I move arm in arm with Balzac and Dumas, where smiling men and welcoming women glide in gilded halls....I summon Aristotle and Aurelius and what soul I will, and they come all graciously with no scorn nor condescension."[13] His epigraphic wedding, in *The Souls of Black Folk*, of fragments from Goethe, Swinburne, and spirituals attests to a formidable range very few of his contemporaries could match. So long as he remained in America he argued forcibly for the mass; but his sense of isolation remained vivid. An Ivy League activist, he was an anomaly.

The conflict early assumed an ironic pattern. In his *Autobiography* Du Bois recounts increasingly ambitious projects—the study of a Philadelphia ward, a rural Georgia town, the Atlanta region, the entire South—only to see them fall to bureaucratic infighting or jealousy over his prominence. Twice the problem arises at Atlanta University, where Du Bois presided over a series of sixteen sociological studies designed not only to yield decennial "photographs" of black Americans but "to make the laws of social living clearer, surer, and more definite" (*A* 217). Friction with Booker T. Washington, however, to whom the university trustees deferred, killed not only the project but Du Bois's connection with the school. He returned in the 1940s with even bigger plans for "a continuous and intensive study of the Negroes of each Southern State," "becoming, as funds and facilities increase, more and more intensive and comprehensive, until at last it virtually means a checking of every Negro family...including their activities, institutions and organizations" (*A* 314, 315). Yet on the verge of the plan's inauguration, Du Bois was abruptly retired, probably because of the young college president's petty jealousy. The pattern is repeated in the NAACP, where Du Bois builds *The Crisis* into a national voice but is chastised for his editorial positions, and during the McCarthy era, when his efforts on behalf of world peace earn him a federal indictment. The action drives him overseas; but as he attacks America, he cannot help enacting its rituals. Now a citizen of the communist—non-imperialist—world, he attempts once again to subsume humanity within his formidible intellect, proposing to Khrushchev a Soviet institute "for the study of Pan-African history, sociology, ethnography, anthropology and all cognate studies," conducting research "into all the activities, past and present, of the peoples of Africa" (*A* 33–34). Combining an almost breathtaking faith in scientific study with an equally breathtaking faith in himself, Du Bois could justify the entire enterprise on universal claims: that all knowledge, like all Africa, was one.

But this visionary desire for community, however hostile to America itself, remains firmly within the American orbit. For as Du Bois glories in his communist brethren around the world—the industrious Russians and Slovaks and Chinese who accept him without prejudice—he is projecting an old national dream upon a wider audience. The people, capable of infinite growth in an indefinitely progressive future, "walk and boast":

> they follow their leaders because these leaders have never deceived them. Their officials are incorruptible, their merchants are honest, their artisans are reliable, their workers who dig and haul and lift do an honest day's work and even work overtime if their state asks it, for they are the state. (*A* 51)

Despite Du Bois's denials, this evocation of China is thoroughly utopian—less in the manner of Marx than of Franklin. The virtuous order of modest tastes, hard work, and just rewards, the order in which intellectuals would be the true aristocrats (36), survives intact from Great Barrington, freed of its capitalist incrustrations. As he seeks community, the harried democrat confirms an ethos. The isolate becomes a universal soul.

Notes

EPIGRAPH

1. Cited in Avrom Fleishman, *Figures of Autobiography: The Language of Self-Writing in Victorian England* (Berkeley: University of California Press, 1983), p. 4.

CHAPTER 1

1. "Drafts for a Critique of Historical Reason," in *Selected Writings*, ed. and trans. H. P. Rickman (Cambridge: Cambridge University Press, 1976), p. 215.

2. *Autobiography: Essays Theoretical and Critical* (Princeton: Princeton University Press, 1980). Parenthetical references in the main text are to this edition.

3. For another version of this theme, see Olney's *Metaphors of Self: The Meaning of Autobiography* (Princeton: Princeton University Press, 1972), pp. 6, 34. See also Jonathan Loesberg, "Autobiography as Genre, Act of Consciousness, Text," *Prose Studies* 4:2 (September 1981): 169–85; Candace Lang, "Autobiography in the Aftermath of Romanticism," *Diacritics* 12:4 (Winter 1982): 2–4 and passim; Paul Jay, "What's the Use? Critical Theory and the Study of Autobiography," *Biography* 10:1 (Winter 1987): 43 and passim; and Janet Varner Gunn, *Autobiography: Toward a Poetics of Experience* (Philadelphia: University of Pennsylvania Press, 1982), pp. 3–8.

4. "Drafts for a Critique of Historical Reason," p. 215. See also Russell Reising, *The Unusable Past: Theory and Study of American Literature* (New York: Methuen, 1986), esp. pp. 13–37. Olney's approach is a good example of what Frank Lentricchia has called "the antihistorical impulses of formalist theories of literary criticism" (*After the New Criticism* [Chicago: University of Chicago Press, 1980], p. xvi).

5. For the figure of the labyrinth as it relates to autobiography, see Jacques Derrida, *The Ear of the Other: Otobiography, Transference, Translation*, ed. Christie V. McDonald, trans. Peggy Kamuf (New York: Schocken, 1985), p. 11.

Olney's "metaphors" are more ontological than linguistic; his emphasis in *Metaphors of Self* is on "the focus through which an intensity of self-awareness becomes a coherent vision of all reality, the point through which the individual succeeds in making the universe take on his own order" (30).

6. See Benveniste's essays "The Nature of Pronouns," p. 219, and "Subjectivity and Language," pp. 223, 226, in *Problems in General Linguistics*, trans. Mary E. Meek (Coral Gables: University of Miami Press, 1971). See also Roland Barthes, "To Write: An Intransitive Verb?" in *The Structuralist Controversy: The Languages of Criticism and the Sciences of Man*, ed. Richard Macksey and Eugenio Donato (Baltimore: Johns Hopkins University Press, 1972), p. 140. See also Derrida's response, p. 155.

7. Michel Foucault, "What Is an Author?" trans. James Venit, *Partisan Review* 42:4 (1975): 609.

8. *Ecce Homo*, vol. 6, pt. 3, of *Nietzsche Werke: Kritische Gesamtausgabe*, ed. Giorgio Colli and Mazzino Montinari (Berlin: Walter de Gruyter, 1969), p. 266; my translation. Parenthetical references (denoted *KG*) in the main text are to this edition.

9. Critics assuming the subject's unity include Barret John Mandel, "Full of Life Now," in *Autobiography: Essays Theoretical and Critical*, ed. Olney, pp. 73–83, and "The Autobiographer's Art," *Journal of Aesthetics & Art Criticism* 27:1 (Fall 1968): 215–26; Elizabeth Bruss, *Autobiographical Acts: The Changing Situation of a Literary Genre* (Baltimore: Johns Hopkins University Press, 1976); William Howarth, "Some Principles of Autobiography," in *Autobiography*, ed. Olney, pp. 84–114; and Roy Pascal, *Design and Truth in Autobiography* (Cambridge, MA: Harvard University Press, 1960).

Those assuming multiplicity include Michel Foucault, "What Is an Author?" 603–19; Roland Barthes, "The Death of the Author," in *Image Music Text*, trans. Stephen Heath (New York: Hill and Wang, 1977), pp. 142–48, *Writing Degree Zero and Elements of Semiology*, trans. Annette Lauers and Colin Smith (1953; rpt. Boston: Beacon Press, 1967), and *Roland Barthes*, trans. Richard Howard (New York: Hill & Wang, 1977); Jeffrey Mehlman, *A Structural Study of Autobiography: Proust, Leiris, Sartre, Lévi-Strauss* (Ithaca: Cornell University Press, 1974); and (in a change of heart) Bruss, "Eye for I: Making and Unmaking Autobiography in Film," in *Autobiography*, ed. Olney, pp. 296–320.

Critics advocating difference include Derrida, *The Ear of the Other*, and "Coming into One's Own," in *Psychoanalysis and the Question of the Text: Selected Papers from the English Institute* (Baltimore: Johns Hopkins University Press, 1978), pp. 114–48; Paul de Man, "Autobiography as De-Facement," *MLN* 94:5 (December 1979): 919–30, *Allegories of Reading* (New Haven: Yale University Press, 1979), pp. 103–18, 160–87; Paul Jay, *Being in the Text: Self-Representation from Wordsworth to Roland Barthes* (Ithaca: Cornell University Press, 1984); Paul John Eakin, *Fictions in Autobiography: Studies in the Art of Self-Invention* (Princeton: Princeton University Press, 1985); William Beatty Warner, *Chance and the Text of Experience: Freud, Nietzsche, and Shakespeare's Hamlet* (Ithaca: Cornell University Press, 1986); Jonathan Loesberg, "Autobiography as Genre, Act of Consciousness, Text," *Prose Studies* 4:2 (September 1981): 169–85; Rodolphe Gasché, "Self-Engendering as a Verbal Body," *MLN* 93:4 (May 1978): 677–94; Louis Marin, "The Autobiographical Interruption: About Stendhal's *Life of Henri Brulard*," *MLN* 93:4 (May 1978): 597–617.

For another—by far the largest—group of critics, the problem of the subject is less decisive than the cultural disclosures of autobiography, an approach that stems from the work of Dilthey and Georg Misch. These writers treat the relation of texts to culture precisely as advocates of unity treat the relation of subject to text: language becomes a transparent medium, disclosing the prior dominance of historical subjects. Studies in this group include Alfred Kazin, "The Self as History: Reflections on Autobiography," in *The American Autobiography: A Collection of Critical Essays*, ed. Albert Stone (Englewood Cliffs, NJ: Prentice-Hall, 1981), pp. 31–43; Robert Sayre, "The Proper Study: Autobiographies in American Studies," *American Quarterly* 29:3 (Bibliographical Issue 1977): 241–58; Karl Weintraub, "Autobiography and Historical Consciousness," *Critical Inquiry* 1:4 (June 1975): 821–48, and *The Value of the Individual: Self and Circumstance in Autobiography* (Chicago: University of Chicago Press, 1978); Patricia Meyer Spacks, "Stages of Self: Notes on Autobiography and the Life Cycle," in *The American Autobiography*, ed. Stone, pp. 11–30; Janet Varner Gunn, *Autobiography*; Mutlu Konuk Blasing, *The Art of Life: Studies in American Autobiographical Literature* (Austin: University of Texas Press, 1977); Georges Gusdorf, "Conditions and Limits of Autobiography," in *Autobiography*, ed. Olney, pp. 28–48.

10. Quoting Kierkegaard, *Repetition* (1941; rpt. New York: Harper and Row, 1964), p. 126.

11. *On the Genealogy of Morals: A Polemic*, trans. Walter Kaufmann (New York: Random House, 1967), I.13, p. 45.

12. *The Will to Power*, trans. Walter Kaufmann and R. J. Hollingdale (New York: Random House, 1968), §488, p. 270. Parenthetical references (denoted *WP*) in the text are to this paperback edition.

13. "The Question of Self in Nietzsche During the Axial Period (1882–1888)," *Boundary 2* 9:3 & 10:1 (Spring/Fall 1981): 56.

14. *Beyond Good and Evil: Prelude to a Philosophy of the Future*, trans. R. J. Hollingdale (Harmondsworth: Penguin, 1973), §231, p. 143; *Thus Spoke Zarathustra: A Book for Everyone and No One*, trans. R. J. Hollingdale (Harmondsworth: Penguin, 1961), p. 62; *Beyond Good and Evil*, §231, p. 143. Parenthetical references to *Zarathustra* (denoted *Z*) and to *Beyond Good and Evil* (denoted *BGE*) in the text are to these paperback editions.

15. *Ecce Homo: How One Becomes What One Is*, trans. Walter Kaufmann (New York: Random House, 1967), pp. 287–88. Parenthetical references (denoted *EH*) in the main text are to this paperback edition.

16. Students of Nietzsche reflect the same approaches to subjectivity as do critics of autobiography. Those advocating unity as the goal of historical development include Corngold, "The Question of Self"; Alexander Nehemas, *Nietzsche: Life as Literature* (Cambridge, MA: Harvard University Press, 1985); David Booth, "Nietzsche on 'The Subject as Multiplicity,' " *Man and World* 18:2 (1985): 121–46; and Joan Stambaugh, *Nietzsche's Thought of the Eternal Return* (Baltimore: Johns Hopkins University Press, 1972). Advocates of the subject as multiplicity include Werner Hamacher, " 'Disgregation of the Will': Nietzsche on the Individual and Individuality," in *Friedrich Nietzsche*, ed. Harold Bloom (New York: Chelsea House, 1987), 163–92; J. Hillis Miller, "The Disarticulation of Self in Nietzsche," *The Monist* 64 (1981): 247–61; and Michel Haar, "La critique nietzschéenne de la subjectivité," *Nietzsche Studien* 12 (1983): 80–110. Those seeing the Nietzschean subject as a resultant of difference include Hugh Silverman, "The Autobiographical Textuality of Nietzsche's *Ecce Homo*,"

Boundary 2 9:3 & 10:1 (Spring/Fall 1981): 141–51; Derrida, *The Ear of the Other*, pp. 3–19; William Beatty Warner, *Chance and the Text of Experience*; and Michael Ryan, "The Act," *Glyph 2: Johns Hopkins Textual Studies* (Baltimore: Johns Hopkins University Press, 1977), pp. 64–89. Rodolphe Gasché ("Autobiography as *Gestalt*: Nietzsche's *Ecce Homo*," *Boundary 2* 9:3 & 10:1 [Spring/Fall 1981]: 271–90) also adheres to this third view—with important qualifications. See below, notes 17 and 39.

17. See R. J. Hollingdale's preface to *Ecce Homo*, p. 7. Derrida maintains that the text challenges us to see life in a different way—as situated neither in a transcendent self nor in mere textuality, but on the border between them (*Ear*, p. 14). Gasché's subtler analysis (drawing in part on Derrida) claims that *Ecce Homo* portrays an alternative to Romantic autobiography by refusing to sanction the self as a function of consciousness and history. The "Nietzsche" of *Ecce Homo* is a "type" constantly overcoming itself, to be grasped, if at all, only through the deep structures of the unconscious ("Autobiography as *Gestalt*," pp. 281–87).

18. *The Ear of the Other*, p. 11.

19. *The Book of My Life*, trans. Jean Stoner (New York: Dutton, 1930).

20. *A History of Autobiography in Antiquity*, vol. 1 (London: Routledge & Kegan Paul, 1950), p. 7.

21. Nietzsche refers to Wagner in twenty-three of the text's seventy sections—and excised several more passages from the final draft. The best treatment of Nietzsche's complex relation with Wagner appears in Ronald Hayman, *Nietzsche: A Critical Life* (London: Weidenfeld and Nicolson, 1980), pp. 107 ff., and especially pp. 190–209. Hollingdale considers the break Nietzsche's second great crisis—the first attending his abandonment of theology in 1865; the third his break with Salomé in 1879; and the last, consummating in madness, in 1889 (*Nietzsche* [London: Routledge & Kegan Paul, 1973], pp. 44–45).

22. *Ecce Homo: Faksimileausgabe der Handschrift*, transkription von Anneliese Clauss (Wiesbaden: L. Reichert Verlag, 1985), p. 59, l. 22. Parenthetical references (denoted *MS*) in the text are to this edition. References include page and line numbers.

23. The most sensitive treatment of the break with Salomé is William Warner's *Chance and the Text of Experience*, p. 116 ff. Warner views *Zarathustra* as "an act of defense, revenge, mourning, and revision" for the failed relationship (201). In a more general sense, one might see this revisionary impulse as a continuous one, associated with the autobiographical act itself.

24. See R. J. Hollingdale's introduction to *Thus Spoke Zarathustra*, pp. 28–29, for a strong, if suspect, statement of this contention.

25. I am indebted to Walter Kendrick for help in translating this and other manuscript fragments.

26. Cf. Derrida, *The Ear of the Other*, pp. 8–10.

27. *The Gay Science*, trans. Walter Kaufmann (New York: Random House, 1974), §337, pp. 268–69.

28. Sigmund Freud, "The 'Uncanny,' " in vol. 17, *The Standard Edition of the Complete Works of Sigmund Freud*, trans. James Strachey (London: Hogarth Press, 1955), p. 233. Definitions are drawn from this essay and from *Deutsches Wörterbuch von Jacob und Wilhelm Grimm* (1936; rpt. München: Deutschen Taschenbuch Verlag, 1984).

29. Derrida discusses the significance of the feminine in Nietzsche in *The*

Ear of the Other, pp. 16–18, and in *Spurs: Nietzsche's Styles*, trans. Barbara Harlow (Chicago: University of Chicago Press, 1979), where he links references to women to the undecidability of truth.

30. Gasché, from a slightly different standpoint, discusses the impossibility of self-engendering in Antonin Artaud's "The Theater and the Plague." See "Self-Engendering as a Verbal Body," 683–84 *et seq*.

31. Cf. Derrida, *Of Grammatology*, trans. Gayatri Spivak (Baltimore: Johns Hopkins University Press, 1976), pp. 141–64.

32. On the significance of Nietzsche's animal imagery in *Ecce Homo*, see Margo Norris, *Beasts of the Modern Imagination: Darwin, Nietzsche, Kafka, Ernst, and Lawrence* (Baltimore: Johns Hopkins University Press, 1985), pp. 73–98.

33. *Freud and Philosophy* (New Haven: Yale University Press, 1970), p. 411. The citation appears in Paul de Man, *Allegories of Reading*, p. 174.

34. For a different view of Nietzsche's rereading, stressing literary coherence, see Nehemas, *Nietzsche*, p. 195. See also Gunn, *Autobiography*, pp. 21–22.

35. Although, to my knowledge, no one has studied revision as a principle of autobiographical construction, several critics have considered aspects of the problem. For an appraisal of the multiple autobiographies of Frederick Douglass and Gertrude Stein, see G. Thomas Couser, *American Autobiography: The Prophetic Mode* (Amherst: University of Massachusetts Press, 1979), pp. 51–61, 148–63. Marc Eli Blanchard considers the "time of the subject writing" in "The Critique of Autobiography," *Comparative Literature* 34:2 (Spring 1982): 109, 111. Most sensitive is Paul John Eakin, who treats the revisions of Mary McCarthy, Henry James, and Jean Paul Sartre in pursuit of autobiographical fiction (*Fictions in Autobiography*, pp. 11–55, 88 ff., 128 ff.). Eakin, however, relies heavily on the psychoanalytic theories of Erik Erikson, for whom identity arises through a series of life crises not easily identifiable in many autobiographies. His model emphasizes an evolving but essentially stable self, one that manipulates but masters its language.

36. See Ferdinande de Saussure, *Cours de linguistique générale*; edition critique, ed. Rudolf Engler (Wiesbaden: Otto Harrassowitz, 1967), 2:253, verso.

37. In "The Intoxicated Song," Zarathustra expresses this synecdochic relationship in universal terms:

> Did you ever say Yes to one joy? O my friends, then you said Yes to all woe as well. All things are chained and entwined together, all things are in love;
>
> if ever you wanted one moment twice, if ever you said: "You please me, happiness, instant moment!" then you wanted *everything* to return.
>
> (*Thus Spoke Zarathustra*, pp. 331–32)

38. Cf. Gilles Deleuze, *Nietzsche and Philosophy*, trans. Hugh Tomlinson (New York: Columbia University Press, 1983), pp. 39–72.

39. Although Gasché argues that Nietzsche deconstructs self-representation as type, by opposing Heracleitean becoming to Parmenidean being, he does not consider the divided nature of the *typos* itself, a division that may serve not necessarily the dissolution of subjectivity, but its constant fluctuation between self, text, and reader during the (re)production of the text. See "Autobiography as *Gestalt*," pp. 271, 274. See also Gasché, "*Ecce Homo* or the Written Body," *Oxford Literary Review* 7:1–2 (1985): 3–23.

40. Henry George Liddell, *Greek-English Lexicon* (1940; rpt. Oxford: Clarendon Press, 1961).

41. *The Ear of the Other*, p. 11.

42. "Autobiography as De-Facement," p. 921.

43. Dominick LaCapra, *Rethinking Intellectual History: Texts, Contexts, Language* (Ithaca: Cornell University Press, 1983), pp. 39, 44.

CHAPTER 2

1. *Autobiography and Literary Essays*, ed. John Robson and Jack Stillinger (Toronto: University of Toronto Press, 1981), p. 139. Parenthetical references (denoted *A*) in the text are to this edition.

2. *The Earlier Letters of John Stuart Mill, 1812–1848*, ed. Francis E. Mineka (Toronto: University of Toronto Press, 1963), p. 30.

3. *Democratic Vistas & The 1855 Preface to Leaves of Grass, Prose Works 1892*, vol. 2, ed. Floyd Stovall (New York: New York University Press, 1964), pp. 448, 449. Parenthetical references in the text are to this edition.

4. *Specimen Days, Prose Works 1892*, vol. 1, ed. Floyd Stovall (New York: New York University Press, 1963), p. 32. Parenthetical references (denoted *SD*) in the text are to this edition.

5. *The Correspondence*, ed. Haviland Miller (New York: New York University Press, 1961), 1:204, 205.

6. Although many critics have attested to the centrality of the mental crisis in the *Autobiography*, few have situated that crisis in Mill's recurring struggle to assert mastery in the text. For a general discussion of Mill's textual concerns see Eugene August, "Mill's *Autobiography* as Philosophic Commedia," *Victorian Poetry* 11:2 (Summer 1973): 143–62. Most discussions stress Mill's conduct with his father and wife, asserting that what he rejected in the former he rediscovered in the latter. See, for example, James Olney's *Metaphors of Self*, pp. 232–60, and Bruce Mazlish, *James and John Stuart Mill: Father and Son in the Nineteenth Century* (New York: Basic Books, 1975). Mazlish, following A. W. Levi ("The 'Mental Crisis' of John Stuart Mill," *Psychoanalytic Review* 32 [January 1945]: 86–101), explores Mill's Oedipal rebellion, suggesting that the infantile crisis colored all Mill's later life. For a countervailing, if incomplete, treatment of the *Autobiography* as a natural outcome of Mill's (largely passive) associational psychology, see Jonathan Loesberg, *Fictions of Consciousness: Mill, Newman, and the Reading of Victorian Prose* (New Brunswick, NJ: Rutgers University Press, 1986), pp. 46 ff.

7. For a similar discussion, see August, "Mill's *Autobiography*," p. 153.

8. Arthur Beatty, *William Wordsworth: His Doctrine and Art in Their Historical Relations, University of Wisconsin Studies in Language and Literature* 17: (1922), p. 109.

9. See Levi, "The 'Mental Crisis' of John Stuart Mill," and Mazlish, *James and John Stuart Mill*, esp. pp. 209–13.

10. Both Mazlish, pp. 224, 228, 229, and Loesberg, p. 56, suggest a similar point.

11. *Leaves of Grass: A Textual Variorum of the Printed Poems*, vol. 1: *Poems, 1855–1856* (New York: New York University Press, 1980), 4.75–79, p. 5. Parenthetical references in the text are to this edition.

12. *Allegories of Reading*, pp. 177–78.

13. Whitman's autobiography has received relatively little attention from critics. The best work has been done by William Aarnes, " 'Free Margins': Iden-

tity and Silence in Whitman's *Specimen Days*," *ESQ* 28:4 (1982): 243–60; and "Withdrawal and Resumption: Whitman and Society in the Last Two Parts of *Specimen Days*," *Studies in the American Renaissance* 1982, 401–32. See also Linck C. Johnson, "The Design of Walt Whitman's *Specimen Days*," *Walt Whitman Review* 21:1 (March 1975): 3–14; and Richard Chase, *Walt Whitman Reconsidered* (New York: William Sloane, 1955), pp. 166–76.

14. The structure was suggested by Aarnes, "Withdrawal and Resumption," p. 402. Aarnes, however, is primarily interested in the social significance of Whitman's experience. I stress the private consequences.

15. *Correspondence* 1:69.

16. Cited in *Walt Whitman's Civil War*, ed. Walter Lowenfels (New York: Knopf, 1960), p. 16. For other appraisals of Whitman's hospital experience, see Gay Wilson Allen, *The Solitary Singer: A Critical Biography of Walt Whitman* (New York: Macmillan, 1955), pp. 287 ff., and Justin Kaplan, *Walt Whitman: A Life* (New York: Simon and Schuster, 1980), pp. 278 ff.

17. *Correspondence* 1:81–82.

18. See Aarnes, "Withdrawal and Resumption," pp. 405 ff.; Allen, *Solitary Singer*, p. 479; and Kaplan, *Walt Whitman*, pp. 371 ff.

19. "Starting from Paumanok," *Leaves of Grass: A Textual Variorum of the Printed Poems*, vol. 2: *Poems 1860–1867*, ed. Scully Bradley, Harold Blodgett, Arthur Golden, William White (New York: New York University Press, 1980), 7.95–97, p. 278.

20. David Cavitch, in *My Soul and I: The Inner Life of Walt Whitman* (Boston: Beacon Press, 1985), offers a striking parallel to the *Döppelganger* who produced *Ecce Homo*. Just as Nietzsche bore the corpse of his father in the living body of his mother, so Whitman, struggling against a remote father (who died in 1855, shortly after the appearance of *Leaves of Grass*), claimed that "his mother produced the [early] poetry, writing through him in a creative process that he disclaimed as his own gift" (8). And, much like Nietzsche, Whitman's subsequent identification with his father proved "a crucial step in [his] emergence" as a mature poet (18–19).

21. For a reading of the *Autobiography* as transposed conversion, see Avrom Fleishman, *Figures of Autobiography*, pp. 138–54, and esp. pp. 144 ff.

22. See Owen Watkins, *The Puritan Experience; Studies in Spiritual Autobiography* (New York: Schocken, 1972), pp. 18–36 and passim; Charles Lloyd Cohen, *God's Caress: The Psychology of Puritan Religious Experience* (New York: Oxford University Press, 1986), pp. 137 ff.; Patricia Caldwell, *The Puritan Conversion Narrative: The Beginnings of American Expression* (Cambridge: Cambridge University Press, 1983), pp. 45–80 and passim; George Starr, *Defoe and Spiritual Autobiography* (Princeton: Princeton University Press, 1965), pp. 3–50; and Paul Delany, *British Autobiography in the Seventeenth Century* (London: Routledge & Kegan Paul, 1969), pp. 27–104.

23. Quoted in Watkins, *The Puritan Experience*, p. 231.

24. Raymond Williams, *The Long Revolution* (New York: Columbia University Press, 1961), p. 73. For additional citations see Starr, pp. 13 ff.; Watkins, pp. 226 ff.; and Delany, pp. 56, 89.

25. *Memoirs of the Life of David Ferris* (Philadelphia: Merrihew & Thompson, 1855), p. 20; Thomas Shepard, *Autobiography*, in *God's Plot; the Paradoxes of Puritan Piety; Being the Autobiography & Journal of Thomas Shepard*, ed. Michael McGiffert (Amherst: University of Massachusetts Press, 1972), p. 43; Richard Jordan, *A Journal of the Life and Religious Labours of Richard Jordan*, in

The Friends' Library (Philadelphia: Joseph Rakestraw, 1860), 12:316; Richard Rogers, *The Diary of Richard Rogers*, in *Two Elizabethan Puritan Diaries*, ed. M. M. Knappen (Chicago: American Society of Church History, 1933), p. 75. Parenthetical references to Shepard's *Autobiography* (denoted *A*) in the text are to this edition.

26. Quoted in Watkins, *The Puritan Experience*, pp. 12–13.

27. *The Puritan Origins of the American Self* (New Haven: Yale University Press, 1975), p. 19. For an alternative reading, stressing the cohesiveness implied by Puritan confessions, see Cohen, *God's Caress*, pp. 201 ff.

28. Morris Golden, *The Self Observed: Swift, Johnson, Wordsworth* (Baltimore: Johns Hopkins University Press, 1972), pp. 12 ff., 39 ff.

29. *"The Stranger Within Thee": Concepts of the Self in Late-Eighteenth-Century Literature* (Pittsburgh: University of Pittsburgh Press, 1980), pp. 24, 32.

30. *A Treatise on Human Nature and Dialogues Concerning Natural Religion*, ed. T. H. Green and T. H. Grose (London: Longmans Green, 1878), 1:534.

31. *The Prelude or The Growth of a Poet's Mind*, VIII 665–75, in *The Poetical Works of Wordsworth*, ed. Thomas Hutchinson, rev. Ernest de Selincourt (1904; rpt. London: Oxford University Press, 1964), p. 555.

32. Quoted in John Clubbe and Ernest J. Lovell, Jr., *English Romanticism: The Grounds of Belief* (De Kalb: Northern Illinois University Press, 1983), p. 138.

33. Quoted in Cox, *"The Stranger Within Thee,"* p. 133.

34. Golden, *The Self Observed*, p. 105.

35. Ibid., p. 142.

36. Quoted in Clubbe, *English Romanticism*, p. 138.

37. Quoted in Patricia Ball, *The Central Self: A Study in Romantic and Victorian Imagination* (London: Athlone Press, 1968), p. 20.

38. Ibid., p. 21.

39. *Past and Present*, Centenary Edition (London: Chapman and Hall, 1897), p. 146.

40. *On Liberty*, in *Utilitarianism, Liberty, and Representative Government* (New York: E. P. Dutton, 1957), pp. 159, 167, 173.

41. *Poetical Works*, ll. 62–65, 143–46, pp. 460, 461.

42. *Sartor Resartus*, Centenary Edition (London: Chapman and Hall, 1898), pp. 132, 151.

43. *Johnson's Wonder-Working Providence, 1628–1651*, ed. J. Franklin Jameson (New York: Charles Scribner's Sons, 1910), pp. 58–59.

CHAPTER 3

1. *The Parable of the Ten Virgins* (Boston: Doctrinal Tract and Book Society, 1852), p. 17. Parenthetical references (denoted *V*) in the text are to this edition.

2. For a reading of Shepard's intellectual life before and after the Migration, see Andrew Delbanco, "Thomas Shepard's America: The Biography of an Idea," *Studies in Biography* (Cambridge, MA: Harvard University Press, 1978), pp. 159–82.

3. *The Puritan Origins of the American Self*, p. 117.

4. *Spiritual Autobiography in Early America* (Princeton: Princeton University Press, 1968), pp. 145–46.

5. Recent studies of the psychology of conversion and grace, as embodied

in confessions, meditative handbooks, and the like, have stressed the growing confidence of saints. While it is undeniable that Shepard found great comfort in Christ, scrutiny of his texts (more accessible than his psyche) suggests the considerable repression such confidence cost. For a more benign view of Puritan spirituality, see Cohen, *God's Caress*, passim, and Charles Hambrick-Stowe, *The Practice of Piety: Puritan Devotional Disciplines in Seventeenth-Century New England* (Chapel Hill: University of North Carolina Press, 1982).

6. See Paul Christianson, *Reformers and Babylon: English Apocalyptic Visions from the Reformation to the Eve of the Civil War* (Toronto: University of Toronto Press, 1978), pp. 102 ff.

7. Quoted in Jesper Rosenmeier, " 'With My Owne Eyes': William Bradford's *Of Plymouth Plantation*," in *Typology and Early American Literature*, ed. Sacvan Bercovitch (Amherst: University of Massachusetts Press, 1972), pp. 82, 79–80.

8. *The Clear Sun-Shine of the Gospel Breaking Forth upon the Indians in New England* (1648), in *Collections of the Massachusetts Historical Society*, vol. 4, 3rd ser., 1843, p. 60.

9. Mason Lowance, *The Language of Canaan: Metaphor and Symbol in New England from the Puritans to the Transcendentalists* (Cambridge, MA: Harvard University Press, 1980), p. 17.

10. Quoted in Lowance, p. 49.

11. *A Brief Exposition with Practical observations upon the whole book of Canticles never before printed* (London: Ralph Smith, 1655), pp. 236–37, 222.

12. Ernest Tuveson, *Redeemer Nation: The Idea of America's Millennial Role* (Chicago: University of Chicago Press, 1968), p. 30. See also James Davidson, *The Logic of Millennial Thought: Eighteenth-Century New England* (New Haven: Yale University Press, 1977).

13. *The New England Mind: The Seventeenth Century* (1939; rpt. Cambridge, MA: Harvard University Press, 1954), pp. 478–79.

14. *An Apologie of the Churches in New-England for Church-Covenant* (London: Benjamin Allen, 1643), p. 5.

15. Rosenmeier, " 'With My Owne Eyes,' " p. 85.

16. Davidson, *The Logic of Millennial Thought*, pp. 97, 114.

17. *Ideology and Utopia: An Introduction to the Sociology of Knowledge* (1936; rpt. New York: Harcourt, Brace & World, 1968), p. 184.

18. See Norman Cohn, *The Pursuit of the Millennium: Revolutionary Millenarians and Mystical Anarchists in the Middle Ages* (1957; rpt. New York: Oxford University Press, 1970); Yonina Talmon, "Pursuit of the Millennium: The Relation between Religious and Social Change," *Archives Européens de Sociologie* 3:1 (1962): 625–48; Allan Graham, "A Theory of Millennialism: The Irvingite Movement as an Illustration," *British Journal of Sociology* 25:3 (September 1974): 296–311; Michael Barkun, *Disaster and the Millennium* (New Haven: Yale University Press, 1974).

19. George Rosen, "Emotion and Sensibility in Ages of Anxiety: A Historical Review," *American Journal of Psychiatry* 124: 6 (December 1967): 781; Talmon, "Pursuit of the Millennium," p. 136; Henri Desroche, *The Sociology of Hope*, trans. Carol Martin-Sperry (London: Routledge & Kegan Paul, 1979), p. 103; Barkun, *Disaster and the Millennium*, p. 56.

20. *The Day of Trouble Is Here* (Cambridge, MA: Marmaduke Johnson, 1674), p. 12. Parenthetical references in the text are to this edition.

21. See William McLoughlin, *Revivals, Awakenings, and Reform: An Essay on Religion and Social Change in America, 1607–1977* (Chicago: University of Chicago Press, 1978), p. xiv: "American history is ... best understood as a millennarian movement." Scholars have now documented that claim for nearly all periods of American history. For the seventeenth century, see Aletha Gilsdorf, "The Puritan Apocalypse: New England Eschatology in the Seventeenth Century" (Diss., Yale University, 1965); and James Holstun, *A Rational Millennium: Puritan Utopias of Seventeenth-Century England and America* (New York: Oxford University Press, 1987). For the eighteenth century, see Ruth Bloch, *Visionary Republic: Millennial Themes in American Thought, 1756–1800* (New York: Cambridge University Press, 1985); Nathan Hatch, *The Sacred Cause of Liberty: Republican Thought and the Millennium in Revolutionary New England* (New Haven: Yale University Press, 1977); and James Davidson, *The Logic of Millennial Thought*. For the nineteenth century, see James Moorhead, *American Apocalypse: Yankee Protestants in the Civil War* (New Haven: Yale University Press, 1978); and Ernest Tuveson, *Redeemer Nation*.

22. Quoted in Davidson, *The Logic of Millennial Thought*, pp. 145–46.

23. Aaron Burr, *The Watchman's Answer to the Question, What of the Night, &c.*, 3rd ed. (Boston: Kneeland, 1757), pp. 31, 32; Jonathan Parsons, *Sixty Sermons on Various Subjects* (Newbury-Port, MA: John Mycall, 1779–80), 1:380.

24. (Boston: Harris, 1692), p. 36.

25. *Things to be Looked for; Discourses on the Glorious Characters, with Conjecture on the Speedy Approaches of that State, Which is Reserved for the Church of God in the Later Dayes* ... (Boston: Samuel & Barth Green, 1691), p. 25.

26. Cited in Mason Lowance, "Typology and Millennial Eschatology in Early New England," *Literary Uses of Typology from the Late Middle Ages to the Present*, ed. Earl Miner (Princeton: Princeton University Press, 1977), p. 245.

27. "Cotton Mather," in *Major Writers of Early American Literature*, ed. Everett Emerson (Madison: University of Wisconsin Press, 1972), pp. 105, 143, 144.

28. Like Whitman's *Specimen Days*, the *Journal* is more than a series of "diary-scraps and memoranda." As a "public Friend," Woolman had a duty to address public incidents; hence his extended, often dry accounts of ministerial travels. Yet, as I shall try to show, the *Journal* contains a powerful subtext of private anxiety and doubt that sharply questions Woolman's official role. It is the tension between these two attitudes, I believe, that caused Woolman to revise so extensively—a tension that makes this work central to American autobiography.

29. William Hedges, "John Woolman and the Quaker Utopian Vision," in *Utopias: The American Experience*, ed. Gairdner Moment and Otto Kraushaar (Metuchen, NJ: Scarecrow Press, 1980), p. 97.

30. *The Kingdom of God in America* (1937; rpt. New York: Harper and Row, 1959), p. 134.

31. All citations are from Woolman's original manuscripts; following the parenthetical reference is the corresponding page in the authoritative edition by Phillips P. Moulton (New York: Oxford University Press, 1971). (Unlike Moulton, I have retained Woolman's original spelling and punctuation throughout.) Most citations are from the revised MS B (chapters 1–10) and from

MS S, both in the possession of the Friends Historical Library, Swarthmore College. Certain passages that Woolman neglected to transcribe are cited from MS A, in the possession of the Pennsylvania Historical Society. For a list of the *Journal's* various drafts, see Moulton, pp. 283–87.

32. Quoted in Janet Whitney, *John Woolman, American Quaker* (Boston: Little Brown, 1942), pp. 393–94.

33. *The Autobiography of Benjamin Franklin: A Genetic Text*, ed. J. A. Leo Lemay and P. M. Zall (Knoxville: University of Tennessee Press, 1981), p. 186. Parenthetical references in the text are to this edition.

CHAPTER 4

1. *The Literary Life of the Early Friends, 1650–1725* (New York: Columbia University Press, 1932), pp. 157, 158.

2. *Image Music Text*, p. 142.

3. D. H. Lawrence, *Studies in Classic American Literature* (New York: Thomas Seltzer, 1923), p. 19; J. A. Leo Lemay, "Benjamin Franklin," in *Major Writers of Early American Literature*, p. 240; James Sappenfield, *A Sweet Instruction: Franklin's Journalism as a Literary Apprenticeship* (Carbondale: Southern Illinois University Press, 1973), p. 204.

4. *The Evolution of American Society, 1700–1815: An Interdisciplinary Analysis* (Lexington, MA: D. C. Heath, 1973), pp. 96–98.

5. *Cities in the Wilderness: The First Century of Urban Life in America, 1625–1742* (New York: Ronald Press, 1938), pp. 221, 224, 226, 226.

6. Quoted in Bridenbaugh, *op. cit.*, pp. 226–27.

7. *The Papers of Benjamin Franklin*, ed. Leonard Larabee, William Wilcox, et al. (New Haven: Yale University Press, 1959–), 1:278. Parenthetical references (denoted *P*) in the text are to this edition.

8. "Corruption and Power in Provincial America," *The Development of a Revolutionary Mentality* (Washington, D.C.: Library of Congress, 1972), p. 63.

9. Quoted in Gordon Wood, *The Creation of the American Republic, 1776–1787* (Chapel Hill: University of North Carolina Press, 1969), pp. 95, 107.

10. *Cato's Letters* (London: T. Wilkins, T. Woodward, J. Walthoe, and J. Peele, 1723–24), 1:266.

11. Nathan Fiske, *Remarkable Providences to be Gratefully Recollected* (Boston: Thomas and John Fleet, 1776), p. 25.

12. *The Complete Works of Benjamin Franklin*, ed. Joel Bigelow (Boston: Charles Little and James Brown, 1851–56), 9:14.

13. Phillips Payson, *Sermon Preached Before the Honorable Council ... at Boston, May 27, 1778*, in *The Pulpit of the American Revolution: or, the Political Sermons of the Period of 1776*, ed. John W. Thornton (Boston: Gould and Lincoln, 1860), p. 337; Jonathan Mason, *An Oration Delivered March 6, 1780, at the Request of the Inhabitants of the Town of Boston, to Commemorate the Bloody Tragedy of the Fifth of March 1770* (Boston: John Gill, 1780), pp. 8–9; John Adams, *The Works of John Adams* (Boston: Little and Brown, 1851–56), 6:218.

14. Norman Fierig, "Benjamin Franklin and the Way to Virtue," *American Quarterly* 31:2 (Summer 1978): 213; Alfred Aldridge, *Benjamin Franklin and*

Nature's God (Durham, NC: Duke University Press, 1967), p. 53; Sacvan Bercovitch, "The Ritual of American Autobiography: Edwards, Franklin, Thoreau," *Revue Française d'Etudes Américaines* 7:14 (May 1982): 141, 142; Richard D. Brown, *Modernization: The Transformation of American Life, 1600–1865* (New York: Hill and Wang, 1976), p. 95.

15. Aldridge, *Benjamin Franklin and Nature's God*, p. 54.

16. Hugh Dawson, "Fathers and Sons: Franklin's 'Memoirs' as Myth and Metaphor," *Early American Literature* 14:3 (Winter 1979/80): 284.

17. Payson, *Sermon*, p. 342; Levi Hart, *Liberty Described and Recommended* (Hartford: Eben. Watson, 1775), p. 11; Wood, *The Creation of the American Republic*, pp. 59–60; Samuel Adams, *Writings of Samuel Adams*, ed. Henry Cushing (1907; rpt. New York: Octagon Books, 1968), 3:266; Smith cited in James Madison, *Madison Papers*, ed. William Hutchinson and William Rachal (Chicago: University of Chicago Press, 1962–85), 1:208.

18. *Cotton Mather and Benjamin Franklin: The Price of Representative Personality* (Cambridge: Cambridge University Press, 1984), p. 179.

19. Carl Bridenbaugh, *Cities in Revolt: Urban Life in America, 1743–1776* (New York: Knopf, 1955), p. 109.

20. Carl Becker, *The Heavenly City of the Eighteenth Century Philosophers* (New Haven: Yale University Press, 1932), p. 129; Sacvan Bercovitch, *The American Jeremiad* (Madison: University of Wisconsin Press, 1978), pp. 93–94, 111; Joseph Priestley, *An Essay on the First Principles of Government, and on the Nature of Political, Civil, and Religious Liberty* (London: J. Johnson, 1771), pp. 4–5.

21. Quoted in Adrienne Koch, ed., *The American Enlightenment: The Shaping of the American Experiment and a Free Society* (New York: George Braziller, 1965), p. 91. See also Robert Nisbet, *History of the Idea of Progress* (New York: Basic Books, 1980), p. 200.

22. *Poor Richard's Politics: Benjamin Franklin and His New American Order* (New York: Oxford University Press, 1965), p. 16.

23. Quoted in Bernard Bailyn, *The Ideological Origins of the American Revolution* (Cambridge, MA: Harvard University Press, 1967), p. 90.

24. Samuel Sherwood, *The Church's Flight into the Wilderness* (New York: S. Loudon, 1776), p. 44.

25. "Events in the Life and the Text: Franklin and the Style of American Autobiography," *Revue Française d'Etudes Américaines* 7:14 (May 1982): 193.

26. Breitwieser, *Cotton Mather and Benjamin Franklin*, pp. 265, 270.

27. "Benjamin Franklin, Cotton Mather, and the Outward State," *Early American Literature* 6:3 (Winter 1971–72): 228.

28. Davis, "Events in the Life and the Text," p. 144.

29. An important study of Franklin's shaping hand in the *Autobiography* is Robert Sayre's *The Examined Self: Benjamin Franklin, Henry Adams, Henry James* (Princeton: Princeton University Press, 1964).

30. "A Portrait of the Autobiographer as an Old Artificer," in *The Oldest Revolutionary: Essays on Benjamin Franklin*, ed. J. A. Leo Lemay (Philadelphia: University of Pennsylvania Press, 1976), pp. 57–58.

31. Sappenfield, *A Sweet Instruction*, p. 179.

32. Breitwieser, *Cotton Mather and Benjamin Franklin*, p. 171.

33. *Works* 1:66.

CHAPTER 5

1. *The Columbian Orator*, ed. Caleb Bingham, 2nd ed. (Boston: Manning and Loring, 1799), pp. 68, 64. Parenthetical references (denoted *CO*) in the text are to this edition.

2. *The Frederick Douglass Papers*, ed. John W. Blassingame, et al., 1st ser., vol. 2 (New Haven: Yale University Press, 1982). Parenthetical references (denoted *P*) in the text are to this edition.

3. *Our National Centennial Jubilee* (New York: E. B. Treat, 1876). Parenthetical references in the text are to this edition.

4. Philip Foner, *Essays in Afro-American History* (Philadelphia: Temple University Press, 1978), p. 141.

5. *The American Jeremiad*, p. 148.

6. *Narrative of the Life of Frederick Douglass, an American Slave; Written by Himself* (Boston: Anti-Slavery Society, 1846), pp. 39–40. Parenthetical references (denoted *N*) in the text are to this edition.

7. Dickson J. Preston, *Young Frederick Douglass: The Maryland Years* (Baltimore: Johns Hopkins University Press, 1980), pp. 100, 153; Philip Foner, *Frederick Douglass* (New York: Citadel Press, 1964), p. 18.

8. *My Bondage and My Freedom* (New York: Miller, Orton & Mulligan, 1855), p. 358. Parenthetical references (denoted *BF*) in the text are to this edition.

9. Quoted in Foner, *Frederick Douglass*, pp. 52, 58–59, 314.

10. *Roll, Jordan, Roll: The World the Slaves Made* (New York: Pantheon, 1974), pp. 437–38.

11. For a discussion of young Douglass's complicated relations with his white masters, see Preston, *Young Frederick Douglass*, pp. 54–56.

12. *Black Skin White Masks*, trans. Charles Markmann (1952; rpt. New York: Grove Press, 1967), p. 18.

13. *The Journey Back: Issues in Black Literature and Criticism* (Chicago: University of Chicago Press, 1980), pp. 31, 39, 43.

14. *Dissemination*, trans. Barbara Johnson (Chicago: University of Chicago Press, 1981), p. 77. Parenthetical references in the text are to this edition.

15. "The Dilemma of Frederick Douglass: The Slave Narrative as Literary Institution," *Essays in Literature* 10:2 (Fall 1983): 223.

16. *The Narrative of William W. Brown, a Fugitive Slave* (Reading, MA: Addison-Wesley, 1969), pp. 43, 46.

17. See John Thompson, *The Life of John Tompson, A Fugitive Slave; Containing His History of 25 Years in Bondage and His Providential Escape, Written by Himself* (New York: Negro Universities Press, 1968); J. W. C. Pennington, *The Fugitive Blacksmith, or Events in the History of James W. C. Pennington*, in *Great Slave Narratives*, ed. Arna Bontemps (Boston: Beacon Press, 1969); Josiah Henson, *The Life of Josiah Henson, Formerly a Slave, Now an Inhabitant of Canada, as Narrated by Himself* (Boston: Arthur D. Phelps, 1849), and *Truth Stranger than Fiction; Father Henson's Story of His Own Life* (1858; rpt. New York: Corinth Books, 1962); William and Ellen Craft, *Running a Thousand Miles for Freedom, or The Escape of William and Ellen Craft from Slavery*, in *Great Slave Narratives*. Parenthetical references to the Crafts' text are to this edition.

18. Several critics have stressed this important, if limited, aspect of Douglass's authority. See Albert Stone, "Identity and Art in Frederick Douglass's

Narrative," CLA Journal 17:2 (December 1973): 204–7; Robert Stepto, *From Behind the Veil: A Study of Afro-American Narrative* (Urbana: University of Illinois Press, 1979), pp. 16–26; Lucinda MacKethan, "From Fugitive Slave to Man of Letters: The Conversion of Frederick Douglass," *Journal of Narrative Technique* 16:1(Winter 1986): 55–71.

19. *The Journey Back*, pp. 29, 30.

20. On this point, see Thomas de Pietro, "Vision and Revision in the Autobiographies of Frederick Douglass," *CLA Journal* 27:4 (June 1983): 387–89; Couser, *American Autobiography*, pp. 52–53, 56, 60; MacKethan, "From Fugitive Slave."

21. Quoted in Joel Porte, *Representative Man: Ralph Waldo Emerson in His Time* (New York: Oxford University Press, 1979), p. 319.

22. Quoted in Philip Foner, *The Life and Writings of Frederick Douglass* (New York: International Publishers, 1950–55), 2:448. Parenthetical references (denoted *LW*) in the text are to this edition.

23. "The Poet," *Essays, Second Series* (Boston: James Munroe, 1844), p. 5.

24. Albert Stone points to this influence—incorrectly, I think—as a source of the text's diminished power. See "Identity and Art," p. 212.

25. Cited in Philip Fisher, *Hard Facts: Setting and Form in the American Novel* (New York: Oxford University Press, 1985), p. 105.

26. *American Notes for General Circulation* (New York: Wilson and Company, 1842), p. 24.

27. *Uncle Tom's Cabin: Or, Life Among the Lowly* (Boston: John P. Jewett, 1851), p. 8.

28. Preston, *Young Frederick Douglass*, pp. xv, 54–56, 81, 91, 110, 140.

29. See, for example, Jean F. Yellin, *The Intricate Knot: Black Figures in American Literature, 1776–1863* (New York: New York University Press, 1972), p. 179, and Stone, "Identity and Art," p. 212.

30. *The Mind of Frederick Douglass* (Chapel Hill: University of North Carolina Press, 1984), p. 276.

31. *The Autonomy of the Self from Richardson to Huysmans* (Princeton: Princeton University Press, 1982), p. 162.

32. "Vision and Revision," p. 391.

33. Quoted in Foner, *Frederick Douglass*, pp. 146–47, 145.

34. *Shadow and Act* (1953; rpt. New York: Random House, 1964), p. 162.

35. Quoted in Paul Zweig, *Walt Whitman: The Making of the Poet* (New York: Basic Books, 1984), p. 216. Parenthetical references in the text are to this edition.

36. Quoted in Zweig, *op. cit.*, pp. 272–73.

37. William Agee, "Franklin and Crèvecoeur: Individualism and the American Dream in the Eighteenth Century" (Diss., University of Minnesota, 1969), pp. 5–6.

38. See Bushman, *From Puritan to Yankee: Character and the Social Order in Connecticut, 1690–1765* (Cambridge, MA: Harvard University Press, 1967), pp. 267, 287; James Henretta, *The Evolution of American Society*, p. 134; and Kenneth Lockridge, *A New England Town: The First Hundred Years* (New York: W. W. Norton, 1970), p. 145.

Scholarly opinion on this issue, as Michael Zuckerman notes ("The Fabrication of Identity in Early America," *William and Mary Quarterly* 3rd ser. 34:2 [April 1977]: 183–214), varies widely, and it is possible to locate nascent individualism in virtually any period. Those who see Puritanism as a force in modernization tend to credit New England with protoindividualism; see Zuckerman, "Fabrication"; and David Flaherty, *Privacy in Colonial New England* (Charlottesville: University of Virginia Press, 1972). Lawrence Stone sees a broad trend toward individualism manifested in politics, sexuality, architecture, economics—even funerary monuments—through the seventeenth and eighteenth centuries in Europe and America (*The Family, Sex and Marriage in England 1500–1800* [London: Weidenfeld and Nicolson, 1977], pp. 223–62). Other students of nineteenth-century American individualism include George Frederickson, *The Inner Civil War: Northern Intellectuals and the Crisis of the Union* (New York: Harper and Row, 1965), esp. pp. 7–16, 39 ff.; Quentin Anderson, *The Imperial Self: An Essay in American Literary and Cultural History* (New York: Knopf, 1971); James Martin, *Men Against the State: The Expositors of Individualist Anarchism in America, 1827–1908* (1953; rpt. Colorado Springs: Ralph Myles, 1970); Rush Welter, *The Mind of America, 1820–1860* (New York: Columbia University Press, 1975), esp. pp. 94 ff., 137–57; and, preeminently, Yehoshua Arieli, *Individualism and Nationalism in American Ideology* (Cambridge, MA: Harvard University Press, 1964). A few writers emphasize American communalism, particularly in the eighteenth century. See Alan Heimert, *Religion and the American Mind: From the Great Awakening to the Revolution* (Cambridge, MA: Harvard University Press, 1966), pp. 102, 114, 136–37; and Michael Zuckerman, *Peaceable Kingdoms: New England Towns in the Eighteenth Century* (New York: Knopf, 1970).

39. Samuel Richardson's *Pamela*; quoted in Jay Fliegelman, *Prodigals and Pilgrims: The American Revolution against Patriarchal Authority, 1750–1800* (Cambridge: Cambridge University Press, 1982), p. 27.

40. Lockridge, *A New England Town*, p. 16; see also Henretta, *The Evolution of American Society*, p. 21, and Bushman, *From Puritan to Yankee*, pp. 142, 190.

41. See Eric Foner, *Tom Paine and Revolutionary America* (New York: Oxford University Press, 1976), pp. 147–73.

42. William McLoughlin, in the introduction to Charles Grandison Finney, *Lectures on Revivals of Religion*, ed. McLoughlin (Cambridge, MA: Harvard University Press, 1960), p. xviii. Subsequent references to Finney are from this edition.

43. "Romantic Reform in America, 1815–1865," *American Quarterly* 17:4 (Winter 1965): 673.

44. *Essays, Second Series*, pp. 280, 292.

45. See Lawrence Buell, *Literary Transcendentalism: Style and Vision in the American Renaissance* (Ithaca: Cornell University Press, 1973), p. 269.

46. See Lewis Perry, *Radical Abolitionism: Anarchy and the Government of God in Antislavery Thought* (Ithaca: Cornell University Press, 1973).

47. The word is used by Stanley Elkins in *Slavery: A Problem in American Institutional and Intellectual Life*, 2nd ed. (Chicago: University of Chicago Press, 1968), p. 165.

48. See Richard D. Brown, *Modernization*, p. 95, and Elkins, *op. cit.*, pp. 29–34, 165.

49. Alexis de Tocqueville, *Democracy in America*, ed. Phillips Bradley (New York: Vintage, 1945), 2:144–45.

50. Quoted in Koenraad Swart, " 'Individualism' in the Mid-Nineteenth

Century (1826–1860)," *Journal of the History of Ideas* 23:1 (January–March 1962): 84.

51. "The Course of Civilization," *The United States Magazine and Democratic Review* 6:21 (September 1834): 209, 213.

52. *Social Statics, or, the Conditions Essential to Human Happiness Specified and the First of Them Developed* (London: John Chapman, 1851), p. 434.

53. *Life and Times of Frederick Douglass* (Hartford, CT: Park, 1882). Parenthetical references (denoted *LT*) in the text are to this edition.

54. Quoted in Moorhead, *American Apocalypse*, pp. 59, 64.

55. *Frederick Douglass' Monthly*, 2 vols. (New York: Negro Universities Press, 1969), June 1861, pp. 473, 485; August 1862, p. 690; March 1862, p. 613.

56. Quoted in Foner, *Frederick Douglass*, pp. 172, 172–73.

57. "Self-Made Men; Address Before the Students of the Indian Industrial School, Carlisle, Pa.," n.d., Frederick Douglass Papers, container 24, reel 18, Library of Congress. Parenthetical references in the text are to this microfilmed pamphlet.

58. See Foner, *Frederick Douglass*, p. 328.

59. Ibid., p. 326.

60. *The Souls of Black Folk: Essays and Sketches* (Chicago: A. C. McClurg, 1903), pp. 9, 10.

61. *Life and Times of Frederick Douglass*, rev. ed. (Boston: De Wolfe, Fiske & Co., 1892). Parenthetical references in the text are to this edition.

62. Draft version of *Life and Times*, Douglass Papers, container 34, reel 21, Library of Congress.

63. Quoted in Foner, *Frederick Douglass*, p. 354.

CHAPTER 6

1. Quoted in Ernest Samuels, *Henry Adams: The Major Phase* (Cambridge, MA: Harvard University Press, 1964), p. 320.

2. *The Education of Henry Adams*, ed. Ernest Samuels (Boston: Houghton Mifflin, 1973), pp. 457–58. Parenthetical references (denoted *EHA*) in the text are to this edition.

3. Quoted in Samuels, *op. cit.*, p. 320.

4. "Composition as Explanation," in *Selected Writings of Gertrude Stein*, ed. Carl Van Vechten (1945; rpt. New York: Random House, 1962), p. 517. Parenthetical references (denoted *C*) in the text are to this edition.

5. James Cox also makes this association between the two writers, but chooses to see Adams as the prophet, and Stein the embodiment of modernism. See "Autobiography and America," *Virginia Quarterly Review* 7:2 (1971): 276–77. See also John Malcolm Brinin, *The Third Rose: Gertrude Stein and Her World* (Boston: Little Brown, 1959), who places Stein in the "sunset phase" of the nineteenth century (xiv).

6. *Picasso* (London: B. T. Batsford, 1938), p. 49. Parenthetical references (denoted *P*) in the text are to this edition.

7. *Everybody's Autobiography* (New York: Random House, 1937), p. 99. Parenthetical references (denoted *EA*) in the text are to this edition.

8. (New York: Random House, 1945), p. 62. Parenthetical references (denoted *WIHS*) in the text are to this edition.

9. *First Principles* (1864; rpt. Osnabruck: Otto Zeller, 1966), p. 438. Parenthetical references (denoted *FP*) in the text are to this edition.

10. *Outlines of Cosmic Philosophy Based on the Doctrine of Evolution, with Criticisms on the Positive Philosophy*, vol. 4 (1874; rpt. Cambridge, MA: Riverside Press, 1902), pp. 171, 176.

11. *Social Statics*, p. 64.

12. Quoted in David W. Marcell, *Progress and Pragmatism: James, Dewey, Beard, and the American Idea of Progress* (Westport, CT: Greenwood Press, 1974), p. 109.

13. *The Destiny of Man Viewed in the Light of his Origin*, 20th ed. (Boston: Houghton Mifflin, 1893), pp. 118–19.

14. *Principles of Psychology*, 2 vols. (1890; rpt. New York: Dover Publications, 1950). Parenthetical references in the text are to this edition. For other assessments of James's influence on Stein see Wendy Steiner, *Exact Resemblance to Exact Resemblance: The Literary Portraiture of Gertrude Stein* (New Haven: Yale University Press, 1978), pp. 29–63; Steiner, "The Steinian Portrait," in *Critical Essays on Gertrude Stein*, ed. Michael Hoffman (Boston: G. K. Hall, 1986), pp. 130–39; Lisa Ruddick, "William James and the Modernism of Gertrude Stein," in *Modernism Reconsidered*, ed. Robert Kiely (Cambridge, MA: Harvard University Press, 1983), pp. 47–63; Michael Hoffman, *The Development of Abstractionism in the Writings of Gertrude Stein* (Philadelphia: University of Pennsylvania Press, 1965), pp. 175–97, 207–15; Shirley Neuman, *Gertrude Stein: Autobiography and the Problem of Narration* (Victoria, Canada: University of Victoria Press, 1979), pp. 34, 36–37, 46, 62, 70; and Donald Sutherland, *Gertrude Stein: A Biography of Her Work* (New York: Hafner, 1949), p. 41.

15. "The Dilemma of Determinism," in *Essays in Pragmatism*, ed. Alburey Castell (New York: Hafner, 1949), p. 41.

16. *Time and Free Will: An Essay on the Immediate Data of Consciouness*, trans. F. L. Pogson (1910; rpt. London: George Allen & Unwin, 1959), p. 131. Parenthetical references (denoted *T*) in the text are to this edition.

17. *La pensée et le mouvant; essais et conferences* (1903; rpt. Paris: Librairie Felix Alcan, 1934), p. 202; my translation.

18. *The Origin of Species by Means of Natural Selection, or the Preservation of Favored Races in the Struggle for Life* (New York: Appleton, 1876), p. 63. Parenthetical references in the text are to this edition.

19. *The Descent of Man, and Selection in Relation to Sex* (New York: Appleton, 1876), p. 128.

20. Ibid.

21. *Being in the Text*, pp. 156–57. See also John Carlos Rowe, *Henry Adams and Henry James: The Emergence of a Modern Consciousness* (Ithaca: Cornell University Press, 1976), esp. pp. 93–131.

22. *The Making of Americans: Being a History of a Family's Progress* (Paris: Contact Editions, 1925). Parenthetical references (denoted *MOA*) in the text are to this edition.

23. For Weininger's influence on *The Making of Americans*, see Leon Katz, "Weininger and *The Making of Americans*," *Twentieth Century Literature* 24:1 (Spring 1978): 8–26. Katz, however, while tracing important filiations, overstates the impact of this text on Stein's career. See also Wendy Steiner, *Exact Resemblance*, pp. 37–38.

24. "The Gradual Making of the Making of Americans," in *Selected Writings*, p. 255. Randa Dubnick makes a similar point in *The Structure of Obscurity: Gertrude Stein, Language, and Cubism* (Urbana: University of Illinois Press, 1984), p. 92.

25. *Gertrude Stein in Pieces* (New York: Oxford University Press, 1970), p. 89. I am indebted to Bridgman throughout this discussion.

26. In *Matisse Picasso and Gertrude Stein with Two Shorter Stories* (Paris: Plain Edition, 1923). Parenthetical references (denoted *LGB*) in the text are to this edition.

27. In *Selected Writings*. Parenthetical references (denoted *TB*) in the text are to this edition.

28. *The Making of a Modernist: Gertrude Stein from Three Lives to Tender Buttons* (Amherst: University of Massachusetts Press, 1984), p. 136. I cannot agree, however, with Walker's further claim that the loosely associative structure of *Tender Buttons* represents a Derridean deconstruction, "unseating both the subject and Western logic as privileged centers and guarantors of truth" (p. 141). On the contrary, Stein's associations shielded the self from an alien language by demonstrating that textuality could not restrict the elusive core of consciousness. As Stein herself acknowledges, to write is to "practice the sign that means that really means a necessary betrayal" (*TB* 468; quoted in Walker, p. 142). Stein was a phenomenologist, not a deconstructor.

29. "Gertrude Stein as Post-Modernist: The Rhetoric of *Tender Buttons*," in *Critical Essays on Gertrude Stein*, p. 119. For other linguistic assessments of *Tender Buttons*, see Walker, *The Making of a Modernist*, pp. 136–42, and Marianne de Koven, "Gertrude Stein and Modern Painting," in *Critical Essays on Gertrude Stein*, pp. 171–83. Allegra Stewart's decoding on the basis of root words and Jungian motifs is fascinating, but unconvincing. See *Gertrude Stein and the Present* (Cambridge, MA: Harvard University Press, 1967), pp. 69–139. For an assessment of *Tender Buttons* similar to my own, see Brinin, *The Third Rose*, p. 162.

30. *The Structure of Scientific Revolutions*, 2nd ed. (Chicago: University of Chicago Press, 1970), pp. 84, 149.

31. *Literary Relativity: An Essay on Twentieth-Century Narrative* (Lewisburg, PA: Bucknell University Press, 1982), p. 20.

32. Robert Wohl, *The Generation of 1914* (Cambridge, MA: Harvard University Press, 1979), p. 212.

33. Quoting Gottfried Benn, in James McFarlane, "The Mind of Modernism," included in *Modernism 1890–1930*, ed. Malcolm Bradbury and James McFarlane (Harmondsworth: Penguin, 1976), p. 86. Parenthetical references (denoted *M*) in the text are to this paperback edition.

34. Quoted in Paul Jay, *Being in the Text*, p. 37.

35. Mark Roskill, *The Interpretation of Cubism* (Philadelphia: Art Alliance Press, 1972), p. 30. Parenthetical references (denoted *I*) in the text are to this edition. See also Brinin, *The Third Rose*, pp. 111, 138–40.

36. *Fluctuant Representation in Synthetic Cubism: Picasso, Braque, Gris, 1910–1920* (New York: Garland, 1976), p. 23. Parenthetical references in the text are to this edition.

37. *Picasso*, p. 16. for other discussions of Stein's work and cubism, see Marilyn Gaddis Rose, "Gertrude Stein and the Cubist Narrative," *Modern Fiction Studies* 22:4 (1976–77): 534–44; Jo Anna Isaak, *The Ruin of Representation*

in Modernist Art and Texts (Ann Arbor, MI: UMI Research Press, 1986), pp. 99–101, 112–13, 117–19; L. T. Fitz, "Gertrude Stein and Picasso: The Language of Surfaces," *American Literature* 45:2 (May 1973): 228–37; Earl Fendelman, "Gertrude Stein Among the Cubists," *Journal of Modern Literature* 2:4 (November 1972): 481–90; Carolyn Copeland, *Language and Time and Gertrude Stein* (Iowa City: University of Iowa Press, 1975), pp. 81–84; Randa Dubnick, *The Structure of Obscurity*, esp. pp. 3–44; and Brinin, *The Third Rose*, pp. 126–51, 157–65. Although they do not explore the cultural milieu, two studies link Stein's experiments with cubist ambiguity: Marjorie Perloff, "Poetry as Word-System: The Art of Gertrude Stein," *American Poetry Review* 8:5 (1979): 33–43; and Wendy Steiner, *Exact Resemblance*, pp. 144–45.

38. *The Autobiography of Alice B. Toklas* (New York: Harcourt, Brace, 1933), p. 106. Parenthetical references (denoted *ABT*) in the text are to this edition.

39. See Bridgman, *Gertrude Stein in Pieces*, pp. 241–42, 260–88. Leon Katz makes a similar point about Stein's "nineteenth-century dilemmas concerning loss of uniqueness" and the everlasting feeling. See "Weininger and *The Making of Americans*," p. 15. Estelle Jelinek also sees Stein as "a woman of her era"—the nineteenth century—"despite her avant-garde friends and literary experimentation." See *The Tradition of Women's Autobiography from Antiquity to the Present* (Boston: Twayne, 1986), p. 134.

40. *Paris France* (London: B. T. Batsford, 1940), p. 32. Parenthetical references (denoted *PF*) in the text are to this edition.

41. Quoted in *Gertrude Stein in Pieces*, p. 215.

42. Cf. Shirley Neuman, *Gertrude Stein*, pp. 14–15, and Estelle Jelinek, *The Tradition of Women's Autobiography*, pp. 134 ff.

43. MS, *The Autobiography of Alice B. Toklas*, Stein Collection, Yale Collection of American Literature, Beinecke Library, Yale University.

44. *Portraits and Prayers* (New York: Random House, 1934), p. 21.

45. In "Visual Rhetoric in *The Autobiography of Alice B. Toklas*" (*Critical Inquiry* 1:4 [June 1975]: 849–81), Paul Alkon argues that the photographs conspire to collapse the distinction between image and text. The ambiguous cross-references between the two question all assumptions of linguistic priority, as text and image continuously exchange places. Alkon is less explicit, though, about the subliminal argument the photographs make for the *stasis* of Stein's inner experience, her use of these images as a refuge from change.

46. For a similar discussion, see James E. Breslin, "Gertrude Stein and the Problems of Autobiography," in *Critical Essays on Gertrude Stein*, pp. 149–59. Breslin, too, notes Stein's "inner stillness"; but he is mistaken, I believe, in contending that stillness allows her "to respond to external pressures with serenity" (155). Rather, her composure masks a pervading anxiety, a determined *retreat* from such pressures.

47. For alternative viewpoints, see Neuman, *Gertrude Stein*, pp. 15 ff., and 29–32. Neuman, too, sees flaws in the *Autobiography*, but for her they arise from Stein's inability to cast off the historical past for a thoroughly continuous present. Estelle Jelinek argues that, rather than confront, Stein's intent was to protect her relationship from the encroaching world. See *The Tradition of Women's Autobiography*, 136 ff.

48. *Lectures in America* (New York: Random House, 1935), p. 63. Parenthetical references (denoted *LIA*) in the text are to this edition.

49. *Narration* (Chicago: University of Chicago Press, 1935), p. 60. Parenthetical references (denoted *N*) in the text are to this edition.

50. *The Geographical History of America or the Relation of Human Nature to the Human Mind* (New York: Random House, 1936), p. 8. Parenthetical references (denoted *GHA*) in the text are to this edition.

51. Shirley Neuman also treats the work as "meta-autobiography," but in the context of Stein's quest to insulate the writing self from temporal intrusions. See *Gertrude Stein*, pp. 47 ff.

52. Quoted in James Mellow, *Charmed Circle: Gertrude Stein & Company* (New York: Praeger, 1974), p. 144.

53. See "Composition as Explanation," p. 514.

54. G. Thomas Couser makes a similar point in *American Autobiography*, p. 159.

55. *Writing Degree Zero*, p. 16.

56. Quoted in Samuels, *Henry Adams*, p. 295.

CONCLUSION

1. *The Autobiography of W. E. B. Du Bois: A Soliloquy on Viewing My Life from the Last Decade of Its First Century* (1968; rpt. New York: International Publishers, 1986), p. 415. Parenthetical references (denoted *A*) in the text are to this paperback edition.

2. *Memories of a Catholic Girlhood* (New York: Harcourt Brace Jovanovich, 1955). Parenthetical references in the text are to this paperback edition.

3. Paul Eakin devotes a perceptive chapter to McCarthy in *Fictions in Autobiography*, pp. 3–55, and esp. pp. 35 ff.

4. *Three: An Unfinished Woman; Pentimento; Scoundrel Time* (Boston: Little, Brown, 1979), p. 9. Parenthetical references (denoted *UW* for *An Unfinished Woman*) in the text are to this edition.

5. See Patricia Meyer Spacks, *The Female Imagination* (New York: Knopf, 1975), p. 183.

6. *Maybe* (Boston: Little, Brown, 1980), pp. 51–52.

7. See Jelinek's "Introduction: Women's Autobiography and the Male Tradition," in *Women's Autobiography: Essays in Criticism*, ed. Jelinek (Bloomington: Indiana University Press, 1980), pp. 1–20. The Spacks citation is taken from her essay "Selves in Hiding" in the same volume, pp. 112–32. For a comprehensive survey of women's autobiographies, see Jelinek, *The Tradition of Women's Autobiography*. See also the essays in *The New Feminist Criticism: Essays on Women, Literature, and Theory*, Elaine Showalter, ed. (New York: Pantheon, 1985).

8. *I Know Why the Caged Bird Sings* (1969; rpt. New York: Bantam, 1985), p. 3. Parenthetical references (denoted *CB*) in the text are to this paperback edition.

9. *Singin' and Swingin' and Gettin' Merry Like Christmas* (1976; rpt. New York: Bantam, 1981), p. 179.

10. *The Heart of a Woman* (New York: Bantam, 1981), pp. 230–33.

11. *All God's Children Need Traveling Shoes* (New York: Vintage, 1986), pp. 102–3. Parenthetical references (denoted *AGC*) in the text are to this paperback edition.

12. *Dusk of Dawn: An Essay Toward an Autobiography of a Race Concept* (1940; rpt. New York: Schocken, 1968), p. viii.

13. *The Souls of Black Folk*, p. 109.

Index